Lecture Notes
in Business Information Processing   124

Series Editors

Wil van der Aalst
  Eindhoven Technical University, The Netherlands
John Mylopoulos
  University of Trento, Italy
Michael Rosemann
  Queensland University of Technology, Brisbane, Qld, Australia
Michael J. Shaw
  University of Illinois, Urbana-Champaign, IL, USA
Clemens Szyperski
  Microsoft Research, Redmond, WA, USA

Christina Keller
Mikael Wiberg
Pär J. Ågerfalk
Jenny S. Z. Eriksson Lundström (Eds.)

Nordic Contributions in IS Research

Third Scandinavian Conference
on Information Systems, SCIS 2012
Sigtuna, Sweden, August 17–20, 2012
Proceedings

 Springer

Volume Editors

Christina Keller
Jönköping International Business School, Sweden
E-mail: christina.keller@jibs.hj.se

Mikael Wiberg
Uppsala University, Sweden
E-mail: mikael.wiberg@im.uu.se

Pär J. Ågerfalk
Uppsala University, Sweden
E-mail: par.agerfalk@im.uu.se

Jenny S. Z. Eriksson Lundström
Uppsala University, Sweden
E-mail: jenny.eriksson@im.uu.se

ISSN 1865-1348   e-ISSN 1865-1356
ISBN 978-3-642-32269-3   e-ISBN 978-3-642-32270-9
DOI 10.1007/978-3-642-32270-9
Springer Heidelberg Dordrecht London New York

Library of Congress Control Number: 2012943578

ACM Computing Classification (1998): J.1, H.4.1, H.3.5, K.4.3, K.6, D.2

Typesetting: Camera-ready by author, data conversion by Scientific Publishing Services, Chennai, India

Printed on acid-free paper

Springer is part of Springer Science+Business Media (www.springer.com)

Preface
Designing the Interactive Society

Information technology has undoubtedly become a ubiquitous technological underpinning to communication and collaboration that permeates our personal and professional lives. Recent developments in social media, commons-based peer production, and information infrastructuring emphasize this more than ever. The society of today is an interactive society shaped by ever-increasing participation in online conversations. The digitization of society's information and communication structures has fundamentally changed everyday life, economy, business, and society. Internet and mobile technology has resulted in information and services, accessible by all regardless of time and place, being taken for granted. Globalization and new open forms of collaboration continue to change the playing field at an ever-increasing rate. Although the rapid evolution of the information society is shaped by digital technology and media convergence, contemporary societal processes of openness, responsibility, democratization, and global communication are also shaping that very same technology. How then, can information systems as an academic yet pragmatic discipline contribute to this endeavor – to the designing of the interactive society? Clearly, the Scandinavian IS tradition with its emphasis on engaged scholarship, action research, and socially embedded design have a lot to contribute to this journey.

To fuel the discussions, we invited two distinguished keynote speakers to SCIS 2012, namely, Alan Hevner and Shirley Gregor. They were asked to provide their respective views of the conference theme and also to introduce their ongoing collaborative efforts to clarify and elaborate a number of critical issues in relation to artifact design and construction of design theory.

SCIS 2012 attracted 33 submissions from the Scandinavian community of information systems researchers, which was a considerable improvement compared to the previous year. Ten submissions were accepted to the conference. The increasing interest for the conferences was also evident in that the Program Committee attracted 49 members. This is the largest number ever in the history of SCIS.

Two themes emerged among the accepted submissions; the interactive society and design. In the interactive society theme, Giulia Nardelli presents a comprehensive literature review resulting in a conceptual typology on the complex relationship between ICT and innovation in services. Bendik Bygstad and Peter Axel Nielsen propose a framework to analyze interaction between software development processes and organizational change processes. A multiple case study by Sune Dueholm Müller, Pernille Kræmmergaard, and Anja Reinwald presents a descriptive model of the dynamic relationships between IT managers and line managers in public organizations consisting of the four archetypes of craftsmanship, entrepreneurship, partnership, and companionship. Furthermore,

Tone Bratteteig and Guri Verne analyze tax authorities from a citizen autonomy perspective and discuss it as a sociomaterial entanglement. Dan Harnesk and John Lindström discuss the intertwined relationship between organizational security objectives, technology, and employees' security behavior in the context of elderly care. The two themes of the interactive society and design are blended in Margunn Aanestad's paper on the challenge of dealing with interdependencies in design, with healthcare as an illustrative example. Heikki Lempinen constructs and refines a framework for dashboard design, as well as principles for design and development of the system. Pertti Järvinen adds to the design theme by discussing how to evaluate (models and instantiations) criteria for goodness that are applicable within different research approaches. Furthermore, Jonas Hedman and Stefan Henningsson present their work on information systems integration in the food industry and finally, John Krogstie presents opportunities of bridging research and innovation by applying Living Labs to perform design science research.

We thank all authors who submitted papers to SCIS 2012. We also thank the Program Committee for excellent contributions as reviewers.

June 2012   Christina Keller
                                                   Mikael Wiberg
                                                   Pär J. Ågerfalk
                                        Jenny Eriksson S.Z. Lundström

Organization

Conference Chair

Pär J. Ågerfalk   Uppsala University, Sweden

Organizing Chair

Jenny Eriksson S.Z. Lundström   Uppsala University, Sweden

Program Chairs

Christina Keller   Jönköping International Business School, Sweden

Mikael Wiberg   Uppsala University, Sweden

SCIS 2012 Program Committee

Margunn Aanestad, Norway
Parisa Aasi, Sweden
Peter Axel Nielsen, Denmark
Karin Axelsson, Sweden
Pernille Bertelsen, Denmark
Pernille Bjørn Rasmussen, Denmark
Claus Bossen, Denmark
Tone Bratteteig, Norway
Christer Carlsson, Finland
Mikael Collan, Finland
Jan Damsgaard, Denmark
Gunnar Ellingsen, Norway
Frode Guribye, Norway
Dan Harnesk, Sweden
Erling Havn, Denmark
Karin Hedström, Sweden
Ola Henfridsson, Sweden
Jonny Holmström, Sweden
Helena Holmström Olsson, Sweden
Pertti Järvinen, Finland
Fredrik Karlsson, Sweden
Erkki Koponen, Finland
Pernille Kræmmergaard, Denmark
John Krogstie, Norway
Katarina Lindblad-Gidlund, Sweden

Rikard Lindgren, Sweden
Jan Ljungberg, Sweden
Ulf Melin, Sweden
Judith Molka-Danielsen, Norway
Bjørn Erik Munkvold, Norway
Jacob Nørbjerg, Denmark
Samuli Pekkola, Finland
Andrea Resmini, Sweden
Anne Persson, Sweden
Tero Päivärinta, Sweden
Matti Rossi, Finland
Mikko Ruohonen, Finland
Lazar Rusu, Sweden
Hannu Salmela, Finland
Kurt Sandkuhl, Sweden
Ulrike Schultze, USA
Lars Svensson, Sweden
Carsten Sørensen, United Kingdom
Bjørnar Tessem, Norway
Virpi Tuunainen, Finland
Vivian Vimarlund, Sweden
Pirkko Walden, Finland
Geoff Walsham, United Kingdom
Liisa von Hellens, Australia

Table of Contents

The Complex Relationship between ICT and Innovation in Services: A Literature Review

Giulia Nardelli

Roskilde University, Department of Communication, Business and Information Technologies,
Hus 44.1, Roskilde University, DK-4000 Roskilde, Denmark
nardelli@ruc.dk

Abstract. Recent literature reveals the increasingly important role of ICT within innovation in services. The heterogeneity of existing literature on the topic makes it harder to identify the main problem areas and to spot the critical knowledge gaps when planning and executing research on ICT and innovation in services. This paper aims at outlining how scholars have investigated the relationship between ICT and innovation in services so far, by analyzing the fragmented body of knowledge available on the topic, to strengthen the problem area as field of study and support its progress. The results of the literature review were derived through a concept-centric analysis of the existing research on ICT and innovation in services. The outcome of the literature review is a conceptual typology that organizes and summarizes the body of knowledge on ICT and innovation in services, and reveals the critical knowledge gaps along with an agenda for future research.

Keywords: ICT, service, innovation, integration, open innovation.

1 Introduction

Innovation has become a crucial element of survival for organizations within every industry due to the crucial changes that are affecting modern economies [1]. With the advent of Information and Communication Technologies (ICT), services have become an important locus on innovative activity [2]. Recent innovation literature has dedicated extensive attention to the link between ICT and New Product Development (NPD). According to the last stream of research, however, NPD models are only partially appropriated for services [3–5]. More and deeper knowledge on the relationship between ICT and innovation in services is still needed to cover theoretical gaps [5] and to support practitioners in their quest for value creation.

A preliminary literature review around the terms "ICT", "service" and "innovation" shows that scholars have looked at these topics from several angles and with diverse scopes and objectives. Since 2008, when Tether and Tajar outlined the need for more knowledge in this problem area, many researchers have dedicated their attention to ICT and service innovation [6–8]. Nevertheless, the heterogeneity of the existing literature makes it harder to identify the main problem areas within the field,

C. Keller et al. (Eds.): SCIS 2012, LNBIP 124, pp. 1–24, 2012.

but also to spot critical knowledge gaps when planning and executing research on ICT and innovation in services.

This paper aims at presenting a thorough literature review on the relationship between ICT and innovation in services, by analyzing the fragmented body of knowledge available on the topic and by considering the many facets of the connection. The outcome of the literature review is a conceptual typology that organizes existing literature on ICT and innovation in services. Moreover, it enables (a) identifying the main problem areas when considering ICT and innovation in services, by outlining five umbrella themes in the body of knowledge; (b) spotting critical research gaps that might guide future inquiries within the field.

The literature review focuses on the following research question:

How has previous literature investigated the relationship between ICT and innovation in services?

By answering the research question, this literature review might contribute both to service innovation research and Information Systems (IS) research by outlining the nature of the relationship between ICT and innovation in services. Moreover, it might contribute to IS research, by addressing Webster and Watson's (2002) call for more literature reviews to strengthen IS as a field of study and to support its progress, by creating a firm foundation for advancing knowledge [9]. I classified the collected body of knowledge under five umbrella themes, which represent the multi-faceted relationship between ICT and innovation in services. According to my analysis, the integration of processes and the multiple opportunities for cooperation are the most relevant aspects of this relationship.

The paper is organized as follows. The introduction presents an overview of the research area and highlights the research question. The second section is dedicated to the definition of ICT and innovation in services. It delineates the problem area and outlines the key concepts and variables of the following analysis. Moreover, it sets the scope and boundaries of the study. I then describe the methodology that I applied for the literature review. The main section of the paper is the analysis of findings from the literature search with the subsequent discussion, within which I present the conceptual typology. Finally, the conclusions answer explicitly the research question; highlight the gaps in the existing literature along with the opportunities for future research.

2   Laying the Foundation: ICT, Services and Innovation

2.1   Information and Communication Technologies: Definitions and Roles

Without stating an explicit definition of ICT, several studies focus on the economic impact of ICT and distinguish between their role as product or within organizational processes [10–12]. In 1998, OECD countries agreed on the industry-based definition of the ICT sector, which includes that: (a) for manufacturing industries, the products must fulfill the function of information processing and communication or must use electronic processing to detect, measure and/or record physical phenomena or control a physical process; (b) for service industries, the products must enable the function of information processing and communication by electronic means [10]. Given the scope of this literature review, I will limit my attention to such broad definition of both ICT manufacturing and services industries, which includes more specific classifications according to context dependent aspects.

Schreyer highlights two main differences in the way OECD researchers treat ICT: (a) the difference between ICT industries and their contribution to growth, and the role of ICT as capital inputs in all parts of the economy; (b) the difference between ICT effects on labor and on multifactor productivity. From this distinction he derives three aspects of the impact of ICT on economic growth: (1) ICT production; (2) ICT as a capital input; (3) ICT as a special capital input [12]. In the first case, scholars consider ICT as a product, and look at ICT relevance in terms of the role of ICT products in the GDP of the economy. The second and third aspects, on the other hand, emphasize the role of ICT by measuring their contribution on productivity growth. When looking at ICT as a capital input, researchers consider their direct and observable impact on outcome and on labor productivity growth, but do not observe side effects, i.e. spillovers and externalities. ICT as capital inputs are one of the types of physical resources in which an organization chooses to invest, and that are combined with other capital (financial resources) and labor (human resources) to produce output [13]. Their impact is thus measured in terms of Return On Investment (ROI) [12]. However, several scholars argued and empirically proved the existence of spillovers and externalities in ICT development and implementation within organizations [5, 6, 10, 14]. This makes it necessary to emphasize the nature of ICT as special capital input [12, 15], which is also what I do in my analysis. The concept of ICT as a special capital input is based on the claim that ICT produce benefits that go beyond those occurring to investors and owners, i.e. ROI. Such externalities are harder to measure, but improve overall productivity and aggregate incoming growth [12].

2.2   Innovation in Services

The full diversity of services and the complexity of their inner attributes make it difficult to determine a single definition of service providing [16]. Rather than proposing a comprehensive definition, the best way to clarify the nature of services, given the aim and the scope of this work, seems to be looking at their distinguishing characteristics as compared to tangible goods. Although the differentiation is much more blurred in the actual practice than in theory, services tend to involve customer participation in the service process and to be: (a) simultaneously produced and consumed; (b) perishable; (c) intangible; and (d) heterogeneous [17]. Each service is characterized by a unique combination of these attributes and relative degrees [14, 18].

Not only services are achieving increasing importance in the eyes of the researchers, but also it has become clear that a large share of innovative effort in contemporary economies relates to service innovation and to New Service Development (NSD) [14, 19]. Scholars distinguished between product and process innovation, to then recognize the importance of organizational and technological innovation [1, 20]. According to den Hertog, four main dimensions describe a new service: (1) new service concept; (2) new client interface; (3) new service delivery system; (4) technological options. Any service innovation involves a certain blend of these dimensions. Chesbrough and Rosenbloom [21] outline the importance, in modern economies, of business model innovation, which they define as focusing device that mediates between technology development and economic value creation [22]. Building on Schumpeterian theories on innovation, Barras provides the foundation for the theory of innovation in services by actually starting with the analysis of the process of adoption of new technologies within a traditional NPD model. He argues that in the service industry the innovation process is actually originated by the adoption of the new technology itself, which subsequently drives to service innovation [23]. More recently, Jong and Vermeulen recognize that service innovation is possible without technological innovation, but, nevertheless, the actual practice involves a wide range of relationships between technology and innovation in services [19]. Jong et al. show that technology especially impacts on service innovation in the process of service delivery. Furthermore they demonstrated how correct adoption and use of Information Technologies (IT) not only can increase efficiency, but also have a positive impact on innovation in services by: (a) facilitating idea generation for new and/or improved services; (b) accelerating the development of the time-to-market of new services; and (c) easing interactions within and between stakeholders [14].

Scupola and Tuunainen distinguish three main roles of ICT within innovation in services [8]. They draw on previous literature [24, 25] to outline the role of ICT as: (1) enabler of service innovation, as service innovations often derive from the introduction of a new technology or from the different use of an existing one, i.e. banking and e-government services [23]; (2) support infrastructure for service innovation, i.e. online help desk; (3) utility for service innovation, when ICT adoption and use aim at reducing costs while increasing coordination of inter- and intra-organizational activities [8]. In the latter case, service innovation does not derive from R&D but rather from the development and implementation of ICT to facilitate and improve business processes [26]. By applying this distinction to organizational research, it is possible to associate these roles to different types of organizations. Explorative and exploitative organizations are respectively characterized by the first two roles, while ambidextrous entities present all three roles [8].

Recently, innovation literature has shown interest in the shift from the closed to an open innovation model, which is related, among other things, to technological changes [27]. According to Chesbrough, this shift characterizes to various degrees many companies in the modern economies. In the open innovation model, a leaky boundary separates the company from its surrounding environment, and allows knowledge and ideas to move around the two [27]. Several scholars show that innovation in services takes place due to the interaction of internal and external factors and agents [4, 28, 29]. Tether and Tajar outline that NSD involves multiple combinations of intra-organizational, Business To Consumer (B2C) and Business To Business (B2B) interactions. They show the prominence of an organizational cooperation mode of innovation within European service firms, which confirms Chesbrough's statement that the open innovation model is recognizable in service innovation, other than in tangible products [27]. By considering the case of Amazon.com, Chesbrough shows how ICT can support the open innovation model in services, but only considers B2C interactions.

2.3   Setting the Boundaries

The preliminary literature review outlined above defines the problem area of this study and represents the foundation of the literature search and analysis of findings. It is evident that a significant body of knowledge is available on ICT, services and innovation, whose relationship delimitates the scope of this research. Many scholars consider in various ways some aspects of such relationship.   The heterogeneity of existing research on ICT and innovation in services, however, calls for the conceptualization of the preliminary review to guide the extraction and discussion of the findings. From the research discussed so far I was able to derive three main concepts, which constitute the ground of my analysis: (1) type of ICT involvement; (2) type of innovation; (3) inter-/intra-organizational dynamics. Table 1 offers a visual summary of the preliminary literature review organized around these three main concepts and the derived variables, with reference to the authoring scholars. This table also represents the analysis scheme, which guided my examination.

Please notice that the table reports the distinction between type of ICT involvement by referring to involvement in the (a) product; (b) process. The latter includes the concept of ICT as a special capital input [12], which I adapted to the scope of my

Table 1. Analysis scheme – concepts, variables and authors

Concept	Variable		Author(s)
Type of ICT involvement	Product		OECD, 2004; Schreyer, 1999
	Process	Enabler	Broadbent, Weill & Neo, 1999; Mele, Spena & Colurcio, 2010; Scupola and Tuunainen, 2011
		Support	
		Utility	
Type of innovation	Technology innovation		Barras, 1986; Fagerberg et al., 2006; Jong & Vermeulen, 2003; Jong et al., 2003; den Hertog, 2000
	Organizational innovation		Atilgan-Inan, Büyükküpcü & Akinci, 2012; Fagerberg et al., 2006
	Business model innovation		Chesbrough & Rosenbloom, 2002
	Innovation in the offering	New service	Jong & Vermeulen, 2003; Jong, Bruins, Dolfsma & Meijaard, 2003; den Hertog, 2000
		New delivery	den Hertog, 2000
Inter-/intra-organizational dynamics	Open innovation		Chesbrough, 2003; Tether & Tajar, 2008
	Buyer-seller relationship	B2C	Sundbo, 1997; Teece, 1986; Tether, 2002; Tether & Tajar, 2008
		B2B	
	Intra-organizational dynamics		Sundbo, 1997; Teece, 1986; Tether, 2002; Tether & Tajar, 2008

analysis. In fact, the variable ICT as a special capital input synthesizes the directly measurable impact of ICT on organizational processes – ICT as a capital input – but also spillovers and externalities – ICT as a special capital input – with emphasis on those that make ICT enabler, support and utility for innovation [8, 24, 25].

3   Research Methodology

"A coherent literature review emerges only from a coherent conceptual structuring of the topic itself" (Bem, 1995, p.175 as in Webster and Watson, 2002, p.xiv), especially when the aim is to create a firm foundation for advancing knowledge. Webster and Watson (2002) describe the two main types of reviews, centered on: (a) a significant existing body of knowledge in the problem area, whose review results in a conceptual model that synthesizes and extends existing research; (2) an emerging issue, whose review offers fresh theoretical foundations through a conceptual model [9]. A thorough literature review on the relationship between ICT and innovation in services is still missing despite the availability of a consistent body of knowledge on the topic. It is therefore possible to recognize the review presented in this paper as of the first type, which specifically aims at offering a coherent structure to the problem area.

Four steps compose the research methodology for this literature review: (1) identification of the problem area and of the research question; (2) definition of the key variables and setting of the boundaries; (3) search and identification of the relevant literature; and (4) analysis of the collected literature and discussion of findings. Each step calls for dedicated research methods and strategies, which I describe in the following paragraphs.

3.1   Identification of the Problem and the Research Question

In this step, I first conducted a literature search on ICT, services and innovation separately, whose results allowed me to identify the problem area and the research question, along with the scope of the study. Moreover, the results of this search enabled me to elaborate a preliminary literature review (Section 2: Setting the grounds), which collects and presents the general theories and the main streams of research on the topics of interest: ICT, services and innovation. From the preliminary literature review I then derived the concepts and variables that constitute the foundation of the knowledge on ICT and innovation in services. The analysis scheme shown in table 1 displays the concepts and variables, which I later on used to organize the literature on ICT and innovation in services and to extract findings.

3.2   Definition of the Key Variables and Setting of the Boundaries

Following Webster and Watson's guidelines (2002), I adopted a concept-centric approach by building a concept matrix based on the analysis scheme, and I let concepts and variables determine the organizing framework of the literature review [9]. Once I gained an overview of the problem area through the preliminary literature review, I was able to identify three main concepts, which have a central role in determining the relationship between ICT and innovation in services: (1) type of ICT involvement; (2) type of innovation; (3) inter-/intra- organizational dynamics. The first concept – type of ICT involvement – included the role of ICT as a product and as a special capital input (adapted from Schreyer, 1999). The latter is in turn differentiated into ICT impact as an enabler, facilitating structure or utility for innovation [8, 24, 25]. The dedicated literature helped me indentify the different types of innovation: (a) technology innovation [14, 19–21, 23]; (b) organizational innovation [1, 20]; (c) business model innovation [22]; and (d) innovation in the service offering – new service [14, 19, 21] and new delivery [21]. Finally, the concept inter- and intra-organizational dynamics involves the variables: (a) open innovation [5, 27]; (b) buyer-seller relationship [4, 5, 28, 29] and (c) intra-organizational dynamics [4, 5, 28, 29].

The concept matrix (Appendix I), which I filled in after I completed the search and identification of the relevant knowledge on ICT and innovation in services, synthesizes the literature through a discussion of concepts and variables within each examined article.

3.3   Search and Identification of the Relevant Literature

To collect and identify the relevant literature to answer the research question, I used (a) a literature search strategy; (b) selection criteria for the studies to be included in the analysis; and (c) an analysis scheme outlining the documentation and coding of the collected body of knowledge [30]. For the literature search strategy I took inspiration from Webster and Watson (2002), and adopted a structured approach based on a search by topic, instead of by journal. To make sure to include all major contributions, which are likely to be found in major journals, I selected ABI Inform as main data source. Moreover, I searched Scopus and ISI Web of Knowledge to include relevant conference proceedings and make sure the literature review is up-to-date.

I considered both the research question and the scope of the literature review to outline the selection criteria. Therefore I limited my inquiry to those studies that reported "ICT", "servic*" and "innovat*" among the keywords, and searched for the combination of these three terms in all databases. Appendix II reports a detailed description of criteria and results from the literature search. I narrowed my results to a number lower than 60 articles in each database with the available search tools, and I created a database to collect the 131 abstracts that resulted from my search. By reading the abstracts I excluded those studies that clearly did not match with the scope of my study and I obtained a total amount of 86 articles. I then created an overview table with the 86 articles to summarize the collected body of knowledge according to the analysis scheme. To outline the most researched areas I included a section in the overview table dedicated to the technologies and sectors touched upon by each study. Finally I classified the articles according to the levels of analysis they adopted: (a) micro level, meaning individuals and sub-units of organizations, such as teams, departments and divisions; (b) meso level, meaning organizations considered as a whole; (c) macro level, meaning systemic entities, such as sectors, industries and networks, along with local, national and global organisms [30].

3.4   Analysis of the Collected Literature and Discussion of Findings

I started the analysis of the collected literature by deriving concepts and variables from the preliminary literature review to build the concept matrix as prescribed by Webster and Watson (2002). From the concept matrix I found out that 43 articles did not fit the scope of the study, and I thus excluded them from the analysis. Appendix I reports the concepts matrix with the 43 papers that I finally included in the analysis. An excellent start for building the concept matrix has been provided by the approach for understanding ICT by Schreyer (1999). Schreyer shows the three aspects of the impact of ICT on economic growth according to OECD researchers: (1) ICT production; (2) ICT as a capital input; (3) ICT as a special capital input. When I started my analysis I noticed that (a) many scholars demonstrated the existence of spillovers and externalities in ICT contributions to productivity growth [5, 6, 10, 14]; and (b) the studies that resulted from my literature search, when looking at ICT impact on productivity growth, all took into consideration these spillovers and externalities. I therefore divided the body of knowledge according to whether they emphasized the aspect of ICT as (1) product or (2) special capital input with regards to innovation.

I then looked for relationships between and among concepts and variables found in the existing literature on ICT and innovation in services to: (a) define and conceptualize the relationship between ICT and innovation in services; (b) identify umbrella themes to organize the body of knowledge and outline research gaps. The concept matrix thus provided me with an overview of the concepts and variables discussed in each article, which facilitated the clustering into themes. The clustering involved a series of subsequent steps. I divided the body of knowledge according to the adaptation of Schreyer's classification (1999) and carried out a detailed analysis of the articles that emphasized each variable of the analysis scheme, which allowed me to recognize similarities, dissimilarities and overlapping areas. Through a detailed examination of identified similarities, dissimilarities and overlapping areas I grouped the studies into sub-themes and finally into umbrella themes. The five umbrella themes that emerged from the analysis of the literature are: (1) management of ICT-based technological innovation; (2) management of organizational innovation resulting from ICT adoption; (3) NSD and innovation in service delivery; (4) business model innovation; and (5) relationship between ICT and innovation in services.

4   The Relationship between ICT and Innovation in Services – Analysis and Findings

Through the analysis of 43 studies I spotted the relationships between and among variables and concepts within the existing literature on ICT and innovation in services and identified five umbrella themes. Table 2 shows the umbrella themes along with the corresponding authors. I ordered the themes according to the variables in the concept matrix, and present them in detail in the following paragraphs.

Table 2. Themes and corresponding authors

	Theme	Level of analysis	ICT as product	ICT as special capital input	ICT as product and as special capital input
1	Management of ICT-based technological innovations	Micro	Campos, Jantunen, & Prakash, 2007; Cocosila & Archer, 2010; Gilbert & Han, 2005; Norum, Grev, Moen, Balteskard, & Holthe, 2003; Ram, Anbu, & Kataria, 2011; Wirth, von Pape, & Karnowski, 2008		Lee, Trimi, Byun, & Kang, 2011
		Meso	Constantinides, 2006; Drozdová, 2008; Jetter, Satzger, & Neus, 2008; Mangan & Kelly, 2009		Bygstad, 2010; Bygstad & Aanby, 2010; Lyytinen & Rose, 2003
		Macro	Chen & Watanabe, 2006; Chen, Watanabe, & Griffybrown, 2007; Shareef, Kumar, Kumar, & Dwivedi, 2011		Ayres & Williams, 2004; S. Lee, Kim, & Park, 2009; Sharif, 2010
2	Management of organizational innovation in ICT-based services	Micro	Beynon-Davies, 2005		
		Meso	Arduini, Belotti, Denni, Giungato, & Zanfei, 2010; Drozdová, 2008		
		Macro	Paskaleva-Shapira, Azorín, & Chiabai, 2008; Shareef et al., 2011		
3	Business model innovation	Micro			
		Meso			Drozdová, 2008; Jetter et al., 2008; Yovanof & Hazapis, 2008
		Macro			

Table 2. (*Continued*)

Theme	Level of analysis	ICT as product	ICT as special capital input	ICT as product and as special capital input
4 NSD and innovation in service delivery	Micro			
	Meso	Bygstad & Lanestedt, 2009; Leon & Davies, 2008; Moller, Rajal, & Westerlund, 2008		
	Macro	Paskaleva-Shapira et al., 2008; Ritala, Hurmelinna-Laukkanen, & Blomqvist, 2009; Siddiquee, 2008; Tuunainen & Tuunanen, 2011		
5 Relationship between ICT and innovation in services	Micro			
	Meso		Gago & Rubalcaba, 2006; Gambarotto & Cammozzo, 2010; Hidalgo Nuchera, López Rodríguez, Heras, & Tafur Segura, 2008; Jbilou, Landry, Amara, & El Adlouni, 2008	
	Macro	Bauer, 2010; R. Williams et al., 2011	Hempell, 2005	

4.1   Theme 1: Management of ICT-Based Technological Innovations

The majority of studies look at the impact of ICT-based technological innovation on different types of service providing organizations. The focus on ICT as a product predominates within this theme. The innovation is the ICT itself, whose adoption and implementation processes generate various consequences in the organization. The studies collected under Theme 1 share the interest for understanding these consequences and the related reactions. In some cases, scholars consider also ICT-based technological innovations' role as special capital input, and study their impact on the innovation processes of the organization. The studies take into consideration many different technologies and focus on various service sectors.

The first sub-set of studies within theme 1 aims at understanding the reasons for adoption of ICT-based technological innovation within services. The analyses show that (a) awareness of the technology and its functionalities [31]; (b) acceptance and appreciation of the technological innovation [32]; and (c) availability of extra-services motivate potential users to adopt the technological innovation [33]. Conversely, the perception of financial, psychological and privacy risk acts as a repellent for adoption. Service providers should therefore create trust among their potential target to ease adoption of ICT-based technological innovations [32, 34].

Going on in the adoption process, some scholars concentrate on the management of organizational consequences of ICT-based technological innovations within services, such as the networks of interdependencies and strategies of negotiation between institutional arrangements, people, technological developments and work practices [35]. Organizations should also ensure user satisfaction [36] and adapt to the specific circumstances and target users [37], which means flexibility and innovativeness. To ease the process of organizational change originated by the adoption of an ICT-based innovation within ICT-based service sectors, Wirth, von Pape, and Karnowski (2008) and Gilbert and Han (2005) suggest considering the different patterns of adoption of ICT-based technological innovations among users. Two studies reveal the need to implement changes in the business model as a result of ICT-based technological innovation [40, 41].

Finally, a sub-set of studies demonstrates the existence of a self-reinforcing innovation mechanism, which seems to be an inner feature of ICT-based technological innovation in different situations and circumstances. Scholars observe this mechanism both when considering ICT only as a product [42, 43], and when recognizing also their role as special capital input [44–50].

4.2   Theme 2: Management of Organizational Innovation Resulting from ICT Adoption

The second theme collects those works that focus on the management of the organizational innovation, when needed because of ICT adoption. Here the emphasis is not on the technology itself, but on the impact the technology has on organizational innovation within services. Theme 2 in fact collects three studies that, while looking on the adoption of ICT to provide e-Government services, emphasize the organizational innovation rather than the technological innovation. Although sector specific, the findings can be applied to other ICT-based services with the relative adaptations.

In particular, within this theme scholars highlight some strategic solutions that might support organizational innovation, such as customer orientation and integration of front-end and back-end systems [51], along with cooperative participation of all stakeholders [52]. Moreover, they recall what already said about technological innovation: different types of organizations in different settings require a different set of support tools [53].

4.3   Theme 3: Business Model Innovation

Theme 3 collects the few works that pay attention to business model innovation. Here scholars adopt a meso level of analysis and the focus is on both ICT as product and as capital input. Drozdová (2008) and Jetter et al. (2008) study the impact of ICT- based technology innovation on service providers, and postulate the consequent need for business model innovation. Drozdová (2008) argues for the strong interconnection between the business model and the IS, which makes it necessary to adapt the business model according to ICT-based innovation. The new business model should take into consideration both structural and infrastructural tasks, and adapt to the specific circumstances in which the technology innovation takes place [40]. Similarly, Jetter et al. (2008) recommend constantly monitoring improvements in the technology and being ready for innovating the business model according to the dynamics of the market [41].

The findings of Yovanof and Hazapis (2008) go in the same direction as they present the concept of business model innovation as a tool for taking advantage of disruptive technologies. They argue that ICT convergence is the cause of a paradigm shift with innovation effects that are both effective and disruptive. In turn, this calls for equally disruptive business models that reshape the innovation strategy [54]. According to their study, the driving forces behind this transformation are: (a) end- users demand, which get more and more sophisticated and challenging for ICT-based service providers; (b) increased global competition, which leads to more efficient global markets; and (c) technological advances that become also more affordable for customers due to the increased competition. As a consequence, organizations should orient their strategies towards more dynamic business models that reflect market dynamics [54].

Among the causes of the need for organizations to implement business model innovation due to ICT-based technological innovation the analyzed works outline: (1) the more sophisticated and challenging user demand [41, 54]; (2) the increased global competition [54]; and (3) the advances and disruptions in ICT [40, 41, 54]. Regarding the management of business model innovation, the studies outline some of the elements that service providers should take into consideration when adapting their business model to ICT-based technological changes and innovations, such as (i) the interconnection between the business model and the IS infrastructure [40, 41, 54]; (ii) the differences between organizations and circumstances [40]; (iii) the need to integrate structural and infrastructural tasks of the business model [40, 41]; (iv) the need to be flexible and adapt to the changes of dynamic markets [41, 54].

4.4   Theme 4: ICT in NSD and Innovation in Service Delivery

Theme 4 – ICT in NSD and innovation in service delivery – collects the studies, whose emphasis is on innovation in the offering, both in terms of NSD an service delivery innovation, within ICT-based services. Again, the focus is on ICT as a product. This theme outlines (1) how to manage ICT-based NSD and service delivery innovation process and (2) the critical factors of success of service offering and service delivery innovation.

The management of service offering and service delivery innovation processes results very similar to the management of organizational innovation. First, the integration of all the front-end and back-end activities related to ICT-based NSD and service delivery innovation processes [55, 56], recalls Beynon-Davies (2005), who postulated the same with regard to organizational innovation. In the latter case integration is necessary to ensure – among users belonging to the service providing organization – the understanding and usability of the system that is at the basis of the organizational innovation. Similarly, within NSD and service delivery innovation such integration supports (a) ease-of-use and (b) motivation to adopt for the final customers [55, 56]. Second, the issue of cooperation between stakeholders emerges again, this time both as integrated element of the management of ICT-based innovation processes [52, 56, 57] and as critical factor of success for new services and/or service delivery innovation [56].

The other critical factors of success for NSD and service delivery innovation are (1) a comprehensive, well-functioning and easy-to-use infrastructure [55, 56, 58]; (2) awareness of the new service and/or service delivery, and motivation to switch to it [56, 58]; (3) sufficient ICT skills among the potential target (-s) of the innovation [58]

4.5   Theme 5: The Relationship between ICT and Innovation in Services

Theme 5 includes eight articles, which more generally aim at understanding the relationship between ICT and innovation in services from various angles. Most works look at ICT as a special capital input, and investigate their impact on innovation in services from various perspectives. Nevertheless, there are two studies that look at ICT-based service sectors to reveal which conditions favor innovation. The set of articles within theme 5 addresses (1) the factors that influence the relationship between ICT and innovation in services; (2) the impact of ICT as a special capital input on innovation in services.

Among the factors that influence the relationship between ICT and innovation in services, Bauer (2010) and Williams et al. (2011) highlight the importance for centralized institutions to develop formalized standards and regulations as support for the innovativeness of ICT-based service sectors [59, 60]. When looking at ICT as a special capital input, scholars recognize their sustaining role with regards to innovation in services. As a consequence of the co-producing nature of services, the studies recognize the importance of both B2B and B2C interactions among stakeholders [15, 61]. The enhanced market competition that is an inner characteristic of modern economies results also a driver of the positive influence of ICT towards innovation in services. On the other hand, ICT as a special capital input seems to lack the self-reinforcing mechanism that scholars postulated when referring to ICT both as a product and as a capital input within theme 1 [42–49]. Organizations have to invest complementary assets and innovative efforts to benefit from ICT as a special capital input with regards to innovation in services [61–63]. Especially important is innovative experience: service providers with long-term innovation strategy result more likely to benefit from the impact of ICT as special capital input on innovation [63]. Employee silence harnesses the potential benefits of ICT, as it contrasts knowledge sharing and collaborative value creation [62]. An important element for organizations to take into consideration is also the diversification of cases and circumstances, which require the adaptation of strategies, management and policies related to ICT and innovation in services [59, 60, 62, 64]. For what concerns the impact of ICT as a special capital input on innovation in services, scholars consider three types of innovation: (1) organizational innovation [15], with a special eye on outsourcing decision making processes [60]; (2) business model innovation [15]; (3) innovation in the service offering, both in terms of new services and new service delivery [15, 63].

4.6   Discussion: The Conceptual Typology

The analysis above provides a conceptual representation in form of a typology of the multifaceted relationship between ICT and innovation in services, shown in figure 1.

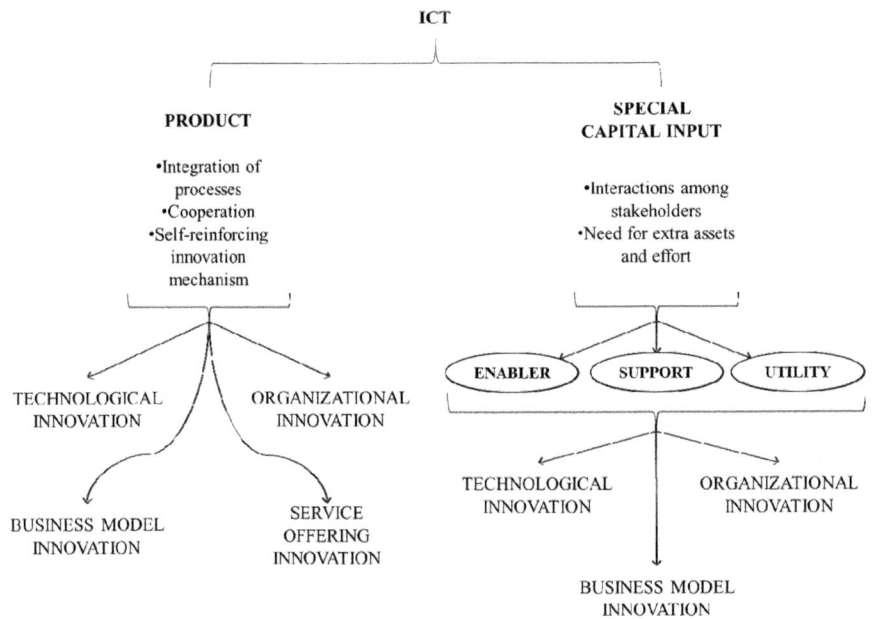

Fig. 1. The conceptual typology

Service innovation research on ICT as product highlighted how these technologies allow (1) the integration of organizational and innovation processes [35, 40, 41, 51, 55, 56]; and (2) the cooperation among internal and external agents [6, 35, 52, 56–58, 65]. Moreover, scholars recognize a (3) self-reinforcing innovation mechanism that impacts on innovation in services in various ways [42–50]. ICT as product can therefore be considered as technological innovation, but also in relation with other types of innovation. The activation of the self-reinforcing mechanism, in fact, is due to the enhanced connection opportunities, which, in turn, generate new possibilities for ICT-based services and products, but also for organizational structures and business models. Similarly, ICT impact as special capital input on innovation in services in terms of technological innovation, organizational innovation and business model innovation. However, when not involved also as product, ICT lack the self-reinforcing mechanism [63]: they require complementary assets and innovative effort to produce externalities and spillovers to positively influence innovation [61–63]. In particular, it is important to always adapt the ICT to the specific cases and circumstances to benefit from externalities and spillovers [59, 60, 62, 64]. This confirms and extends what found out in the preliminary literature review: the relationship between technology and innovation in services can positively impact on innovation in services if managed correctly [14, 19]. Whereas Jong et al. (2003) limited the impact on innovation in the service offering, further research extends it to technological, organizational and business model innovation.

Another important aspect of the relationship between ICT and innovation in services is related to the open innovation model by Chesbrough (2003). Many studies mention the co-productive nature of services as particularly close to the cooperation opportunities offered by ICT. Even though no study openly refers to Chesbrough's framework (2003), scholars report the enhanced cooperative innovation that directly steams from ICT, when considered both as product and as special capital input [15, 61]. The analyses indirectly refer to strongly enhanced B2C, as well as B2B interactions thanks to ICT, which become crucial drivers of knowledge sharing and collaborative value creation [15, 47, 57, 66]. The collected body of knowledge therefore extends Chesbrough's case on Amazon (2003), by showing the important role that ICT might play on both B2B and B2C interactions.

5   Conclusions, Limitations and Agenda for Future Research

The purpose of this literature review was to organize the fragmented work on the relationship between ICT and innovation in services to advance knowledge in the field and support future research. I answered the research question – How has previous literature investigated the relationship between ICT and innovation in services? – by identifying five umbrella themes under which I categorized the collected articles. The identified umbrella themes reflect the different facets of the relationship and are: (1) Management of ICT-based technology innovation; (2) Management of organizational innovation that result from the adoption of ICT; (3) Business model innovation; (4) ICT in NSD and service delivery innovation; (5) Relationship between ICT and innovation in services.

The results of the analysis allowed me to build a conceptual typology that summarizes the multi-faceted relationship between ICT and innovation in services, and may therefore be used as a support to plan and execute future research on ICT and innovation in services. First, the typology outlines the three main aspects of the link between ICT as product and innovation in services that have been identified from the analysis: (1) the integration of organizational and innovation processes; (2) the cooperation among internal and external agents; and (3) the self-reinforcing innovation mechanism that characterizes ICT as a product. Second, as special capital input, ICT impact on technological, organizational and business model innovation, but lack the self-reinforcing mechanism. Nevertheless, ICT as a special capital input might enhance the interactions among stakeholders and facilitate open innovation models, such as the one postulated by Chesbrough (2003).

The implications for organizations include the need to invest additional innovative effort and complementary capital inputs to benefit from ICT externalities and spillovers. The study has implications for IS, innovation and service researchers as well. Such implications are centered on the need to consider the differentiation between ICT as product and special capital input. In fact, this differentiation determines the character of the relationship between ICT and innovation in services and should be considered when addressing the issue.

The results of the literature review also highlight the most critical knowledge gaps within the problem area: (1) business model innovation related to ICT within service sectors; and (2) open innovation and ICT in practice. In the first case, further analysis is needed to better understand how ICT can better sustain business model innovation within services. Similarly, scholars should investigate further on the role of ICT within open innovation in services, as existing knowledge on the topic still lacks validation and specificity.

To conclude, this study is not free of limitations. The conceptual typology is the result of the analysis of a fragmented body of knowledge and thus requires additional work to add details on the many facets of the relationship between ICT and innovation in services. This study also needs empirical investigation of the conceptual typology in the service industry to explore its correspondence with reality.

Nonetheless, this paper provides a thorough literature review on the relationship between ICT and innovation in services, which allows outlining an agenda for future research. One of the main objectives of future research is the assessment of the causality of interactions between ICT and innovation in service, for example by developing a conceptual framework. Such framework should represent the causal links between and among the various elements of the relationship between ICT and innovation in services.

References

1. Atilgan-Inan, E., Büyükküpçü, A., Akinci, S.: A Content Analysis of Factors Affecting New Product Development Process. Business and Economics Research Journal 1, 87–100 (2010)
2. Metcalfe, J.S., Miles, I.: Innovation systems in the service economy: measurement and case study analysis. Kluwer Academic, Boston (2000)
3. Gallouj, F., Weinstein, O.: Innovation in services. Research Policy 26, 537–556 (1997)
4. Sundbo, J.: Management of Innovation in Services. The Service Industries Journal 17, 432–455 (1997)
5. Tether, B.S., Tajar, A.: The organizational-cooperation mode of innovation and its prominence amongst European service firms. Research Policy 37, 720–739 (2008)
6. Bygstad, B., Lanestedt, G.: ICT based service innovation – A challenge for project management. International Journal of Project Management 27, 234–242 (2009)
7. Chesbrough, H.: Bringing Open Innovation to Services. MIT Sloan Management Review 52, 85–90 (2011)
8. Scupola, A., Tuunainen, V.K.: Open innovation and role of ICT in business-to-business services–Empirical Evidence from Facility Management Services. In: Pre-ICIS Workshop Sigsvc 2011, Shangai (2011)

9. Webster, J., Watson, R.T.: Analyzing the past to prepare for the future: Writing a literature review. MIS Quarterly 26, xiii–xxiii (2002)
10. OECD: The Economic Impact of ICT. OECD Publishing (2004). National Center for Biotechnology Information, http://www.ncbi.nlm.nih.gov (retrieved January 5, 2012)
11. OECD: OECD Science, Technology and Industry Scoreboard - Statistics - OECD iLibrary, http://www.oecd-ilibrary.org/science-and-technology/oecd-science-technology-and-industry-scoreboard_20725345 (retrieved February 6, 2012)
12. Schreyer, P.: The contribution of information and communication technology to output growth. Statistical Working Party (99) (1999)
13. Grant, R.: Contemporary strategy analysis. Blackwell Publishing, Oxford (2005)
14. Jong, J.P.J.D., Bruins, A., Dolfsma, W., Meijaard, J.: Innovation in service firms explored: what, how and why? Business study. EIM – Business and Policy Research, Zoetermeer (January 2003)
15. Gago, D., Rubalcaba, L.: Innovation and ICT in service firms: towards a multidimensional approach for impact assessment. Journal of Evolutionary Economics 17, 25–44 (2006)
16. Cook, D., Goh, C.: Service typologies: a state of the art survey. Production and Operations 8, 318–338 (1999)
17. Fitzsimmons, J.A., Fitzsimmons, M.J.: New service development: creating memorable experiences. Sage Publications, Thousands Oaks (2000)
18. Fitzsimmons, J.A., Fitzsimmons, M.J.: Service management: operations, strategy, and information technology. McGraw-Hill/Irwin, Ney York (2006)
19. Jong, J.P.J.D., Vermeulen, P.A.M.: Organizing successful new service development: a literature review. Management Decision 41, 844–858 (2003)
20. Fagerberg, J., Mowery, D., Nelson, R.: The Oxford handbook of innovation. Oxford Handbooks Online. Oxford University Press, Oxford (2006)
21. den Hertog, P.: Knowledge-intensive business services as co-producers of innovation. International Journal of Innovation Management 4, 491–528 (2000)
22. Chesbrough, H., Rosenbloom, R.: The role of the business model in capturing value from innovation: evidence from Xerox Corporation's technology spin- off companies. Industrial and Corporate Change 11, 529–555 (2002)
23. Barras, R.: Towards a theory of innovation in services. Research Policy 15, 161–173 (1986)
24. Broadbent, M., Weill, P., Neo, B.: Strategic context and patterns of IT infrastructure capability. Journal of Strategic Information Systems 8, 157–187 (1999)
25. Mele, C., Spena, T.R., Colurcio, M.: Co-creating value innovation through resource integration. International Journal of Quality and Service Sciences 2, 60–78 (2010)
26. Potts, J., Mandeville, T.: Toward an Evolutionary Theory of Innovation and Growth in the Service Economy. Prometheus 25, 147–159 (2007)
27. Chesbrough, H.: The era of open innovation. MIT Sloan Management Review 44, 35–41 (2003)
28. Teece, D.: Profiting from technological innovation: Implications for integration, collaboration, licensing and public policy. Research Policy 15, 285–305 (1986)
29. Tether, B.S.: Who co-operates for innovation, and why: An empirical analysis. Research Policy 31, 947–967 (2002)
30. Leidner, D., Kayworth, T.: A review of culture in Information Systems Research: Toward a theory of Information Technology culture conflict. MIS Quarterly 30, 357–399 (2006)

31. Ram, S., Anbu, J.P., Kataria, S.: Responding to user's expectation in the library: innovative Web 2.0 applications at JUIT Library: A case study. Program: Electronic Library and Information Systems 45, 452–469 (2011)
32. Cocosila, M., Archer, N.: Adoption of mobile ICT for health promotion: an empirical investigation. Electronic Markets 20, 241–250 (2010)
33. Norum, J., Grev, A., Moen, M.A., Balteskard, L., Holthe, K.: Information and communication technology (ICT) in oncology. Patients' and relatives' experiences and suggestions. Supportive Care in Cancer: Official Journal of the Multinational Association of Supportive Care in Cancer 11, 286–293 (2003)
34. Shareef, M.A., Kumar, V., Kumar, U., Dwivedi, Y.K.: e-Government Adoption Model (GAM): Differing service maturity levels. Government Information Quarterly 28, 17–35 (2011)
35. Constantinides, P.: Large-Scale ICT Innovation, Power, and Organizational Change: The Case of a Regional Health Information Network. The Journal of Applied Behavioral Science 42, 76–90 (2006)
36. Campos, J., Jantunen, E., Prakash, O.: Development of a Maintenance System Based on Web and Mobile Technologies. Journal of International Technology and Information Management 16, 1–9 (2007)
37. Mangan, A., Kelly, S.: Information systems and the allure of organisational integration: a cautionary tale from the Irish financial services sector. European Journal of Information Systems 18, 66–78 (2009)
38. Wirth, W., von Pape, T., Karnowski, V.: An Integrative Model of Mobile Phone Appropriation. Journal of Computer-Mediated Communication 13, 593–617 (2008)
39. Gilbert, A.L., Han, H.: Understanding mobile data services adoption: Demography, attitudes or needs? Technological Forecasting and Social Change 72, 327–337 (2005)
40. Drozdová, M.: New business model of educational institutions. Ekonomie and Management 1, 60–68 (2008)
41. Jetter, M., Satzger, G., Neus, A.: Technological Innovation and Its Impact on Business Model, Organization and Corporate Culture – IBM's Transformation into a Globally Integrated, Service-Oriented Enterprise. Business & Information Systems Engineering 1, 37–45 (2008)
42. Chen, C., Watanabe, C.: Diffusion, substitution and competition dynamism inside the ICT market: The case of Japan. Technological Forecasting and Social Change 73, 731–759 (2006)
43. Chen, C., Watanabe, C., Griffybrown, C.: The co-evolution process of technological innovation—An empirical study of mobile phone vendors and telecommunication service operators in Japan. Technology in Society 29, 1–22 (2007)
44. Ayres, R., Williams, E.: The digital economy: Where do we stand? Technological Forecasting and Social Change 71, 315–339 (2004)
45. Lee, S.G., Trimi, S., Byun, W.K., Kang, M.: Innovation and imitation effects in Metaverse service adoption. Service Business 5, 155–172 (2011)
46. Bygstad, B.: Generative mechanisms for innovation in information infrastructures. Information and Organization 20, 156–168 (2010)
47. Bygstad, B., Aanby, H.: ICT infrastructure for innovation: A case study of the enterprise service bus approach. In: Vital And Health Statistics. Series 20 Data From The National Vitalstatistics System Vital Health Stat 20 Data Natl Vital Sta, pp. 257–265 (2010)
48. Lyytinen, K., Rose, G.M.: Disruptive information system innovation: the case of Internet computing. Information Systems Journal 13, 301–330 (2003)

49. Lee, S., Kim, M.-S., Park, Y.: ICT Co-evolution and Korean ICT strategy—An analysis based on patent data. Telecommunications Policy 33, 253–271 (2009)
50. Sharif, A.M.: It's written in the cloud: the hype and promise of cloud computing. Journal of Enterprise Information Management 23, 131–134 (2010)
51. Beynon-Davies, P.: Constructing electronic government: the case of the UK inland revenue. International Journal of Information Management 25, 3–20 (2005)
52. Paskaleva-Shapira, K., Azorín, J., Chiabai, A.: Enhancing digital access to local cultural heritage through e-governance: innovations in theory and practice from Genoa, Italy. Innovation: The European Journal of Social Science Research 21, 389–405 (2008)
53. Arduini, D., Belotti, F., Denni, M., Giungato, G., Zanfei, A.: Technology adoption and innovation in public services the case of e-government in Italy. Information Economics and Policy 22, 257–275 (2010)
54. Yovanof, G.S., Hazapis, G.N.: Disruptive Technologies, Services, or Business Models? Wireless Personal Communications 45, 569–583 (2008)
55. Leon, N., Davies, A.: Managed service paradox. IBM Systems Journal 47, 153–166 (2008)
56. Tuunainen, V.K., Tuunanen, T.: Mobile Service Platforms: Comparing Nokia OVI and Apple App Store with the IISIn Model. In: Mobile Business (ICMB), pp. 74–83 (2011)
57. Ritala, P., Hurmelinna-Laukkanen, P., Blomqvist, K.: Tug of war in innovation – coopetitive service development. Journal of Services 12, 255–272 (2009)
58. Siddiquee, N.A.: E-government and innovations in service delivery: the Malaysian experience. International Journal of Public Administration 31, 797–815 (2008)
59. Bauer, J.M.: Regulation, public policy, and investment in communications infrastructure. Telecommunications Policy 34, 65–79 (2010)
60. Williams, R., Graham, I., Jakobs, K., Lyytinen, K.: China and Global ICT standardisation and innovation. Technology Analysis & Strategic Management 23, 715–724 (2011)
61. Hidalgo Nuchera, A., López Rodríguez, V., Heras, L.J., Tafur Segura, J.J.: Drivers and Impact of ICT adaptation in the European Transport and Logistic Services (2008), http://oa.upm.es/3562/1/INVE_MEM_2008_55635.pdf
62. Gambarotto, F., Cammozzo, A.: Dreams of silence: Employee voice and innovation in a public sector community of practice. Innovation: Management Policy and Practice 12, 166 (2010)
63. Hempell, T.: Does experience matter? Innovations and the productivity of information and communication technologies in German services. Economics of Innovation and New Technology 14, 277–303 (2005)
64. Jbilou, J., Landry, R., Amara, N., El Adlouni, S.: Combining Communication Technology Utilization and Organizational Innovation: Evidence from Canadian Healthcare Decision Makers. Journal of Medical Systems 33, 275–286 (2008)
65. Moller, K., Rajal, H., Westerlund, M.: Service innovation myopia? A new recipe for client-provider value creation. California Management Review 50, 31 (2008)
66. Nylén, D., Holmström, J.: From Forestry Machines to Sociotechnical Hybrids: Investigating the Use of Digitally Enabled Forestry Machines. In: Chiasson, M., Henfridsson, O., Karsten, H., DeGross, J.I. (eds.) Researching the Future in Information Systems. IFIP AICT, vol. 356, pp. 199–214. Springer, Heidelberg (2011)

Appendix 1: Concept Matrix for Literature Review

#	Author(s)	Year	Micro	Meso	Macro	Sub-unit	Organization	Sector/Industry/Nation	Product	Process	ICT as enabler	ICT as support	ICT as utility for innovation	Technology innovation	Business model innovation	Organizational innovation	Innovation in the offering	Service delivery innovation	New Service Development	Open innovation	Buyer-seller relationship	Intra-organizational dynamics	B2C	B2B
			Level of analysis						ICT involvement					Type of innovation						Inter- and intra-organizational dynamics				
1	Jbilou,J.; Landry,R.; Amara,N.; El Adlouni,S.	2009					X			X								X						
2	Bygstad,B.; Aanby,H.	2010					X		X	X	X	X	X					X	X	X	X	X		
3	Campos,J.; Jantunen,E.; Prakash,O.	2007				X					X					X		X	X					
4	Gago,D.; Rubalcaba,L.	2007					X		X	X	X	X	X	X	X	X	X	X	X	X	X	X		
5	Norum,J.; Grev,A.;Moen,M.;Balteskard,L.;Holthe,K.	2003				X					X							X						
6	Leon,N.; Davis,A.	2008				X					X							X	X					
7	Moller,K.; Rajal, R.; Westerlund,M.	2008				X					X									X	X		X	X

No	Author	Year													
8	Siddique,N.	2008			X	X					X				
9	Paskaleva-Shapira,K.; Azorin,J.; Chaibai,A.	2008			X	X					X	X	X	X	X
10	Ram,S.; Anbu,J.P.; Kataria,S.	2011	X			X			X		X		X		
11	Sharif,A.M.	2010			X	X	X		X		X		X	X	X
12	Constantinides,P.; Barrett,M.	2006		X		X				X	X				X
13	Hempell,T.	2011			X	X	X	X	X		X				
14	Tuunainen,V.K.; Tuunanen,T.; Piispanen,J.	2011			X	X						X	X	X	
15	Hao,H.	2011			X			X			X		X		
16	Nylén,D.; Holmström, J.	2011	X				X			X				X	X
17	Ritala,P.; Hurmelinna-Laukkanen,P.; Blomqvist,K.	2009			X	X						X	X	X	X
18	Potts,J.; Mandeville,T.	2007			X			X	X						
19	Chen,C.; Watanabe,C.; Griffy-Brown,C.	2007			X	X					X			X	X
20	Ayres,R.U.; Williams,E.	2004			X	X	X				X				
21	Lee,S.G.; Trimi,S.; Byun,W.K.; Kang,M.	2011	X				X	X	X	X	X		X	X	
22	Williams,R.; Graham,I.; Jakobs,K.; Lyytinen,K.	2011			X	X	X	X	X			X		X	
23	Jimenez-Zarco,A.I.; Martinez-Ruiz,M.P.; Izquirdo-Yusta,A.	2011	X				X	X			X	X	X	X	X
24	Shareef,M.A.; Kumar,V.; Kumar,U.; Dwivedi,Y.K.;	2011			X	X					X		X	X	

#	Authors	Year														
25	Cocosila,M.; Archer,N.	2010	X		X		X			X			X			
26	Castellacci,F.	2010		X		X	X		X							
27	Gambarotto,F.; Cammozzo,A.	2010		X			X			X						X
28	Arduini,D.; Belotti,F.; Denni,M.; Giungato,G.; Zanfei,A.	2010		X	X				X	X						X
29	Bygstad,B.	2010		X		X	X						X			
30	Kanstrup,A.M.; Bjerge,K.; Kristensen,J.E.	2010	X				X		X		X	X	X			
31	Bauer,J.M.	2010			X	X	X		X	X	X					
32	Hidalgo,A.; Lopez,V.	2009		X			X	X	X							
33	Lee,S.; Kim,M.S.; Park,Y.	2009			X	X	X	X	X	X					X	
34	Bygstad,B.; Lanestedt,G.	2009		X		X						X	X	X	X	
35	Jetter,M.; Satzger,G.; Neus,A.	2009		X		X	X			X	X	X				X
36	Mangan,A.; Kelly,S.	2009		X		X				X		X				X
37	Yovanof,G.S.; Hazapis,G.N.	2008	X	X			X	X	X	X	X	X	X			
38	Wirth,W.; von Pape,T.; Karnowski,V.	2008	X			X				X						
39	Drozdova,M.	2008			X	X	X			X	X	X				
40	Chen,C.J.; Watanabe,C.	2006				X	X			X						
41	Gilbert,A.L.; Han,H.	2005			X		X	X					X			
42	Beynon-davies,P.	2005	X			X						X				X
43	Lyytinen,K.; Rose,G.M.	2003			X	X	X				X					

Appendix 2: Literature Search (Nov. 30th,2011)

1) **ABI Inform – Review and research articles**

- **1321** documents found for: (servic*) AND (innovat*) AND (ICT) AND LN(English)
- **80** documents found for: (servic*) AND SU(innovat*) AND (ICT) AND LN(English)
- **55** documents found for: SU(servic*) AND (innovat*) AND (ICT) AND LN(English)
- **18** documents found for: SU(servic*) AND SU(innovat*) AND (ICT) AND LN(English)
- No documents found for: SU(servic*) AND SU(innovat*) AND SU(ICT) AND LN(English)
- No documents found for: (servic*) AND SU(innovat*) AND SU(ICT) AND LN(English)

2) **SCOPUS – Review and research articles**

- **548** results found for: TITLE-ABS-KEY(innovat* AND servic* AND ict*)
- **489** results found for: TITLE-ABS-KEY(innovat* AND servic* AND ict*) AND SUBJAREA(mult OR ceng OR CHEM OR comp OR eart OR ener OR engi OR envi OR mate OR math OR phys OR mult OR arts OR busi OR deci OR econ OR psyc OR soci)
- **216** results found for: TITLE-ABS-KEY(innovat* AND servic* AND ict) AND SUBJAREA(mult OR arts OR busi OR deci OR econ OR psyc OR soci)
- **17** results found for: KEY(innovat* AND servic* AND ict) AND SUBJAREA(mult OR arts OR busi OR deci OR econ OR psyc OR soci)

3) **ISI – Review and research articles**

- **116** results for Topic=(servic*) AND Topic=(innovat*) AND Topic=(ICT) AND Language=(English)
- **59 results for** Topic=(servic*) AND Topic=(innovat*) AND Topic=(ICT) AND Language=(English)

Refined by: [excluding] Web of Science Categories=(GENETICS HEREDITY OR ENVIRONMENTAL SCIENCES OR HEALTH POLICY SERVICES OR MEDICAL INFORMATICS OR INDUSTRIAL RELATIONS LABOR OR METALLURGY METALLURGICAL ENGINEERING OR AGRICULTURE MULTIDISCIPLINARY OR NEUROSCIENCES OR NURSING OR PHYSIOLOGY OR PLANT SCIENCES OR AGRONOMY OR PSYCHIATRY OR PSYCHOLOGY CLINICAL OR BIODIVERSITY CONSERVATION OR PUBLIC ENVIRONMENTAL OCCUPATIONAL HEALTH OR REHABILITATION OR ENERGY FUELS OR GEOGRAPHY OR ENGINEERING AEROSPACE OR HEALTH CARE SCIENCES SERVICES) AND [excluding] Web of Science Categories=(ENGINEERING INDUSTRIAL OR OPERATIONS RESEARCH MANAGEMENT SCIENCE OR AUTOMATION CONTROL SYSTEMS OR EDUCATION EDUCATIONAL RESEARCH OR BUSINESS FINANCE OR ENGINEERING ELECTRICAL ELECTRONIC OR COMPUTER SCIENCE ARTIFICIAL INTELLIGENCE OR PUBLIC ADMINISTRATION OR ENGINEERING MANUFACTURING OR COMPUTER SCIENCE SOFTWARE ENGINEERING OR ENVIRONMENTAL STUDIES OR COMPUTER SCIENCE THEORY METHODS OR TRANSPORTATION SCIENCE TECHNOLOGY

Understanding and Managing Process Interaction
in IS Development Projects

Bendik Bygstad[1] and Peter Axel Nielsen[2,3]

[1] Norwegian School of IT, Oslo, Norway
[2] Research Centre for Socio-Interactive Design Aalborg University, Denmark
[3] Department of Information Systems, University of Agder, Norway
bygben@nith.no, pan@cs.aau.dk

Abstract. Software-based information systems must be developed and implemented as a part of business change. This is a major challenge, since business change and the development of software-based information systems usually are performed in separate processes. Thus, there is a need to understand and manage the relationship between these two kinds of processes. In this paper we draw on a longitudinal case study. We suggest a framework to analyze the case as interaction between software development processes and organizational change processes. In the analysis we find that the framework enables us to understand critical events in the case, what led to the events, and what the consequences are. We discuss the implications for information systems research and in particular we discuss the contribution to project management of iterative and incremental software development.

Keywords: process interaction, project management, iterative software development, longitudinal process research.

1   Introduction

This paper is about the necessary interaction between two processes; the software development process and planned organizational change. The challenge that comes from the need to align IT and business is not new, but has consistently been at the top five concerns for CIO for the last decade [1-3].

We find that this also has important bearings on how software-based information systems should be developed. There is indication that IS project managers are facing several new challenges; to name a few: (1) The speed of change, driven by globalization, demands that information systems should be delivered in parallel with business change. Often it is no longer an option for the organization to "wait" while a new system is developed [4], and IT is expected to contribute to organizational agility [5] rather than hinder it. (2) The power balance between the organization and the IT departments has changed. Instead of humble users, the IS and software project managers meet powerful organizational actors who are well aware of IS failures and are inquisitive of the value of IT investments [6].

In this paper we are trying to make sense of a large development project where the project managers faced similar challenges. The existing literature is valuable in

C. Keller et al. (Eds.): SCIS 2012, LNBIP 124, pp. 25–43, 2012.
© Springer-Verlag Berlin Heidelberg 2012

explaining the case study, but it also does not explain the core of the problems facing the project manager, namely, how to organize the interaction between the software development and the business change. We suggest in this paper a process view that is intended to provide a perspective on the interaction between software development processes and organizational change processes; or *process interaction* for short. By taking a process view we have a particular focus on what has happened in terms of events, their antecedents and implications [7]. We also bringing to the foreground the *development* processes and leave the issues in the background concerning how software-based information systems may be used in an organization and hence influence that organization.

Altogether, we are in this paper addressing the following two research questions:

- How can we *understand* process interaction, i.e., interaction between software development processes and organizational change processes?
- How can a software project manager of iterative and incremental software development processes *manage* process interaction?

Throughout this paper we take the standpoint of the project manager of software development. The software project manager has roles and responsibilities that are significantly different from managers of organizational change or general managers of the business organization.

2   Software Development and Organizational Change

In this section we provide a brief overview of research that is relevant to the research questions. The scope of the review is that of software *development* and its relationship with organizational *change*. Outside this scope is thus research that addresses information systems and their relationships with organizations or otherwise does not pertain to a development perspective.

We have identified seven related, but different research stream: IS development project management, socio-technical IS development methodologies, Scandinavian systems development, IS implementation, business process innovation, enterprise architecture, and iterative software engineering. For each research stream we present its main concern as well as how it contributes to the issues raised in this paper. Table 1 provides an overview of the literature.

IS Project Management: Normative IS project management research has for a long time addressed organizational issues like business alignment, risk management, and stakeholder analysis [9]. This research tends to be concerned with control. Common issues are: managing the systems life cycle, estimation, modeling, quality, scheduling, and cost. It is hardly surprising that control has become a common denominator given the turbulent history of software project failures. On the other hand, much of the normative software project research gives the impression that software projects are standalone projects starting from scratch.

Table 1. Research streams relevant to process interaction

Research stream	Main concern	Contribution to process interaction
IS project management [8-10]	Controlling the project and its environment's influence on its conditions. Projects should be aligned with business strategy.	The IS project manager has co-responsibility for value produced by the information system.
Socio-technical ISD methodologies [11-13]	Technical development should be part of organizational and human development.	An information system design cannot be separated from the organization design, and it should be developed in an integrated process.
Scandinavian ISD [14-16]	Systems development should be a part of organizational change, and with strong user participation.	The IS project manager should be a change agent for the organizational use of the information system.
IS implementation [17-19]	Mutual adaptation between the organization and the technology is necessary for a good solution.	Both work processes and technology may be modified in a dynamic and emergent process
Business process innovation [20]	Businesses should be organized as processes, not functions.	IT is an enabler of business process innovation.
Enterprise architecture and business process management [21]	Business aims, processes and IT solutions should be treated as an integrated whole.	A modeling approach is useful for integration and better communication.
Iterative software engineering [22-24]	Iterative and incremental development reduces technical and organizational risks.	Developers and business people should work very closely to produce useful solutions.

A recent contribution is the notion of value management, which aims to identify and manage business value in addition to cost in software projects [8, 9]. Value management is based on stakeholder analysis, and thus expands the scope of the project beyond its traditional introvert perspective. Value management is not widely used, and it has so far not been integrated with current software engineering frameworks.

A rather fundamental critique has been raised during the past 15 years against the top-down planning and control approach; that it does not reflect practice. A number of empirical studies of IS development projects find that projects are situated and emergent and require skills like empathy and improvisation rather than managerial control [25-27].

While many of the techniques from IS/software project management research may very well be necessary and useful for project management it is also a limited view.

This stream of research has little to offer on the interaction between the software development process and the organizational change process.

Socio-technical IS Development Methods: The socio-technical tradition within information systems development arose to deal with the single purpose of creating a fit between an organization and the social world on the one hand and the technologies and their employment in information systems on the other [28]. An information system design cannot be separated from the organization design, and it should be developed in an integrated process.

The socio-technical methodologies like ETHICS [13] and Multiview [11, 12] takes this holistic view into IS development. Great care is taken to ensure a correct diagnosis of the organizational problem and to establish real business objectives, to analyze the human and technical aspects of the new solution in an integrated way, to ensure real user participation and to design a socio-technical solution.

However, although the socio-technical approaches criticize a static view of the organizational implementation of information systems, ETHICS and Multiview are primarily concerned with analysis and design and ignores the development of software as the foundation for software-based information systems. Despite improvements the overall image remains; these methodologies have not really addressed the need for process interaction. They are also not much used in practice [29].

Scandinavian Systems Development: Scandinavian systems development research has consistently focused on organizational issues [30], in particular the end users [14]. Dahlbom and Mathiassen [15] described alternative approaches to the organizational issue, and concluded that the systems developer should act as an organizational change agent.

This ambitious program has not been much visible in practice, and one of the reasons is probably that most project managers lack the necessary knowledge and resources to make this happen. Some interesting cases of integrated projects are documented, for example [31] from Norwegian municipalities and Bardram's account of organizational prototyping [32]. However, these examples refer to small and relatively simple projects in terms of organizational complexity. While providing interesting cases they hardly address the more complex challenges of combining large scale systems development and organizational change, which are usually performed as separate processes managed by fundamentally different process models and management cultures [33, 34].

IS Implementation: In IS implementation research the focus has been on human, social and business effects. Leonard-Barton showed that successful organizational implementation of information systems depends on the mutual adaptation of the technology and the organization [18, 35]. Newman and Robey [19] described information systems development as a social process and suggested an integrated process model based on encounters between analysts and users. A different approach was the information infrastructure perspective, focusing on the installed base of social and technical elements, and the dynamics of bootstrapping and scaling [36].

These contributions have documented theoretically and empirically that the organizational impact of an information system is not deterministic on the structuring of work processes, and that both work processes and technology may be modified in a dynamic and emergent process.

While these contributions have provided important insights, they are not very specific in terms of practical guidance for the software project manager. They insist that the process of organizational change and technical change should be holistic and mutually adaptive, but they do not provide sufficient guidelines to solve the challenge of process interaction.

Business Process Innovation: In the early 1990s first Hammer and then Davenport introduced process innovation as a dramatic rethinking of how businesses should be organized; as processes, not functions [37]. Davenport defined the innovation process itself in five steps; identifying processes suited for innovation, identifying opportunities for innovation, develop process vision, understand existing process and design new process prototype. Software-based systems were described as key resources, both as enabler and as implementer of business processes. Davenport paid due respect to IS development methods and emphasized that IS development should fit with the corresponding processes. However, these rather general guidelines were never worked into an integrated methodology for combining IS development and process innovation [34].

Enterprise Architecture and Business Process Management: A more recent approach was enterprise architecture and business process management, which present a holistic view on both the processes and the IT capabilities of the organization, in order to ensure that individual projects can build capabilities – not just fulfill immediate needs [21]. It also emphasizes that a modeling approach is useful for integration of different levels and provides better communication.

While this approach presents an integrative view on information systems and organizational change, it does so on a relatively high level. It does not address how this should be done in more detail, and it does not relate much to the established methods for developing and implementing information systems.

Iterative Software Engineering: Modern software engineering has addressed the challenge of alignment with the organization in several ways. In 1988, as a response to the quality problems of software constructions, Boehm proposed a spiral model for software development with an iterative structure allowing for more frequent interaction with users and customers. The iterative approaches took on the challenge of unstable and changing requirements due to complex organizational issues and changing organizations. Further, both object-oriented methodologies like OOA&D [38] and Rational Unified Process [23] and the agile methodologies like Extreme Programming [39], Crystal Methodologies [40] and Scrum [24] embrace the iterative approaches for these reasons. These approaches are all strong on technical development while organizational issues and development are taken more lightly.

The dominating software engineering methodologies pay lip service to an integrated approach, but concentrate on producing the software product. The organization is seen as very important, but mainly as an arena for eliciting the requirements – not as a target for change.

3   Process Interaction

In this framework we see the organization as a combination of two: a business organization embedded in and supported by an information infrastructure. The business organization includes the formal structure of the organization, its decision and knowledge management processes as well as informal structures and processes. We regard the organization as being supported by an information infrastructure. Following Hanseth and Monteiro we regard the information infrastructure as a heterogeneous network comprising an installed base of technology, organization, culture and work practices [17, 41]. The features of this information infrastructure influence both the opportunities and the constraints. In a successful organization, this information infrastructure is an immensely valuable resource. It constitutes a backbone of the organization. However, in a world of change it is also a barrier to organizational innovation because the information infrastructure is difficult and expensive to change. This is shown in figure 1 as the organization and the information infrastructure forming together a whole and glued together in complex ways.

Planned organizational change is generally accomplished through a top-down intervention to improve the problem-solving abilities of an organization [33, 42]. Organizational change projects often use variants of Lewin's classical stage model. First, the organization is assessed and diagnosed. Then, it goes through an unfreeze stage where old patterns are loosened. In the third stage, the actual changes in routines and roles are performed, while the new structure is re-freezed in the fourth stage [42]. There are other models of organizational change like business process re-engineering [43] or total quality management [44]; but for the purposes in this paper we shall make no further assumption on how organizational change comes about.

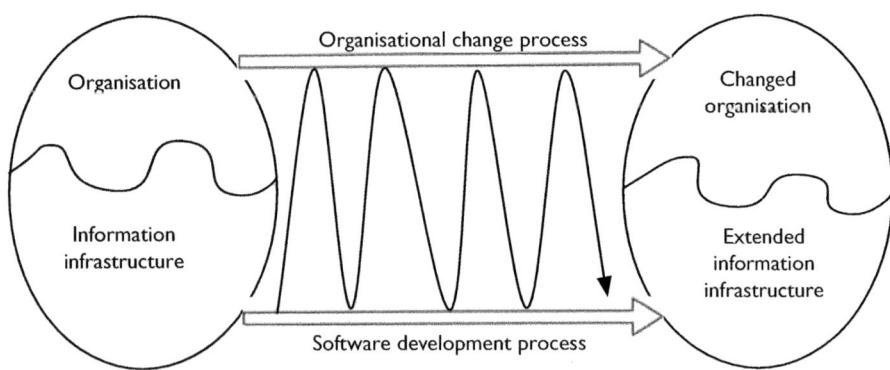

Fig. 1. Process interaction

We apply a process view on organizational change as well as on software development. Our concern here is the interaction between these processes. Following Newman and Robey we think it is not sufficient simply to state that these processes interact [19]. To the left in figure 1 is the existing organization forming a whole with the existing information infrastructure. We then envisage an organizational change initiative with two projects: An organizational change project performed to change the organization and a software development project performed to change the information infrastructure. In the framework, the target for the organization change processes is a changed organization that again forms a whole with the new and modified information infrastructure; but a quite different process, namely the software development process, changes this infrastructure. The software development process produces among all its results and deliverables the software that will be a major part of the extended information infrastructure.

The two processes are quite different in scope, management techniques and structure. The scope of the organizational change processes is to change the organization; while the scope of the software development processes is to develop a software-based information system. The organizational change process is usually based on management interventions on different levels: organization, team or individual [42], while the software development process is focused on an array of methodologies, techniques, tools and models. Most organizational change projects follow a waterfall model while most modern software development projects tend to be iterative and sometimes even agile. To understand and consequently manage the interaction between these processes we need to addresses the different ways that software development processes and organizational change processes interact during the period from beginning to end, as illustrated in figure 1.

4   Research Approach

The research approach is case study of the particular kind called longitudinal process research.

The case is based in the company Airline that is an international airline carrier in Scandinavia. As a part of the Marketing Division, the Airline established an Electronic Direct Channel (EDC), which was responsible for selling airline tickets and hotel reservations on the Internet. Adding sales from other online agents, Internet sales were expected to account for 25% of sales by 2005. Simplified, the tasks of the EDC were: marketing air tickets in different national markets on the Scandinavian website and receiving electronic orders. Feedback mechanisms were to be home page hits and actual bookings.

Acknowledging the commercial potential of web-based booking, the Airline decided to establish a web-based marketing channel in all important markets: Europe, Asia and the Americas. To support this new organization, a new content management and publishing system was needed. A project was initiated with the following objectives:

- To establish a web-based marketing channel in all important markets.
- To enable the editors using an easy tool to publish materials and campaigns.
- To integrate this new information system with the booking systems.

A project group of five (one project manager, one web designer and three programmers) was set up the software development project. Following earlier practice, a parallel customer project was established with an Airline project manager and a user group consisting mainly of web editors.

The case study was planned and carried out using longitudinal process research (LPR). We take LPR to be an intensive research approach that focuses attention on organizational processes as experienced by organizational actors [45-48]. LPR is the study of organizational processes with the intention of developing contextualized theories about them. According to Ngwenyama [46], the researcher conducts an intensive analysis of the context, temporal order and underlying logic of events in the organizational process under study. In our case study, we have studied organizational change processes and IS development processes as they were performed over time in and around a complex project.

LPR is based on three criteria for data collection [46]:

- Engagement with the research site is required to build any substantive theory of organizational processes.
- Participant observation enables the researcher to contextualize in making sense of practices and situations. It also makes the researcher sensitive to organizational insights encoded into actors' actions and language.
- Validity is ensured through: multiple sources of data, systematic data gathering and reliable data recording or transcription. This requires the researcher to gather empirical data so that all perspectives of the organizational processes are covered and findings can be corroborated.

4.1   Data Collection

The data was collected over a period of a year and a half while the software development project being studied lasted for almost a year. The main data source was semi-structured interviews utilizing an interview guide. The interview guide was designed to reflect a particular interest in iterative software development processes. Interviews were conducted at two sites, Stockholm and Oslo, in order to get data from inside the project and from the prospective users and other stakeholders. In addition, project meetings were observed and the findings were discussed with stakeholders. Interviews with international web editors were done by email. A secondary source of data was the huge amount of project documentation comprised of both product documentation and process documentation.

The data collection, which was done in four phases and is summarized in table 2.

Table 2. Data collection

Phase	Activities	Stakeholders	Documents
Phase 1	Initial meeting with management to agree on objectives and procedures in the study, and to collect documentation	Line manager Project managers	Project objectives and plans
Phase 2	Workshop with project and business stakeholders to get the broad picture, and separate interviews	Project manager Project group Business users	Status reports Technical documents: SW architecture, use cases, etc.
Phase 3	Separate interviews with stakeholders to construct full time line in project	Project manager Project group Business users	Status reports Project evaluation report Release notes
Phase 4	Last round of interviews. Validation meeting to confirm and discuss findings.	Line manager Project manager Business users	Case description

4.2 Data Analysis

LPR suggests three modes for data analysis to assist the researcher in closing the gaps between the findings and the empirical data [46]:

- Comprehensive analysis helps to reveal and surface deeper structures of the organizational processes.
- Temporal analysis helps to contextualize findings by placing events and situations in a narrative structure.
- Member verification ensures that interpretations and case descriptions made by the researcher are meaningful to the organizational actors.

Interview summaries and project documents were registered into an Atlas.ti database and coded. Then a systematic search for patterns was conducted using the Atlas.ti search tool. First, a timeline with significant events and iterative phases was produced. Second, iterations, context, actors, and artefacts were modeled graphically as an emerging socio-technical network. Third, a case description was written. The case description was written gradually over time, in a process of learning and also negotiation between the researcher and the stakeholders. The case description was written and rewritten for each phase (cf. table 2) of interviews as both the project stakeholders and the researcher reinterpreted the organizational processes. For example, the challenge of how the software development processes should interact with the organizational change processes was in the background in the first round, but was in the forefront during the problematic period.

The analysis further builds on the idea of critical events [48]. We split the temporal analysis into events that are critical to process interaction. We describe each critical event, its preconditions in terms of what led to the event and its consequence in terms of activities following the event. We then illustrated and explained the kind of process interaction taking place. The analysis of critical events is close to the kind of analysis where Newman and Robey [19] sliced a time scale into incidents and episodes.

5   The Case

Building on the longitudinal process analysis we identified five events particularly critical to the process interaction in the case. The five events occurred in the time order as described and the result of the former event formed the pre-condition for the next. They are described in table 3.

Table 3. Critical events in the case

Pre-condition	Critical event	Following activity	Process interaction
E-business part of airline tickets expected to grow	The Airline decides to establish a decentralized e-marketing organization.	Two projects started: Organizational change Software development	Formal agreement between the two processes
Workshops are held to specify solution	Workshops with marketing editors fail.	Editors withdraw and the project focuses on technical issues	A breakdown of the interaction between processes.
The software project lacks relevant input	The Airline project manager becomes involved in the software development.	The software solution is developed successfully	Organizational process inactive. The software development process isolated
International editors are recruited	New marketing editors enter	After a course in Stockholm, the editors start testing the system. A lot of change requests and technical problems.	Improvised interaction between the two processes.
The technical solution is stabilized	Start-up	The new business organization starts to use the new solution successfully.	The interaction is well structured even into production

Critical event 1: The Airline decides to establish a decentralized e-marketing organization

The Airline decided to establish a web-based marketing channel in all critical markets. Two projects were initiated:

- An organizational project where international editors in the actual markets were recruited, trained and put in charge of the e-business operation, as a part of the marketing division. Part of this project was a group of Scandinavian editors, who represented the Airline in the software project, headed by a project manager.

- A software development project to develop the new content management and publishing solution to be used. This consisted of an experienced project manager and four developers.

The aim of the two projects was to establish a new organizational process supported by an extended information infrastructure, as illustrated in figure 2.

| Event 1:
Airline decided to establish decentralized e-marketing organization.

Result:
Formal agreement between the two processes | 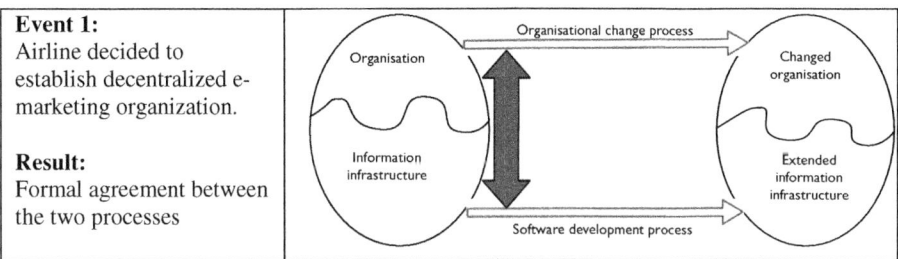 |

Fig. 2. Critical event 1

The two projects were nicely aligned and the new organization and system were planned to go into production in the following summer. However, the projects were not integrated into a common plan; rather they ran in parallel. The process models were also different: the organizational change project followed a waterfall structure, while the software development project followed an iterative and incremental structure using the Rational Unified Process. The software project was planned with five iterations. Each iteration was set up to follow the workflows in the Rational Unified Process starting with a revision of requirements, proceeding with design, coding and testing and ending with an increment, a temporary release, to be validated by the users.

We have characterized the result of this event as a *formal agreement between the two processes*; they were established with a common goal and an intention to interact during the project. This is illustrated by the unbroken arrow, which - as with subsequent figures - is used for illustration purposes and not to suggest a formal syntax.

Critical Event 2: Workshops with Editors Fail

In the two first iterations, the two project groups extended the number of use cases into 20 detailed ones. Then, they started working on a graphical prototype trying to translate the use cases visually. The workshops were not very successful and the participants interpreted them differently: the Airline project manager, who was now elaborating the software requirements specification, was moderately satisfied. According to him:

> "The workshop in the first iteration was OK because it gave the users an impression of the system. The workshop in the second was useful, but we were not able to show the users how the system would work."

Some of the editors felt alienated from the whole concept:

> "We spoke different languages, and they had no idea how we worked. We were polite and there was no conflict, but that was how we felt. We thought we might get it straight later on in the process. Use cases focused on the new system – not on how things were solved today. Development was system oriented, not on the work process."

Later, the developers said:

> "Of course, the graphical prototype should have been a full architectural prototype, but this was not possible because the necessary component from the other project was not ready. In addition, the editors did not really prioritize the workshops."

Not surprisingly, the results were unsatisfying. Nobody felt that the graphical prototype was useful. In addition, the project was held up by an important component from a sister project in Copenhagen that was delayed by six weeks. Thus, by the end of the elaboration phase (the analysis and design phase in the Rational Unified Process) the two main goals had not been reached: the business users and developers did not have a shared view of the system, and the architecture of the system was not stable.

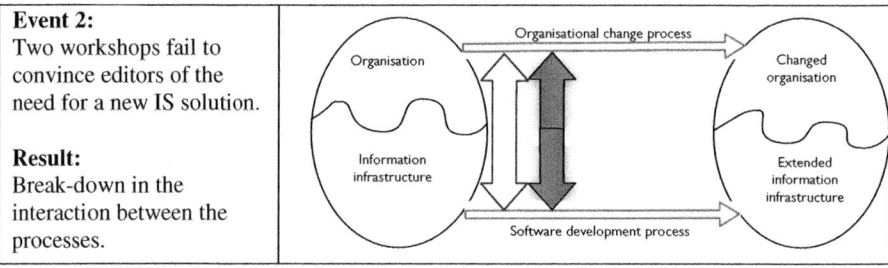

Fig. 3. Critical event 2

The result of event 2 was a break-down in the interaction between the two processes. The marketing editor group was unconvinced about the need for the new system, and the software project group lacked both user input and software components. In figure 3, the discontinuous arrow illustrates this.

Critical event 3: The Airline project manager becomes involved in software development

In the third iteration, the project group got a better grip on the technology and started to work more closely with the Airline project manager, who was now sitting in the same room. This iteration produced the basic functionality, enabling the users to upload content to the content database.

In the fourth iteration, the first release of the necessary component arrived and the crucial functionality of creating web pages was developed. In a few intense and informal work sessions, a design was developed as the application was prototyped. One of the developers commented:

"When the Airline PM really joined the team, the whole atmosphere changed. We were able to experiment with screens and solutions at a practical level. Also, it was important that he really understood the technical difficulties involved. We were sitting long hours together solving real problems. It was very productive and also great fun!"

Event 3: The airline PM gets involved in software development. **Result:** Isolation of the software project.	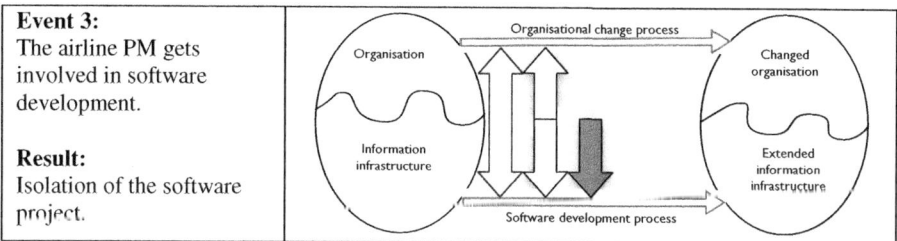

Fig. 4. Critical event 3

Although the software project's spirit and technical results were greatly improved during the third and fourth iterations, the result of event 3 was that the interaction between the two processes stopped. The Scandinavian editors had withdrawn, and the international editors were not yet recruited while the Airline project manager practically had "changed sides". This left the project unintentionally "encapsulated", concentrating on the (quite challenging) technical issues. In figure 4, the half arrow, pointing at the software development process, illustrates this.

Critical event 4: New editors enter

In the winter of 2001 the international marketing editors were recruited. After a period of technical problems during testing, a beta version was presented for the international editors: In a two-day course in Stockholm for all the marketing editors, totaling at that time around 30. Most of them were introduced to the system right there without much preparation. In spite of technical stability problems and long response time due to slow APIs in the Vignette platform, the market organization and the software team perceived the course as rather successful for most of the editors. A few editors were less motivated and lacked the basic IT skills.

After the course, the editors went home and started to load materials into a test database that was later set into production. In this period, the project worked hard with error corrections and use case change orders. The project manager said:

"Many new features were wanted from editors, both Scandinavian and the others, especially navigation features tightly connected to their work processes, page search and design. We were surprised by the volume of change orders."

The result of Critical Event 4 was that the interaction between the two processes was reinitiated. The nature of this interaction was not controlled by the RUP iteration as the previous iterations of the software project had proceeded. Rather, it was characterized by improvisation and problem solving. This is illustrated in Figure 5 by the two arrows pointing towards each other.

Event 4: New marketing editors enter. **Result:** Improvised interaction.	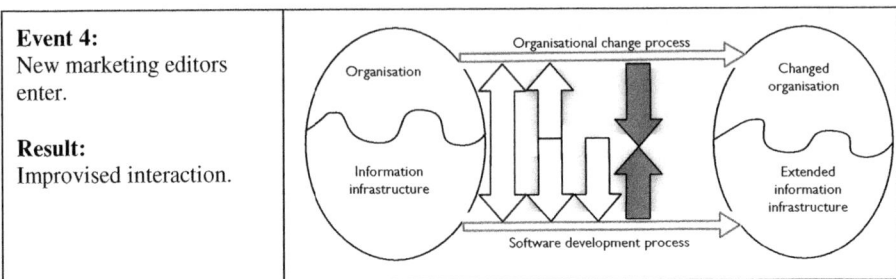

Fig. 5. Critical event 4

Critical event 5: Into production

Eventually all the software went into production. Some technical problems were experienced, but afterwards the technical solution was stable and in use in the new international organization. There were 50-60 users of the system: six editors in Scandinavia, the rest in Europe, USA and Asia. Most of these were part-time editors with main responsibilities in marketing or sales. Campaigns were started at a central Marketing division level or at a national level. The system allows the national editors to tailor their web pages to their local markets. The head of marketing and the editors in cooperation usually planned campaigns with external, creative consultants and bureaus. The day-to-day monitoring of the result of the campaigns was done on two parameters: the Marketing department followed the Internet traffic on the web site, while the Revenue Management monitored the actual booking. The running marketing decisions were taken on the basis of this monitoring.

Although the number of change requests remained high for the first year of operations, the international editors were satisfied. One international editor commented:

> "It aids our communication strategy of distributing information instantly (almost) of developments to the SAS product that affect our customers. It provides a means of tailoring our communication to suit the needs of our customers in Australia."

The international editors reported that the system was relatively easy to use, but that the step-wise structure was time-consuming:

> "Pages are created in steps so once you understand the sequence it's fairly straight forward."

> "... I do find it takes quite some time to load a new page because of all the stages you need to go through combined with the speed of the system."

Setting the system into production was, despite some technical problems, successful, and thus, the result of the 5th critical event was that the two processes interacted as intended. The redesigned organization (decentralized web marketing) was aligned and integrated with the extended information infrastructure including the system's publishing solution. This is illustrated in figure 6 by the unbroken arrow.

Event 5: Into production. **Result:** Organized interaction	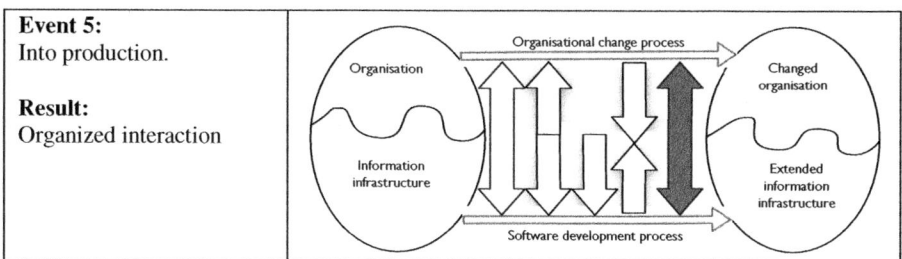

Fig. 6. Critical event 5

6   Discussion

The focus in this paper is on process interaction and we have chosen to focus our presentation on the aspects of the case that relates to this perspective. We think the evidence in this case shows that the basic problem was not poor project management. The two project managers certainly knew they were facing great challenges and they started by forming two projects with a formal agreement between them (critical event #1). The effort to establish a better e-business platform was a high profile project at the time. The Airline had also previously been through similar large projects and had considerable experience with projects of such complexity.

However, between critical event #2 and critical event #4 the two processes, for reasons partly outside the control of the two project managers, lost contact. The process interaction suffered greatly under this and was not rescued until critical event #4 where new stakeholders entered. The new stakeholders, the marketing editors, allocate time and resources to process interaction by providing detailed feedback to the software development project through testing of the software. Thus, the projects were not necessarily poorly managed, but the process interaction was not organised and not managed.

How could the project managers in the case have been improved using the proposed framework? First, the two projects could have been designed to interact better. In this planning, the project managers would have seen that the waterfall structure of the organizational change project was incongruent with the iterative structure of the software development project. The easy intervention would have been to create planned interaction at certain intervals, ensuring that the iterative software development project received the necessary input. Alternatively, and more expensively, the organizational change project could have been designed following an iterative process. Such frameworks for organization change are available [42].

Second, when the critical events occurred, the framework could have been used to assess the situation in much the same way as we have done in the case description. This would provide a better basis for intervening into both the organizational change processes and the IS development processes. At critical event #2 the software development project should have insisted that the feedback on the early prototypes was a necessary condition for getting the requirements right. At critical event #3 the Airline project manager should not have left the organizational change process; but should have insisted that time and resources should be allocated to the organizational change. At critical event #4 the process interaction increases and the only problem with process interaction was that it came very late in the process. This created much turbulence for the software development process at a time when the requirements should have been fixed well before.

We have showed in section 2 that normative IS and software project management research has a strong focus on control [9, 10]. Our framework illustrates the limitations of this perspective. There is a risk that this strong focus on control may constitute a barrier to process interaction. The reason is that the project managers (both the software development project manager and the organizational change project manager) may prefer to maintain internal project control rather than risk the uncertainties of interaction. As illustrated in the case this will increase project control, but also increase the overall risk of the project.

The software engineering frameworks, building on iterative and incremental principles of development processes [23, 40, 49] have improved software development considerably over the last years. We also find that these frameworks have an interesting potential for socio-technical innovation [51].

However, the research on agile software development [24, 40, 49] has a rather limited view on the challenges posed by process interaction . The case shows that there is much more to interaction than user participation and prototyping. To work effectively in a socio-technical context, the software development process is dependent on interaction with the organizational change process. As the case illustrates, this represents a considerable challenge. The first barrier is that there is hardly any awareness on the organizational change side of this need since software development projects are usually seen as merely technical projects. The second barrier is that the structures of the two processes are incongruent. Most organizational change projects follow a waterfall model making frequent interaction much less desirable. Software engineering projects, on the other hand, are iterative and incremental in ways that would not make sense without frequent interaction.

7   Conclusion

In this paper, we propose a framework of process interaction. Process interaction focuses attention on the meeting between the planned organizational change process and the software development process.

The framework consists of the conceptualization of process interaction as depicted in figure 1. The focus is not as much on the organization integrated with the information infrastructure as it is on the two processes leading to a changed organization and an extended information infrastructure, respectively. In particular, we have with this framework drawn attention to how the interaction plays out in an organizational and temporal context.

We have used the framework to analyze a longitudinal case from the airline carrier business and found that it enables us to understand critical events in the case. Altogether, the framework does provide understanding of process interaction and thereby we have addressed the first research question set in the introduction. We have provided a detailed answer to a particular way of addressing the question and we have in sections 4 and 5 shows the usefulness of the framework.

Our findings also lead to the need for further research into the applicability of our framework where both existing and new cases could be analyzed with the framework. A long-term vision would be to extend current software engineering frameworks and software development methodologies to encompass the process interaction.

References

1. Luftman, J., Ben-Zvi, T.: Key issues for IT executives 2010: Judicious IT investments continue post-recession. MIS Quarterly Executive 9 (2010)
2. Luftman, J., Kempaiah, R.: An update on business-IT alignment: "A line" has been drawn. MIS Quarterly Executive 6 (2007)
3. Luftman, J., McLean, E.R.: Key issues for IT executives. MIS Quarterly Executive 3, 89–104 (2004)
4. Stapleton, J.: DSDM: Business focused development. Addison-Wesley, Harlow (2003)
5. Sambamurthy, V., Bharadwaj, A., Grover, V.: Shaping agility through digital options: Reconceptualizing the role of information technology in contemporary firms. MIS Quarterly 27, 237–263 (2003)
6. Carr, N.: IT doesn't matter. Harvard Business Review 81, 41–49 (2003)
7. Markus, M.L., Robey, D.: Information technology and organizational change: Causal structure in theory and research. Management Science 34, 583–598 (1988)
8. Boehm, B.W.: Value-based software engineering. ACM SIGSOFT Software Engineering Notes 28, 112 (2003)
9. Cadle, J., Yeates, D.: Project management for information systems. Prentice-Hall, Harlow (2004)
10. McManus, J., Wood-Harper, A.T.: Information systems project management. Prentice-Hall, Harlow (2003)
11. Avison, D., Wood-Harper, A.T.: Multiview. Blackwell, London (1990)
12. Avison, D., Wood-Harper, A.T., Vidgen, R.T., Wood, J.R.G.: A further exploration into information systems development: The evolution of Multiview 2. Information Technology & People 11, 124–139 (1998)
13. Mumford, E.: Sociotechnical systems design. Manchester Business School, Manchester (1985)
14. Bjerknes, G., Bratteteig, T.: User participation and democracy: A discussion of Scandinavian research in systems development. Scandinavian Journal of Information Systems 7, 73–98 (1995)
15. Dahlbom, B., Mathiassen, L.: Computers in context: The philosophy and practice of systems design. Blackwell, Cambridge (1993)
16. Kyng, M.: User and computers: A contextual approach to design of computer artifacts. Scandinavian Journal of Information Systems 10, 7–44 (1998)
17. Hanseth, O., Monteiro, E.: Inscribing behaviour in information infrastructure standards. Accounting, Management and Information Systems 7, 183–211 (1996)
18. Leonard-Barton, D.: Implementation as mutual adaptation of technology and organization. Research Policy 17, 251–267 (1988)
19. Newman, M., Robey, D.: A social process model of user-analyst relationships. MIS Quarterly 16, 249–266 (1992)

20. Davenport, T.H.: Process innovation: Reengineering work through information technology. Harvard Business School Press, Boston (1993)
21. Ross, J.W., Weill, P., Robertson, D.: Enterprise architecture as strategy: Creating a foundation for business execution. Harvard Business School Press, Boston (2006)
22. Boehm, B.W.: A spiral model of software development and enhancement. IEEE Computer 21, 61–72 (1988)
23. Jacobsen, I., Booch, G., Rumbaugh, R.: The unified software development process. Addison Wesley, Reading (1999)
24. Schwaber, K., Beedle, M.: Agile software development with scrum, vol. 18. Prentice-Hall (2001)
25. Ciborra, C.: From control to drift. Oxford University Press, Oxford (2000)
26. Ciborra, C.: De profundis? Deconstructing the concept of strategic alignment. Scandinavian Journal of Information Systems 9, 67–82 (1977)
27. Orlikowski, W.: Improvising organizational transformation over time: A situated change perspective. Information Systems Research 7, 63–92 (1996)
28. Bostrom, R.P., Heinen, J.S.: MIS problems and failures: A socio-technical perspective, Part 1: The causes. MIS Quarterly 1, 17–32 (1977)
29. Fitzgerald, G.: Evaluating information systems projects: A multidimensional approach. Journal of Information Technology 13, 15–27 (1998)
30. Iivari, J., Lyytinen, K.: Research on Information Systems Development in Scandinavia. In: Currie, W.L., Galliers, R.D. (eds.) Rethinking Management Information Systems, pp. 57–102. Oxford University Press (1999)
31. Pape, T., Thoresen, K.: Evolutionary prototyping in a change perspective: A tale of three municipalities. Information Technology & People 6, 145–170 (1992)
32. Bardram, J.: Organisational prototyping: Adopting CSCW applications in organisations. Scandinavian Journal of Information Systems 8, 69–88 (1996)
33. Christensen, G., Grønland, S.E., Methlie, L.B.: Informasjonsteknologi. Cappelen, Oslo (1999)
34. Giaglis, G.: On the integrated design and evaluation of business process and information systems. Communications of the Association for Information Systems 2 (1999)
35. Munkvold, B.E.: Tracing the roots: The influence of socio-technical principles on modern organisational change practices. In: Coakes, E., Willis, D., Lloyd-Jones, R. (eds.) The New SocioTech: Graffiti on the Long Wall, pp. 13–25. Springer, London (2000)
36. Hanseth, O., Lyytinen, K.: Design Theory for Dynamic Complexity in Information Infrastructures: The Case of Building Internet. Journal of Information Technology 25, 1–19 (2010)
37. Davenport, T.H.: Process innovation. Ernst & Young, Boston (1993)
38. Mathiassen, L., Munk Madsen, A., Nielsen, P.A., et al.: Object-oriented analysis & design. Marko Publishers, Aalborg (2000)
39. Beck, K.: Extreme programming explained: Embrace change. Addison-Wesley, Boston (2000)
40. Cockburn, A.: Agile software development. Addison-Wesley Publishing (2001)
41. Hanseth, O.: From Systems and Tools to Networks and Infrastructures—from Design to Cultivation: Towards a Design Theory of Information Infrastructures (2010) (unpublished manuscript)
42. French, W.L., Bell, C.H.: Organization development. Prentice-Hall, Englewood Cliffs (1998)
43. Hammer, M., Champy, J.: Reengineering the corporation - A manifesto for business revolution. Nicholas Brealey Publishing, London (1993)

44. Hradesky, J.: TQM handbook. McGraw-Hill, New York (1995)
45. Monge, P.R.: Theoretical and analytical issues in studying organizational processes. Organization Science 1, 406–430 (1990)
46. Ngwenyama, O.K.: Groupware, social action and organizational emergence: On the process dynamics of computer mediated distributed work. Accounting, Management and Information Technologies 8, 127–146 (1998)
47. Pettigrew, A.M.: Longitudinal field research on change theory and practice. Organization Science 1, 267–292 (1990)
48. Pettigrew, A.M.: Contextual research and the study of organizational change processes (1985)
49. Larman, C.: Agile and iterative development: A manager's guide. Addison-Wesley, Boston (2004)
50. Bygstad, B., Munkvold, B.E.: Software engineering and IS implementation research: An assessment of current SE frameworks. In: Kirikova, M., Grundspenkis, J., Wojtkowski, W., Wojtkowski, G.W., Wrycza, S., Zupancic, J. (eds.) Information Systems Development: Advances in Methodologies, Components and Management. Kluwer Academic/Plenum Publishers, New York (2002)

Dynamic Relationships in e-Government Initiatives: Craftsmanship, Partnership, Companionship, and Entrepreneurship

Sune Dueholm Müller, Pernille Kræmmergaard, and Anja Reinwald

Aalborg University, Fibigerstræde 3, DK-9220 Aalborg
sdm@dps.aau.dk

Abstract. IS plays an important role in modernization of the public sector, and government agencies increasingly use IT for both innovation purposes and exploitation of existing opportunities. These organizations not only see IS as an enabler of business strategy but also focus on the operational and tactical benefits of IS. However, although IS management has been studied at the strategic level, middle management has not received the same attention. Existing research has, for example, investigated the relationship between the CIO and top management, but no studies have looked at the relationship between IT and middle management in bridging the gulf between the strategic and operational level and bringing about IS benefits to the organization at the tactical level. This article addresses this research gap by exploring the relationship between IT and middle management in government agencies across four Danish municipalities. Based on an exploratory, multiple case study we develop a descriptive model of the dynamic relationships between IT managers and line managers in public organizations. The model describes four archetypes – craftsmanship, entrepreneurship, partnership, and companionship – depending on the level of involvement (arm's-length versus embedded) and the envisioned role of IT (management versus leadership). The model is a powerful vehicle for understanding and possibly changing the relationships depending on the needs and visions of the organization wanting to increase its e-government maturity.

Keywords: e-government, t-government, dynamic relationship, maturity, middle management.

1   Introduction

Since the middle of the 90s information technology has been used within the public sector to support and gradually transform governmental services [1], and with the advent of the internet and the diffusion of the underlying technology interest in e-government has increased dramatically [2, 3]. The prospect of changing public sector organizations from bureaucracies to service organizations better equipped to meet citizens' needs in the new millennium holds great promise [4]. By tapping into the potential behind modern technology, electronic government (e-government) is made possible. According to Weerakkody & Dhillon [1], "e-government is about the

C. Keller et al. (Eds.): SCIS 2012, LNBIP 124, pp. 44–55, 2012.
© Springer-Verlag Berlin Heidelberg 2012

transformation of internal and external processes of government using information and communication technologies to provide efficient and user focused services to citizens, businesses and other stakeholders" [1:2]. E-government is seen as the key to improving efficiency, encouraging participation by citizens, and improving governance [1, 5, 6]. The increased focus on e-government has resulted in a similar increase in research on the subject [2, 7], including research on the various stages of e-government development resulting in different maturity models [8-14].

Siau & Long present a frequently cited stage model describing five maturity levels of e-government. According to the authors, public sector organizations implement different changes moving from one stage of e-government development to the next [8]. The move from stage one (web presence) to stage two (interaction) and from stages two to three (transaction) is technological in nature focusing on automation of existing processes. By comparison, the "jump" between stages three and four (transformation) is cultural in nature[1] whereas the move between stages four and five (e-democracy) is political in nature. The purpose of the latter two is to radically transform government services – a transformation which calls for a higher degree of change within government and in terms of interacting with citizens. Moving from one stage to the next requires changes and entails different challenges. Sarikas and Weerakkody have determined that most change efforts come to a halt at the transaction stage of e-government development [15] despite many government agencies striving toward this maturity level [16]. Due to the difficulties in changing government services and reaching the transformational stage of e-government, or simply t-government, knowledge about how to successfully jump to the transformation stage is of particular interest. T-government redefines the delivery of government services, entails complete transparency and new ways of working, and requires a single point of contact between government agencies and citizens [1, 2, 8, 11, 16, 17]. However, our knowledge about barriers to t-government is limited. Van Veenstra et al. have identified 23 impediments, divided into three categories (Governance, Organisational and managerial, and Technological) blocking public sector organizations from reaching the transformation stage of e-government. Their findings lead the authors to conclude that the impediments have not received sufficient attention in the literature, and that additional knowledge is needed to successfully overcome the impediments and achieve the goal of t-government [18]. Dhillon et al. also identify various challenges confronting government agencies in transforming government services, including lack of senior management commitment [16]. In addition, Reinwald and Kræmmergaard point to stakeholder engagement at various levels as key to moving toward t-government [19].

From the broader Information Systems (IS) literature we know that collaboration between IT and management is crucial to success in IT projects as well as IT-based innovation [20-22]. Existing research has investigated the relationship between the CIO and top management at the strategic level. For example, El Sawy & Pavlou [23]

---

[1] The word "jump" signals an order-of-magnitude change. Rather than supporting, automating, and digitizing existing processes (stages 1-3), the transformation stage changes the way government agencies provide their services [8].

have shown that commitment and a shared mindset between the CIO and top management team "are prerequisites for leveraging digitalization to obtain strategic success" [24:2]. Although the role of top management has been studied, little is known about middle management. No studies have looked at the relationship between IT and middle management in bridging the gulf between the strategic and operational level and bringing about IS benefits to the organization at the tactical level. Yet the literature points to the importance of IT and middle management collaboration. For example, Bassellier et al. state that "the literature supports the notion that partnerships between IT and line management lead to IT success by fostering successful project implementation" [25:323]. Management of IT requires trained IT professionals as well as shared responsibility between line managers and IT professionals to ensure alignment between IT and business objectives [22]. Moreover, in IT-based innovation the involvement of middle management is necessary. Den Hengst and de Vreede (2004) conclude that "there is evidence that it is important to include knowledge and build support from the bottom as well, by inviting the middle managers. Top managers are often isolated from daily practice and therefore, do not understand the business and real issues to the extent middle managers do" [26:87].

The lack of knowledge about the relationships between IT managers and line managers and how it affects e-government implementation and the transformation of government services leads to our research question: How can we empirically describe and understand the relationships between IT managers and line managers in local government? We explore the relationships between these managers in government agencies across four Danish municipalities in an attempt to understand and describe their relationships. We develop a relationship model as a vehicle for understanding and possibly changing the relationships between IT managers and line managers depending on the needs and visions in terms of e-government maturity.

The paper is organized as follows. In the following section we outline our research approach. In section 3 we present our findings in the form of a relationship model. In section 4 we discuss the implications of our research for practitioners as well as researchers.

2   Research Approach

The study presented here is a qualitative, exploratory, multiple case study. The case study method is a well-established research approach within IS [27-29]. We organized our research as a case study for a number of reasons. First, case studies are suited for investigating "a contemporary phenomenon within its real-life context" [30:13] and our goal was to understand the relationship between IT and middle management in government agencies across four Danish municipalities. Second, multiple data sources is a key characteristic of case study research [30], and we had access to very rich data from multiple sources, including interviews, workshops, and written material. Third, the case study method is advantageous in situations where investigators are asking "how" or "why" questions about events over which they have little or no control [30:9]; our investigation was driven by such a question (how can we empirically describe and understand the relationships between IT managers and line managers in local government?) based on our analysis of the working relationships and collaborations between IT managers and line managers in the participating municipalities.

The research took place between September 2010 and June 2011. Figure 1 depicts the research process by means of a timeline. The research was conducted in collaboration with four Danish municipalities. The municipalities (Frederikshavn, Hedensted, Odense, and Viborg) vary in size (61,556, 46,119, 190,103, and 93,745 citizens respectively)[2], are geographically dispersed, are engaged in digitization efforts, and are confronted by the challenges of transforming government services. Such efforts include the implementation of various self-service solutions, secure and encrypted communication between citizens and public employees, and digital signature for accessing online services.

Data collection and analysis was an iterative process involving joint meetings, workshops, interviews, and analyses between events. Table 1 provides an overview of our data sources.

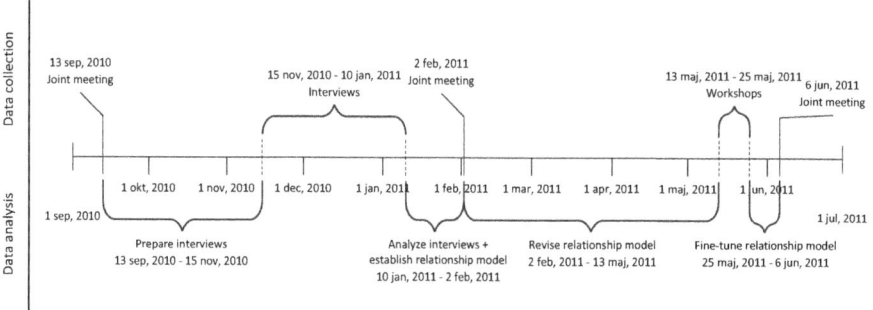

Fig. 1. Case study timeline

Table 1. Data sources

Source	Date	Participants
Joint meeting	Sep. 13, 2010	4
Interviews:		
Frederikshavn	Dec. 6, 2010	4
Hedensted	Dec. 1, 2010, Jan. 10, 2011	5
Odense	Jan. 6, 2011	4
Viborg	Nov. 15, 2010, Nov. 25, 2010	5
Joint meeting	Feb. 2, 2011	6
Workshops		
Frederikshavn	May 19, 2011	14
Hedensted	May 23, 2011	6
Odense	May 25, 2011	6
Viborg	May 13, 2011	19
Joint meeting	June 6, 2011	4

---

[2] According to Statistics Denmark: http://www.statistikbanken.dk/FOLK1

The case study was kicked off with a joint meeting (September 13, 2010) of the municipal IT managers who were asked to describe and exemplify what they consider good and not-so-good relationships with other parts of their organizations. Based on input from that meeting, interview guides were prepared. We conducted 18 interviews (November 15, 2010 – January 10, 2011) with the IT managers, line managers, and IT employees in each municipality, using distinct interview guides [31, 32] for each management level. The guides focused on exploring the research question and facilitated a natural flow of open-ended questioning. The questions were carefully selected based on Saxton [33] who has studied the effects of partner and relationship characteristics (partner reputation, prior affiliation, shared decision making, and similarities between partners) on alliance outcomes. Our approach was thus semi-structured; the interviews lasted from one to two hours and provided comparable data across the four units to support theory development. To facilitate data analysis, we had all the interviews transcribed. The interviewees were selected with the help of the municipal IT managers who were asked to identify exemplary relationships and relationships with improvement potential. All involved in each relationship were interviewed. In the wake of the interviews, we analyzed the empirical data and developed a first draft of a relationship model. The model was subsequently presented and evaluated at a joint meeting (February 2, 2011) of the IT managers and line managers. Based on their feedback, the model was revised and further developed in anticipation of the workshops (May 13, 2011 – May 25, 2011) in each municipality where the model was validated and used as a communication device in discussing the evolvement of existing relationships. The workshop participants debated the future direction of their relationships in support of digitization efforts and transformation of government services. Their input was used to fine-tune the model which was approved at the last joint meeting (June 6, 2011) of the IT managers.

During data analysis we searched for patterns across the four cases and in turn we developed the observed patterns into descriptive theory in the form of a relationship model. We engaged in theory building by juxtaposing insights from the four cases into relationship patterns between IT managers and line managers engaged in digitization efforts. First, we listed similarities and differences among the four cases in order to break simplistic frames and foster sophisticated understanding [34]. We also compared and contrasted the four patterns to deepen our understanding and search for possible explanations [35]. Second, we considered existing e-government literature to generalize each pattern and to integrate them into a comprehensive view of the relationships between IT managers and line managers. In this process of creative thinking and discussion, we sought to develop descriptions of each pattern as a particular type of working relationship. This process – corresponding to Weick's "disciplined imagination" [36] – also involved investigating our theory's comprehensiveness by considering other possible patterns. We concluded each round of data analysis with key informant reviews[3] (during the joint meetings and

---

[3] Key informant reviews is the practice of presenting interviewees and other research subjects with the analysis in order for them to determine the validity of the interpretations [37].

workshops) in which the public employees participating in the research project
provided feedback on our analyses and the relationship model.

3   Findings

Based on our investigation of the relationships between IT managers and line
managers engaged in digitization efforts in four municipalities, we have been able to
discern four interaction patterns which are summarized in the relationship model
shown in Figure 2. The model describes four archetypes – craftsmanship,
entrepreneurship, partnership, and companionship – depending on the level of
involvement (arm's-length versus embedded) and the envisioned role of IT
(management versus leadership). These relationship types are dynamic in the sense
that they have the potential to evolve over time.

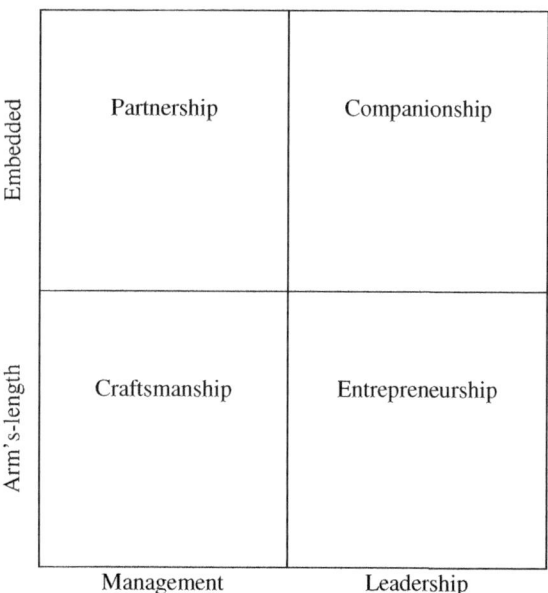

Fig. 2. The mid-level management relationship model

An arm's-length relationship is impersonal and instrumental. Knowledge of the
other party in the relationship is limited, and contact is established only when
problems arise focusing on one's own priorities. Trust and insight into the expertise of
the other party is low. In contrast, a socially embedded relationship is more personal,
trustful, and collaborative. Both sides of the relationship know each other intimately,
accept their mutual dependency, and are committed to working together toward
common goals [38, 39]. A management focused relationship is concerned with
problem-solving activities and doing things right. A leadership focused relationship,
on the other hand, is oriented toward innovation and doing the right things [40, 41].

These two dimensions – arm's-length versus embedded relationships and management versus leadership focused relationships – delineate four archetypes: Craftsmanship, entrepreneurship, partnership, and companionship.

Craftsmanship revolves around operational support. The relationship is limited to solving immediate problems. Experiences from previous encounters have resulted in mistrust and taught line managers to avoid involving IT managers in order not to complicate matters. Whenever they work together, the roles and responsibilities are clearly defined with the line managers calling the shots. Success is measured in terms of helping the line managers provide better and improved services to their clients.

Entrepreneurship is focused on strategic development. The line managers have positive experiences from previous digitization efforts and are willing to experiment with new technologies in supporting and transforming government services. The relationship is characterized by uncertainty in terms of what to expect, and although line managers are reluctant to defer to the IT managers' expertise, roles and responsibilities are unclear as the relationship is constantly evolving. The evolving nature of the relationship also implies that the success criteria are emergent.

Partnership is about collaborating on operational issues but is not limited to problem-solving. Previous experiences have left both sides with positive expectations for the future, and line managers are very open to new ideas, even though the IT managers and their employees place great demands on them. The partners put trust in each other's expertise and intentions which, in turn, results in decisions being taken together. Roles and responsibilities are shared with each partner making specific contributions. Success depends on being able to maintain a portfolio of reliable and efficient systems.

Companionship is centered on strategic development and the utilization of technology for the purpose of changing the way government agencies work and provide services to citizens. Experiences from cross-functional teamwork have taught IT and line managers to use digitization in transforming their organization. The division of roles is unclear as both sides assume responsibility for achieving the strategic benefits of modern technology. The success of the relationship depends on being able to transform IT-based innovations into perceived value for citizens and the organization alike.

Table 2. Relationship characteristics

	Craftsmanship	Entrepreneurship	Partnership	Companionship
Primary activities	Operational support	Strategic support	Joint operational responsibility	Joint strategic responsibility
IT governance structure	Clear division of roles – line managers responsible	Unclear division of roles – shared responsibilities	Clear division of roles – shared responsibilities	Unclear division of roles – shared responsibilities
Critical success factors	Customer satisfaction, efficiency improvements	Emergent	Efficient and reliable systems	IT-enabled innovation and strategic benefits.

Examples of the craftsmanship relation include implementing highly specialized software tools and solving system errors blocking employees from continuing their work. On several occasions software tools had been purchased without consulting the IT strategy or discussing it with the IT departments due to lack of trust, and because the IT employees were not believed to have sufficient specialist knowledge. Examples of such tools include highly specialized systems for monitoring water quality and drainage in Frederikshavn municipality. In Hedensted municipality, such tools include a case management system for servicing unemployed people. However, in both cases the IT department's help was needed to integrate the software with the existing portfolio of systems. Their help was also enlisted whenever system malfunctions or other problems occurred, preventing employees from completing their work assignments. In both instances, the relationship was about firefighting, i.c. solving immediate problems.

The entrepreneurship relation manifested itself when introducing e-learning and labor reducing technologies in Viborg municipality. Competing demands and reorganization within the health and nursing sector highlighted the need for digitization and IT-based solutions. Such solutions had the potential to support and transform government services by relocating and empowering employees to provide care for clients in their own homes rather than at treatment centers. It proved, however, difficult to align expectations between stakeholders. On the one hand, the line manager involved was disappointed with the rate of progress and the IT department's lack of strategic focus on those areas. On the other hand, the IT manager regarded the demands as unreasonable considering his obligations to other parts of the municipality. The misaligned expectations led to a lack of clarity concerning roles and responsibilities. In the end, the goals of the digitization efforts were subject to negotiation.

The partnership relation was expressed in the growing collaboration between the IT department and the line manager of children and youth affairs in Viborg municipality. Awareness about the potential contribution by the IT department had historically been low within that sector and their services had therefore been requested only at the time of implementation. Positive experiences from the last encounter (implementing a system that allows parents to digitally put their children down for childcare and to regularly check waiting lists) during which the IT manager and his employees proved themselves managerially and technically competent resulted in earlier involvement with greater expectations and responsibilities being put on the IT department. As a consequence, the next project (digitization of all communication between parents and schools as well as childcare institutions) was run collaboratively with clearly defined roles and goals. While the line manager was responsible for the pedagogical/teaching strategies, the IT manager was charged with generating ideas (for example, providing news through SMS messaging) for the implementation of the strategies through greater use of IT.

Lastly, an example of the companionship relation was the decision to invite the IT manager to a seminar about the future of public libraries in Odense municipality. IT was only one topic on the agenda, but prior experiences made it natural to involve him as a valued discussion partner. The relationship between the IT manager and the line manager of the municipality's department of culture evolved over time to the point where not only concrete e-government related IT projects but also the more general IT development within the municipality was being debated. In that way, the relationship became a breeding ground for novel ideas with no clear division of roles and responsibilities but with the common goal of reaping the strategic benefits of IT-enabled innovation.

4   Discussion and Implications

Our investigation of the relationships between IT managers and line managers in local government has both practical and research implications. In terms of practical implications, the model is a powerful vehicle for understanding and possibly changing the relationships depending on the needs and visions of the organization wanting to increase their e-government maturity. The model facilitates communication between key stakeholders about existing and future relationships. By using it to describe current relationships within public sector organizations, the model may be used as a basis for discussing the desired level of involvement (arm's-length versus embedded) and the envisioned role of IT (management versus leadership) in supporting and transforming government services. Such discussions help managers determine whether any given relationship impedes or advances ongoing as well as planned digitization efforts to reach higher stages of e-government development. Due to their dynamic nature, it is possible to modify the relationships to better suit the needs of the organization. The workshops in the four municipalities demonstrated the usefulness of the relationship model as a communication device. The model was instrumental in fostering mutual understanding and facilitating discussions about desired future relationships as well as collaborative projects. For example, in Odense municipality, the model was used by their digitization forum, consisting of various line managers and an IT manager from each of the municipality's two IT departments (one focusing on operations and the other on development), to discuss strategic digitization efforts and coordinate cross-disciplinary projects. In that forum, many of the line managers' ideas were tested, and the IT managers were encouraged to come up with ideas for linking technologies to e- and t-government visions of the municipalities. In Viborg municipality, using the model accentuated the need to renegotiate the relationship between the IT department and the various line managers. Subsequently, it was decided to assign an IT contact person to each department. In turn, these contact persons became business agents who were empowered to collaborate with the departments at the strategic level.

In terms of research implications, our relationship model presents interesting prospects for future research. As previously mentioned, e-government is seen as the key to improving efficiency, encouraging participation by citizens, and improving governance [1, 5, 6]. As a consequence, the various stages of e-government development and the barriers to t-government, in particular, have attracted the attention of practitioners and researchers alike [8-16, 18]. Despite our knowledge of various impediments, we still know very little about what it takes to reach the transformational stage of e-government. Previous research has, however, shown that collaboration between IT and management is crucial to success in IT projects as well as IT-based innovation [20, 21, 25], and our case study contributes to that line of research by exploring the relationship between IT and middle management in four municipalities engaged in digitization efforts. More research is nonetheless needed on how the relationships affect both e- and t-government implementation. Preliminary results suggest that the entrepreneurship and companionship relations are needed when confronted by the challenges of transforming government services (i.e. "jumping" to the transformational stage of e-government). We might even speculate that as we move from stage one to stage three the level of involvement tends to increase (from arm's length to embedded relationships), while the jump to stages four and five requires a change in the envisioned role of IT (from management versus leadership focused relationships). Meanwhile, future research is needed to test this proposition. Looking at our four cases, the empirical data lends credence to this claim. In Viborg municipality, information technology has been utilized to restructure and decentralize parts of the organization, moving public employees closer to their clients, and to upskill employees through e-learning. Moreover, within the health and nursing sector, welfare technology has been incorporated into the strategy of enabling the elderly to remain in their own homes for as long as possible. In both instances, the line manager has challenged her IT counterpart to collaborate more closely with her in transforming existing government services through novel use of IT. The relationships between the IT and line managers is, therefore, categorized as entrepreneurship. In Odense municipality, developments within the social services department saw the relationship between the responsible line manager and the IT manager evolve from craftsmanship, over entrepreneurship, to companionship. In the beginning, the relationship centered on systems maintenance and support, but due to the growing use of IT he was selected to spearhead a newly established business development unit with the goal of rethinking the organization and strengthening the collaboration between IT and line management within the municipality.

References

1. Weerakkody, V., Dhillon, G.: Moving from e-government to t-government: A study of process reengineering challenges in a UK local authority context. International Journal of Electronic Government Research 4, 1–16 (2008)
2. Gil-Garcia, J., Martinez-Moyano, I.: Understanding the evolution of e-government: The influence of systems of rules on public sector dynamics. Government Information Quarterly 24, 266–290 (2007)
3. Heeks, R., Bailur, S.: Analyzing e-government research: Perspectives, philosophies, theories, methods, and practice. Government Information Quarterly 24, 243–265 (2007)
4. Wimmer, M.: European perspective towards online one-stop government: the eGOV project. Electronic Commerce Research and Applications 1, 92–103 (2002)
5. Schware, R., Deane, A.: Deploying e-government programs: The strategic importance of "I" before "E". Info: the Journal of Policy, Regulation and Strategy for Telecommunications, Information and Media 5, 10–19 (2003)

6. Lee, S., Tan, X., Trimi, S.: Current practices of leading e-government countries. Communications of the ACM 48, 99–104 (2005)
7. Grönlund, Å., Horan, T.: Introducing e-Gov: History, definitions and issues. Communications of the Association for Information Systems 15 (2004)
8. Siau, K., Long, Y.: Synthesizing e-government stage models – a meta-synthesis based on meta-ethnography approach. Industrial Management & Data Systems 105, 443–458 (2005)
9. Moon, M.: The evolution of e-government among municipalities: Rhetoric or reality? Public Administration Review 62, 424–433 (2002)
10. Lee, J.: 10 year retrospect on stage models of e-government: A qualitative meta-synthesis. Government Information Quarterly 27, 220–230 (2010)
11. Layne, K., Lee, J.: Developing fully functional e-government: A four stage model. Government Information Quarterly 18, 122–136 (2001)
12. Klievink, B., Janssen, M.: Realizing joined-up government – Dynamic capabilities and stage models for transformation. Government Information Quarterly 26, 275–284 (2009)
13. Janssen, M., Veenstra, A.: Stages of growth in e-government: An architectural approach. The Electronic Journal of e-Government 3, 193–200 (2005)
14. Andersen, K., Henriksen, H.: E-government maturity models: Extension of the Layne and Lee model. Government Information Quarterly 23, 236–248 (2006)
15. Sarikas, O., Weerakkody, V.: Realising integrated e-government services: a UK local government perspective. Transforming Government: People, Process and Policy 1, 153–173 (2007)
16. Dhillon, G., Weerakkody, V., Dwivedi, Y.: Realising transformational stage e-government: a UK local authority perspective. Electronic Government, An International Journal 5, 162–180 (2008)
17. Affisco, J., Soliman, K.: E-government: a strategic operations management framework for service delivery. Business Process Management Journal 12, 13–21 (2006)
18. van Veenstra, A., Klievink, B., Janssen, M.: Barriers and impediments to transformational government: insights from literature and practice. Electronic Government, An International Journal, 226—241 (2011)
19. Reinwald, A., Kræmmergaard, P.: Managing stakeholders in transformational government – A case study in a Danish local government. Government Information Quarterly (2011) (accepted for publication)
20. Bashein, B., Markus, L.: A credibility equation for IT specialists. Sloan Management Review 38, 35–44 (1997)
21. Boynton, A., Zmud, R., Jacobs, G.: The influence of IT management practice on IT use in large organizations. MIS Quarterly 18, 299–318 (1994)
22. Bassellier, G., Reich, B., Benbasat, I.: Information technology competence of business managers: A definition and research model. Journal of Management Information Systems 17, 159–182 (2001)
23. El Sawy, O., Pavlout, P.: IT-enabled business capabilities for turbulent environments. MIS Quarterly Executive 7, 139–150 (2008)
24. Hansen, A., Kraemmergaard, P., Mathiassen, L.: Negotiating social alignment in IS leadership: A participatory process model. Submitted to MIS Quarterly Executive (2011)
25. Basselier, G., Benbasat, I., Reich, B.: The influence of business managers' IT competence on championing IT. Information Systems Research 14, 317–336 (2003)
26. den Hengst, M., de Vreede, G.: Collaborative business engineering: A decade of lessons from the field. Journal of Management of Information Systems 20, 85–113 (2004)
27. Benbasat, I., Goldstein, D., Mead, M.: The case research strategy in studies of information systems. MIS Quarterly 11, 369–386 (1987)

28. Cavaye, A.: Case study research: a multi-faceted research approach for IS. Information Systems Journal 6, 227–242 (1996)
29. Lee, A.: A scientific methodology for MIS case studies. MIS Quarterly 13, 33–50 (1989)
30. Yin, R.: Case Study Research: Design and Methods. Sage Publications, Thousand Oaks (2003)
31. Kvale, S.: Interviews: An Introduction to Qualitative Research Interviewing. Sage Publications, Thousand Oaks (1996)
32. Patton, M.: Qualitative Research & Evaluation Methods. Sage Publications, Thousand Oaks (2002)
33. Saxton, T.: The effects of partner and relationship characteristics on alliance outcomes. The Academy of Management Journal 40, 443–461 (1997)
34. Eisenhardt, K.: Building theories from case study research. The Academy of Management Review 14, 532–550 (1989)
35. Miles, M., Huberman, A.: Qualitative Data Analysis: An Expanded Sourcebook. Sage Publications, Thousand Oaks (1994)
36. Weick, K.: Theory construction as disciplined imagination. The Academy of Management Review 14, 516–531 (1989)
37. Mason, J.: Qualitative Researching. Sage Publications, Thousand Oaks (2002)
38. Schultze, U., Orlikowski, W.: A practice perspective on technology-mediated network relations: The use of internet-based self-serve technologies. Information Systems Research 15, 87–106 (2004)
39. Uzzi, B.: Social structure and competition in interfirm networks: The paradox of embeddedness. Administrative Science Quarterly 42, 35–67 (1997)
40. Zaleznik, A.: Managers and leaders: Are they different? Harvard Business Review 82, 74–81 (2004)

Disentangling for Autonomy: Understanding the Sociomaterial Practices of Public Services

Tone Bratteteig and Guri Verne

Department of Informatics, University of Oslo,
P.O. Box 1080 Blindern, 0316 Oslo, Norway
{tone,gbverne}@ifi.uio.no

Abstract. An ambition for a democratic information society is providing services that maintain and even enhance citizens' mastery and control of their environment. Analyzing public services from a citizen autonomy perspective can indicate where the service and its IT-systems do not support user autonomy. We analyze a public service and discuss it as a sociomaterial entanglement. Based on our data on citizens' use of a public service we identify a need to distinguish between entanglements and imbrications and suggest a notion of disentangling in order to characterize the way in which the public service advisors help the citizens. Experiencing the service as an imbrication enables the citizen to see and act, while an entanglement seems impossible to handle without a certain level of competence. Different types of entanglements need different types of competencies to address them. Finally, we discuss how the notion of disentangling tax issues can support citizen autonomy.

Keywords: Sociomateriality, entanglements, imbrications, autonomy, tax.

1 Introduction

In the interactive society information systems are a part of everyday life of all citizens – as infrastructure or as part of citizens' activities or both. The society is profoundly dependent on its technologies, and the technologies are intertwined with how the society is organized. This poses challenges for how government presents itself and acts towards the citizens as well as challenges for the citizens as actors and users of technology-based services. Public agencies increasingly present web-based facades towards the citizens – our concern in this paper is to investigate and discuss if and how public services support users' autonomy, in particular public services that depend on IT systems. An important ambition for a democratic information society is to provide services that maintain and even enhance users' autonomy as citizens. This is the basic assumption in the research project *"Autonomy and Automation in an Information Society for All"* [1] in which this paper is grounded.

The paper reports from an empirical study of how citizen autonomy is challenged and supported by various parts of a public agency. The contribution of the paper is twofold. One is the analytical framework developed to analyze what makes a situation complicated for the citizen. The other is the extension of sociomaterial theory where

C. Keller et al. (Eds.): SCIS 2012, LNBIP 124, pp. 56–75, 2012.

we suggest that the notions of entanglement and imbrication are given different meanings, and that the notion of disentangling is a concept for describing how a sociomaterial entanglement must be addressed to create a space for action and change.

The paper is structured as follows: In this introductory section we present the conceptual background for the paper. In section 2 we present the research approach and methods. Section 3 reports from the empirical material in three examples of taxpayers calling the Tax Agency call center and advisors helping them on the phone. In section 4 we analyze the examples with respect to how and what makes them complicated for the caller and the advisor. The fifth section discusses the theoretical concepts in more detail and in chapter 6 we introduce the notion of *disentangling*, in order to explain how the advisor helped the caller. In section 7 we come back to the concept of autonomy and try to open it up: What does autonomy mean for users of public services, and how can autonomy be supported and enhanced? The last section concludes the paper.

1.1   Background

Our concern in this paper is if and how public services support citizens' autonomy: Do they support citizens acting freely according to their own choices? To act in their own best interest might presuppose knowledge in many areas. We are concerned whether the citizens know and understand enough, and can reason about their choices. Acting requires understanding. But what if the citizens cannot figure out what to do?

The study draws upon sociomaterial theory for the analysis of what makes things complicated for the citizens. The paper argues both empirically and theoretically for the necessity of disentangling a complicated situation to help the caller and support his or her autonomy.

Autonomy

The Concise Oxford Dictionary [2] defines autonomy as "the possession or right of self-government" or "freedom of action". The word comes from Greek *autonomous*, "having its own law". Acting freely means that people should be able to act according to their own norms and plans – their own "law". Without going into a discussion about rational choice [3, 4] we take the view that in order to govern themselves people need to understand their choices and what they imply. Based on this view we see autonomy as something scalable, where people can have more or less autonomy in different situations.

The concept can be defined and interpreted differently [1]. We find, however, that this brief discussion on autonomy is sufficient as an introduction to start our analysis. In Section 7 we discuss the concept more thoroughly on the basis of our analysis.

eGovernment

IT-based public services and eGovernment as research fields both study how the public or citizens and the government workers experience the increasingly automated government. Introducing IT to government work involves both the making of a socio-technical infrastructure for eGovernment and changed work conditions for government workers. Studies of changes in work for government workers and local politicians introduced by IT point to extra work and new work tasks [5, 6].

Some studies point to difficulties of citizen participation in development of eGovernment projects [7, 8], and some to successful participatory design [9]. There are very few studies addressing the whole situation of e-government citizens.

In this paper we focus on the use of eGovernment services by citizens as a way to understand how a service creates and solves problems in their life situation. The starting point of our study is the increasingly smooth façade that the government presents to its citizens as more tasks and citizens' duties are automated by IT, and work is delegated to the citizens by means of online self-services. We investigate the sort of problems citizens experience while managing their tax or fulfilling their civic duties, and how the public agency relate to these problems.

Sociomateriality

Our study of citizens' autonomy in public services is based on a sociomaterial perspective seeing the public service as a sociomaterial assemblage in which the agency of both technology and people are constituted. The intimate tangle of technologies and organization is the focus of scholars studying sociomateriality. Technologies, people and organizations are seen as mutually constituted in an imbrication [10, 11], entanglement [12, 13, 14] or a sociomaterial assemblage [15], where they can be separated only analytically. The sociomaterial perspective is enriching our understanding of the relations between technology, people and organization in that it focuses on the entangled nature of such sociomaterial assemblages.

The recursive intertwining of humans and technologies in practice makes it impossible to talk about technology as an external driving force or that human agency is all that matters when we want to explain modern societies and change [14]. A challenge for researchers has been to understand and describe the dual view of technology and society development without putting too much explanatory power on one or the other side of the dualism. In this perspective autonomy is seen as an outcome of the assemblage rather than a property of humans or artifacts. We can see how autonomy is an effect of ongoing and (more or less) durable sociomaterial practices [15].

Citizen Autonomy in the Information Society

Analyzing public services from a citizen autonomy perspective can help us identify where the smooth façade do not support citizens' mastery of their own situation or even hampers their autonomy. Workers' mastery of technologies used in their work has been a long-standing focus within participatory design [16]. As an example of a public service we focus on tax – also because the tax authorities are in the forefront when it comes to IT support for their services. Tax and its digital presentations can be experienced as entanglements where rules and regulations, electronic services, web forms, paper forms, IT systems etc. cannot easily be separated.

A Brief Introduction to the Norwegian Tax System

The Norwegian tax system is based on the principle that everybody should pay tax according to their means and receive benefits and services according to their needs. The tax includes state and community tax as well as a national insurance contribution for receiving health services if needed. The tax authorities have succeeded in establishing a sociomaterial infrastructure that enables the automation of most of the tax calculations, based on data sent to the tax authorities from employers, banks, insurance companies, social security offices and other public agencies. The employer calculates and pays the predicted tax for the employee: All employees will need to have a tax deduction card, which shows how much tax the employer should deduct from the salary and pay to the Tax Collector. The predicted tax is calculated based on the previous year's economic situation, and sent to all tax payers in March/April every year. The tax payers have the obligation to check that the information basis for the calculation is correct, and to correct or add information if needed. The tax payer does not have to do anything if all information is correct.

On the basis of the tax return at the end of the year, the tax authorities calculate the exact amount of tax to be paid for the previous year. Every citizen receives a tax settlement notice, which provides information about the income, fortune and debt on which the tax is calculated, and information on whether too much or too little tax is paid (by the employer). If too much tax is paid the tax payer receives the excess amount, if too little tax is paid the tax payer has to pay the remaining amount. The tax payer can appeal the tax assessment, but has to pay the outstanding tax while the complaint is being handled by the tax office.

2   Research Method

We base our analysis and discussion on fieldwork from the Tax Information Call Centre (TICC) where citizens can call if they need help with their tax issues, carried out by Verne [17]. The call centre sits in the middle between the Tax Agency and the citizens, situated as a separate unit within the Tax Agency. The study was initiated as an open, exploratory study aimed at understanding the tax issues that citizens calling in experienced as problematic. TICC has offices at several locations nationwide, and we studied one – to protect the anonymity of the callers and the advisors we will not go into more details about where the study has actually been carried out. We report from fieldwork comprising 15 sessions of "co-listening" on the TICC telephone service in addition to interviews and observations of TICC advisors, as well as document studies, over a period of 22 months.

- *Co-listening* involves the researcher sitting together with a tax advisor at his/her desk, with a headset for listening to phone calls and with a position that allows the researcher to see what the advisor is doing on the computer screen and on the desk. The researcher takes (handwritten) notes of what the callers ask about as well as what the TICC advisors answers, what they do to solve problems, and how the IT systems support (or not) the actions of both the TICC advisors and the callers.

- *Interviews.* Eight semi-structured interviews of approximately one hour and a half with tax advisors and their managers have been taped and transcribed.
- *Observation* has taken place as a supporting activity to the co-listening. While being in physical locations of the call center doing co-listening and interviews, the researcher also has observed work practices. In the offices there are several screens and whiteboards that report the daily traffic on the phone, recurrent topics of the calls and about the advisor's work schedules. Field notes have been written immediately after the visit.
- *Document studies.* Various steering documents and annual reports have been read to get an understanding of the strategies, objectives and plans of the TICC.

Co-listening is routinely taking place at the call centers, as a way of training new advisors and improving the answers for all advisors. It is also used for letting case handlers from other units of the agency learn about the kinds of questions people are asking TICC. All people co-listening – including the researcher – have signed non-disclosure agreements to protect the privacy of the callers.

The data analysis started as soon as the data gathering began. Preliminary data analysis has influenced the data gathering inductively. Interviews and notes from the phone conversations have been analyzed and marked, and we have done several rounds of interpreting the data (inspired by [18]). The analysis has been built up inductively from the data.

3   What Do Tax Payers Call for?

In this section we report from three examples of people calling in to the Tax Information Call Center (TICC). The TICC received 2.2 million phone calls in 2010 with an average duration of 3.23 minutes. The three examples we have chosen were among the longer calls as they took between 10 and 20 minutes, indicating that they are more complicated than most calls.

Example 1: Single Father Needs a New Tax Card

A man calls the TICC in late October. He speaks in a low voice, and the connection is bad so the advisor has to ask him to repeatedly explain his situation. It is difficult to get the grip of what he is saying, but slowly a picture emerges that he is a single father of two small children. He is also unemployed, receives unemployment benefits and works part time in a kindergarten. He wants to change his tax card, and be taxed in tax class 2 (like all single parents are entitled to). The call advisor asks for his national identity number and uses this to look up background data for his tax card in the Advance Tax Register. He can see that tax is calculated off the caller's benefits when it should not. This tells the advisor that too much tax has been withheld. The advisor makes some calculations on a small handheld calculator while he is asking some follow up questions. The caller mentions that he became a single father some months ago. The advisor says that "you should preferably tell us such things electronically" but he does not ask him to use the online services himself (as the routine says). Instead he asks the caller to verbally confirm that he is receiving a benefit. When the caller responds adequately to this the advisor change his tax class to 2, enters some new figures in the advance tax database entry for the caller and issues an exemption card: A tax card for low incomes where no tax payment is required. This will free the caller from paying tax for the rest of the year. The exemption card will be sent automatically to the caller from a central print service. The advisor closes the call by stating that he himself "has been nice" and helped the caller, and urges the caller to update the information after the turn of the year so that he receives a correct tax card for next year. Because it was late in the year the updates done by the advisor will not be transferred automatically to the next year.

Comments

By looking up the data in the advance tax database the advisor does not need to understand all that the caller is saying, as the data can tell about erroneous taxation better than the caller can do. The advisor is less vulnerable to errors or misunderstanding about tax issues when s/he checks the facts of the database. S/he gets an impression of the caller's initial understanding of tax by the way the question is presented.

In this case the advisor can issue an exemption card because he understands that this man has overpaid tax so far this year from his small salary and benefit. In sum this father has received less money every month for himself and his children than he should have. The advisor also infers that this man does not have much money for a living, so he makes a quick fix to get his economy balanced immediately and in more accordance with his rights.

The fact that he has received a smaller net income than he should have the current year may have had dramatic consequences for his life situation, and for his possibilities for supporting his children. The unemployment benefit does not give much leeway on a monthly basis. The advisor deviated from the routines to be able to help him immediately, instead of directing the caller to the electronic self-service or paper forms. When we asked why he did so and helped the man by manually updating the database the advisor replied "there are some people that are stuck and I thought he was there".

The income of this taxpayer was lower than it should be, but changing the situation required knowledge about the technical details of the rules and requirements, and the ability to use the electronic self-service to carry out the adequate change. His autonomy was also challenged as he might have a too low income to be able to sustain himself and his children. He was dependent on the tax advisor both to *tell* him how the rules applied to his situation and *fix* the figures and tax class. The tax advisor helped him do the first moves towards a better life situation.

In a tax perspective this situation was not very complicated. The rules are clear and unambiguous, and for the advisor it was easy to see how the rules should be applied in this situation. The advisor helped the caller "untie" the tax knot of sociomaterial entanglement by changing three numbers in the database.

Example 2: Mother Calls for Daughter to Complain about Tax Payment

Our next example is more complicated. The tax rules are still clear and unambiguous but in this case the tax advisor can neither find a root of the problem nor fix it. A woman is calling the TICC. She says she calls on behalf of her daughter, who has underpaid tax last year and has to pay the rest this year. The mother gives her daughter's national identification number and the advisor enters the number in the log system. Her address from the Population Register pops up. We can see from the data on the screen that she is a young adult. The mother explains that the daughter has appealed her tax assessment, and when she received a giro for half of the amount of her outstanding tax some weeks later they both had believed that her complaint was granted and that a compromise was settled. When she recently received a second giro with the same amount both mother and daughter started to think that perhaps the complaint had not been granted, perhaps it was not even handled yet. The mother tells that the daughter had to borrow money to pay the first tax giro, and that she cannot afford the second one.

The daughter has not received any reply letter from the tax office so the mother complains that the case handling is far too slow. She asks how long time it will take before her daughter receives a reply to the complaint. The advisor informs her about the routines and time limits that govern the agency's complaint handling, and it becomes clear that the agency is well within the time limits in this case. The advisor explains the routines, which say that the daughter will have to pay the outstanding tax independent of the handling of the complaint. If the complaint is granted she will get the money refunded from the tax collector next year.

The mother claims that the outstanding tax is a result from the daughter being ill for a period last year: The illness is the main argument in the complaint. The daughter also has claimed deductions because of commuting from home to work. The mother says that the Tax Agency is unreasonable because her daughter does not have so much money and the agency is too slow in settling the case.

The advisor asks if her "daughter's address in the Population Register is correct" because the tax office reply letter could have been sent to the wrong address. The mother tells the advisor that the daughter has moved from home and gives him the new address. This is not the same address as listed in the Population Register. The advisor does not tell her this, instead he asks if the daughter has had more addresses. The mother mentions another address, which also is different from the one listed in the register. They talk about addresses for a while without the mother (or the advisor) mentioning the one registered.

The advisor retrieves the complaint from the electronic archive. It appears that the daughter has used the electronic service for complaining. The advisor is in doubt whether the daughter has filled in the online appeal form correctly and completely, but he does not tell the mother. He says to her "I cannot tell you everything", and adds that a possible reason for the daughter not having received a reply could be that a letter from the tax office asking for documentation of the claims had not been received if the address registered is not the correct one, and thereby documentation may not have been provided by the daughter. He tells her to check with her daughter that she has registered the correct address in the Population Register and tells her that she might need to provide documentation for her claims in the complaint.

Comments

The advisor could not disclose all data he could find in the registers to the mother because of privacy concerns, since the daughter is of full age and legal capacity. A fairly common source of troublesome situations is that people are not listed with the correct address in the Population Register, implying that they will not receive letters from the tax office. There can be many reasons why a young daughter would not want to tell her mother her registered address, in addition to forgetfulness by the daughter from having moved several times. The advisor cannot know which is the case, and he cannot ask the mother directly.

The mother did not sound very content during the call. She was blaming the Tax Agency for slow case handling and for being unreasonable. The situation became a sociomaterial entanglement where the mother did not separate what was the law and regulations, unreasonable practice, the contents of some registers, online services possibly not functioning, a secretive or forgetful daughter, missing documentation, a call advisor that could not fix the problem or cautious privacy routines. There was no quick fix presented to her on the phone, and the help she got implied that she had to sort things out herself with her daughter.

To sort out this entanglement so that the daughter could act autonomously in her own best interest will require some knowledge of the rules and regulations involved, made complicated by IT-systems' strict behavior and the privacy concerns from the advisor.

This situation is not as easy to disentangle as the previous example. The caller cannot provide the advisor with all relevant information, as she does not know how the daughter documented her complaint. The advisor cannot give the caller all the information he has concerning her daughter. He can also not sort out the roots of the problems, and even if he could, that would not help the problem of having to pay the outstanding tax. He can in no way grant the complaint on the phone. He could only help the mother by indicating some steps she can take to start sorting out the case.

In this case there are no clear steps to take that will fix the situation for the caller. Even if the daughter updates the Population Register and provides documentation and sort out all other complications, her complaint may still not get approved. This can put her in an unfavorable economic situation with tax debt at a young age, putting restrictions on her autonomy when it comes to possible education or housing at a later stage.

This case looks like an entanglement that cannot be disentangled at the point of the call. The advisor encourages the mother (and daughter) to do their part of the disentangling as a way to act in the daughter's best interest. Providing the mother with an understanding of the situation as something they can handle adequately will be an important move towards autonomy.

Example 3: A Newly Immigrated Citizen Needs a Tax Card

Our next example turned out as easy, but could have been a lot more complicated had the advisor not been so experienced.

A Norwegian man is calling. He starts by telling that he has married recently and is calling on behalf of his wife. She has recently immigrated from a foreign country, and has received a national identification number. He asks if she can get an exemption card, so that she will not have to pay tax if the income is below the no tax threshold. The advisor says that he can send her a paper form to fill in. The caller asks if she can start to work before she has received the card: "yes, she can", the advisor says, these things are independent.

The caller tells the national identity number of the wife, and the advisor looks her up in the Population Register, where he sees that she is listed with a daughter also with a foreign name. The advisor explains that the wife cannot apply for an exemption card through the simplified online service because she has not yet received PIN-codes in the mail. He tries to look her up but cannot find her in the Advance Tax Register. So even when she gets her PIN-codes she cannot apply electronically.

The advisor then creates two new records in the Advance Tax Register and enters the wife and the daughter, each with name, national identity number and address. He then prints out a blank form, where he marks with a green felt pen the fields she will have to fill in. He puts the form in an envelope and writes the address by hand for mailing it to her, and tells that it is important that she fills out this information since they do not have any data on her.

Comments

It has been an issue of some controversy whether the TICC advisors should be eligible to write in the advance tax database. The routines say that they should not do this except in acute situations. After the call we asked the advisor how he should have handled this case if he could not create a new record in the register. He said that entering new people with blank fields is not outside the routines: no data are actually changed. But young, inexperienced advisors do not feel like using the old-fashioned command-based technology that must be used to write in the database. They instead send a request through their log system to the regional tax office to which the citizen belong and ask for a new person record in the advance tax database. The request will go as an ordinary email and it can take up to three weeks before it is handled by the actual tax region. Without the shortcut the agency would not have been ready to process any filled in form from the wife, and issue an exemption card.

Insecurity about her tax card could hamper the process of getting a job. Getting a job before an exemption card means that a default percentage of the wage (50%) will be withheld by the employer. The excess tax will not get refunded until after the tax assessment next year. It is easy to see that this can put the wife in a less favorable economic situation with possible consequences for her autonomy.

There are lots of requirements for receiving the necessary permits when entering a new country. Among these technical details is the importance of being registered in the necessary registers. In this case the disentangling of the situation depended on the experienced advisor, who knew where to enter the data and just did it, instead of sending a request to another unit in the agency. Hence, autonomy of the tax advisor may be important for providing citizen autonomy. By being able to consider the actual case presented on the phone and act accordingly without a too narrow space of interpretations can help the caller more.

4 Analysis

Understanding these examples and how they got handled requires us to take a step back and consider the taxpayers and the TICC as a part of a larger sociomaterial assemblage. What struck us during the analysis of the data was that most questions did not concern difficult tax problems; most questions were rather simple but they still came out as a very complex mix of formal, technical, social and organizational issues. This entanglement of very different issues was problematic for the taxpayers calling in. We first discuss the role of TICC as a basis for explaining what the advisors do and not do, then we discuss the taxpayers: Who are they and why do they call?

4.1 TICC's Role

The Tax Agency has a web site with information about tax rules and regulations. Some services, like ordering or changing a tax card, are electronically available. Still, people often call and ask questions where the answer is relatively easy to find on the web site. Even if a tax card can be ordered digitally on the web site, many young people, who are experienced users of digital services[1] pick up the telephone in order to ask the agency to send them one. One explanation that easily comes to mind is that the agency web site is to blame. The advisors agree that it is not easy to find the information you need on the web site. Another explanation is that since the agency has the means to exercise power over the taxpayers, and that errors may have pecuniary consequences for them, some tax payers want to double-check their understanding with a human advisor. The reasons may hence be more complicated than being just a personal preference or (in)ability, they may also have to do with the agency's role in the society.

Some users prefer to use the digital service for changing or ordering a tax card when the advisor tells them that this is faster. However, some callers say that they do not have Internet available (their PC has crashed, they are not familiar with using digital services etc.) and many say that they have tried and not succeeded in using the digital service. A caller needs to change some information in his tax card:

Advisor: "Preferably you should use the Internet for this." Caller: "Yes, but I do not understand it."

In such cases the advisor will help them in various ways. However, the agency's official policy is that the advisors should direct the callers to the web site for self-service if this is available for the case at hand. The callers are expected to learn how to use the digital self-service and use it without calling a next time. This is seen as a more long-term help in that the taxpayers can help themselves next year without calling TICC. This instruction often creates a dilemma for the advisor. By letting the callers handle things themselves (e.g. filling in and returning a paper form) the advisor knows that there is a risk that this will not get done, and that they will do nothing or call once more or at a later time. In the first case, the caller

---

[1] It is mandatory to apply to schools in Norway through a public digital service. All young people from secondary school and higher have experienced at least this service.

might experience a less favorable economic situation compared to how things could have been. The objective "Helping the caller towards self-help" is in conflict with the objective "Directing the caller to the online service" in the cases where there is a risk that the caller will get nothing done and carry on with a less favorable economic situation. If the caller has small economic means, this can indeed create a dire life situation with too little net income or even a tax debt.

The advisors' practices differ when it comes to how fast or reluctant they are to carry out services that the callers are able to do themselves. Some advisors are relatively quick to offer help, and some are more eager to explain how this can be carried out on the web page and seem not to notice the callers' doubts as to how feasible this will be. There are many reasons why advisors carry out services that are available on the web site, as one advisor commented: "We cannot expect that the callers make up an average of the population", indicating that the average taxpayers are able to read and make use of the information on the web.

The Tax Agency collects data about the calls. The advisors register the questions, however, the registration system does not include categories for what causes most trouble for the taxpayers. The categories used to classify a question in the agency's registration systems are based on concepts from the inside of the Tax Agency: tax rules, regulations, systems, routines and what the advisors are allowed to do. If a caller tells the advisor that s/he has not succeeded using the online service for ordering a tax card there is no category for the advisor to register this. The Tax Agency expresses an "introvert" attitude towards registering the questions from the callers [19]. Reports and statistics made on the basis of these registrations therefore do not convey any information on how the services are experienced by the taxpayers. Such information could have been used to improve the online services in supporting the taxpayers.

4.2 The Taxpayers Calling In

Who is calling TICC? Early in the call the advisor gets an impression of whether the caller needs extra help or if s/he can handle things with some explanations and directions. This impression is based on a mix of what the caller says and information from the databases.

Our examples – and the empirical material at large – indicate that what is making a question complicated for the caller is not the complexity of the rules alone but the caller's life situation or the *context* of the call situation. The caller cannot find documentation of claims, cannot carry out percentage calculations, does not know what interest cost is, needs her mother to call, cannot use the Internet, does not have the correct address registered, is sick etc. The instructions to the advisors address such problems only superficially.

We can illustrate the relationship between complicated tax rules[2] and complicated life situations or context in a table:

---

[2] We define a complicated tax question to be one where the advisor does not know the answer or otherwise acknowledges the questions as being complicated.

Table 1. Relations between easy and complicated tax questions and contexts/ life situations

Tax rules Contexts	easy	complicated
easy	well suited for online self-help	second line support
complicated	need help	rarely occur

The instructions of directing callers to the online pages do not address callers with a complex context (the lower row). The table illustrates that if the callers' context is not taken into account the table collapses to one row (the upper row) where the only dimension is easy or complicated tax issue. This hides the fact that it is the individual life situation they experience, outside of the Tax Agency, and not the complexity of the tax issue that creates difficulties for people. The complexity of the tax issue does not alone determine whether people can help themselves or need help from an advisor.

Phone calls belonging to the *upper left corner* easily fit the objectives of directing taxpayers to self-service on the web pages. Their autonomy will not be hampered by doing so. Questions belonging to the *upper right corner* can be handled in various ways by the advisor. Some advisors look up the actual rules in a book, ask a colleague or direct the question to second line support through the log system, where the caller normally gets an answer within a day or two. Unless the application of the tax rules have unfortunate consequences for the caller by prescribing heavy taxation this will not inhibit the autonomy of the caller much. These cases are rare in the empirical material: the only type of questions always considered complicated by the TICC advisors are questions about taxation of Norwegians staying abroad or international workers in Norway, they are usually directed to second line support immediately.

The phone calls of the *lower left corner* are the ones that elicit extra help from the advisor. The question and the tax rules involved are simple and unambiguous, so the advisor knows the rules by heart and can easily explain them to the caller. What takes up the advisor's time is to try to understand what the caller wants and needs. The personal situation may vary a lot from caller to caller. As we saw in examples 1 and 2, a complicated life situation can make a simple tax issue appear very complicated.

There are very few phone calls belonging in the *lower right corner* in the empirical material. Whether this indicates that citizens with complicated life situations very rarely run into complicated tax questions or just handle them in other ways than calling the Tax Agency we do not know.

We have one example of a caller who may fit into this category. A woman called and asked if income from selling land property was to be taxed as "personal income" or "capital income". She owned a piece of land close to the city. The municipality was developing the area by building infrastructure for water and sewage and she was charged a part of these costs. She was living off disability pension, and had to sell some of her land to pay the costs. If the income from the sales counted as personal income she risked losing her disability pension. If the income counted as capital income, she risked no such thing. The caller sounded well aware of the rules for her disability pension, but did not know how the sales income would be classified according to the tax rules. The advisor did not know the answer. He tried to look it up in a law book to see if there was a limit on how many pieces of land she could sell without a reduction of her pension. He could not find the answer, and decided to write a note describing the question and send it to second line support. They would check up the rules and call back within 48 hours.

Depending of the answer of the question, this example fits in different corners of the table above. If the sales income is counted as capital income then nothing unfavorable will be expected to happen with the woman's pension: the example fits in the *upper right corner*. If the sales income is counted as person income she risks a reduction in her pension. This can make it necessary for the caller to sell more land to compensate loss of income, hence further deductions in her pension may be a consequence. This can create several cycles of handling a complicated situation, where it is difficult (and outside the scope of this paper) to see what her possibilities for negotiation and solution will be. In this case we categorize it as an example in the *lower right corner* until the answer is known, and the case is settled.

5   Levels of Entanglements

As stated earlier, we were struck by the fact that most phone callers' questions did not concern difficult tax problems but rather simple questions that presented themselves as a complex mix of formal, technical, social and organizational issues. We have found the notion of "entanglement" useful to describe this mix of issues that creates problems for the caller.

"Entangle" means to wrap or twist together or to cause (something) to get caught in or twisted with something else, or it can mean to involve in complicated circumstances [2]. The concept of entanglement was introduced to Information Systems research by Orlikowski [12] in a discussion about the notion of sociomateriality analyzing how technology use involves a close interplay between social and technical issues, the "entanglement of the social and the material – 'a mangling of human and material agencies' [20] or what Suchman calls 'a creative sociomaterial assemblage'." [15:1440]. Barad [21] discusses quantum entanglement[3] building on the Niels Bohr's work, emphasizing that a human observer is not separate from the phenomenon s/he observes, but entangled with the object of observation. Barad's argument is similar to Pickering's [20]: the phenomenon we observe is entangled with the apparatus for observation and ourselves as observers.

"The mangle operate[s] ... at a level of detail not usually accessible to empirical study", says Pickering [20:xi]. Orlikowski describes how technical detail is involved in sociomaterial entanglements, discussing the Google Page Rank algorithm and the Blackberry email push functions as examples [12]. The email push function on the Blackberry phones in the "Plymouth" organization that she studied gets intertwined with the ways in which work is organized and carried out (how the email routines change, which in turn influences the practices of using the email push function: It is the company policy to have it turned on).

---

[3] The term entanglement is used in quantum theory to describe how particles of matter can become correlated to predictably interact with each other regardless of how far apart they are.

In the tax setting we can use the concept of entanglement on two levels. The basic level is to describe and analyze tax and tax rules as entangled with the technology that is used to represent and act upon it. Tax calculation is done by computers on the basis of reports and numbers about taxpayers' economy from other computers in banks, public services (e.g. welfare and pension), insurance companies and employers. When there are no irregularities, or no particular incidents happen that affect a taxpayer's economy, tax will be reported, deducted and paid automatically. However, at this analytical level we also find other public systems that have information needed for or affecting the tax. A taxpayer has a name and address as well as a unique national identification number, and this information is found in the Population Register – which acts as a reference base for correct information. Some welfare payments qualify for no tax while others are seen as income and therefore taxed. Everyone has the right to earn a minimum without paying tax (with an exemption card), but if you earn more you have to pay tax from the whole amount. Single parents are entitled to pay less tax than co-habiting parents (so-called tax class 2), and so on: The tax system is based on a number of rules where different public systems and their information are intertwined and integrated.

The second level of entanglement concerns how the technical-formal entanglement is intertwined with the social. Tax is a way in which society organizes that all citizens and users of the welfare state also contribute by paying for the services – depending on their income and economy rather than on what each person make use of. Every person living and working in the country is therefore a potential taxpayer. For the taxpayers, however, tax affects their personal economy and is therefore intertwined with all other aspects of their lives that depend on their economy – which in our society are most things. Everybody has to pay their share of tax by law. The tax authorities follow general rules like all public services in order to treat everybody the same way. Every taxpayer has to confirm to these rules – the rules have to be followed even when a taxpayer discusses or disagrees with the tax authorities.

A tax issue can be experienced as an inextricably impossible knot, hence the services that TICC (and other public service providers) offer is crucial in order to open the knot and point to possible actions that will solve the problems for the citizens. To be able to analyze how the advisors help the callers we need the notion of *disentangling*. It seems useful to look at the work of the TICC advisors as disentangling of the tax entanglement for and on behalf of citizens and taxpayers.

6   Imbrications

The disentanglements can be done in many different ways – as demonstrated in the examples from TICC. Some entanglements are more complicated to disentangle, if at all possible. We suggest a second concept for talking about entanglements that are possible to disentangle: "*imbrications*". Imbrication refers to:

> "*the interweaving of human and material agencies … To imbricate means to arrange distinct elements in overlapping patterns so that they function interdependently. The verb "imbricate" is derived from names of roof tiles used in ancient Roman and Greek architecture.*

The tegula and imbrex were interlocking tiles used to waterproof a roof. The tegula was a plain flat tile laid on the roof and the imbrex was a semi-cylindrical tile laid over the joints between the tegulae.". [11:150].

Fig. 1. Roof tiles in Port Grimaud, France

Leonardi suggests seeing human and material agencies as imbrications producing routines and technology, where "those agencies are weaved together to produce empirically distinct figurations" [11:9] in different ways.

"Thus, sometimes, human and material agencies interweave in ways that create or change routines, and other times, they weave together in ways that produce or alter technologies." [11:10].

The concept of imbrication suggests that it is the interweaving of the agencies that produce the result, and the result maintains that there is a difference between the two. The notion also refers to patterns or durable results ("organizational residue" [11:10]). The results of earlier imbrications stay and act as conditions for further imbrications "though in a non-deterministic way" [11:13]. In this way imbrications constitute what Star and Ruhleder [22] call infrastructure, providing conditions for (further) actions.

We let the notion of *imbrication* stand for an entanglement that can be disentangled by a stepwise sequence of choices and actions, by seeing how the elements are woven together as a basis for, or pointing to, steps of actions, or addressing them separately but still as parts of a complex interplay. Disentangling implies changing the understanding of an entanglement into that of an imbrication, where it will be possible to see the different agencies producing the result. This will open up a space for negotiation, choice, action and change.

Types of Disentangling

The three examples in section 3 illustrate that the formal, technological and social are intertwined and that clear causal relationships are difficult to establish. However, there are fundamental differences between the types of entanglements and these differences can point to useful distinctions for addressing the entanglements – and for the disentanglements – with far-reaching consequences for human autonomy. Going back to table 1 we find that the four types of situations necessitate different types of entanglements that need to be handled differently:

1. Easy tax rules and easy to handle context: the entanglement is addressed as an imbrication from both the taxpayer and the TICC side, where the taxpayer "misses one of the tiles" that easily can be provided by TICC. In many cases the tax web site could have been used by the taxpayer to provide the missing "tile". In these cases TICC most often help the taxpayer navigate on the web site so that they manage to get what they need themselves.
2. Easy tax rules and complicated context: The entanglement is mainly due to a mix of social and technical issues on the taxpayer side. Most of our examples are in this category. It seems that the disentanglement carried out by the TICC advisors often aims to reduce the complexity to an imbrication of social and technical "tiles" where the TICC advisor either explains to the taxpayer what s/he has to do to correct what is wrong or provide the missing parts for the imbrication to be correct. In some situations the TICC advisor leave it to the taxpayer to do his/her part, in other situations the TICC advisor carries out some of the steps (the "missing tiles") until the taxpayer can do the rest him/herself. The explanation of the composition and workings of the imbrications and the decision of how much of the work should be left to the taxpayer varies from advisor to advisor: Some seem more reluctant to address the socio-technical entanglements on the taxpayer side.
3. Complicated tax rules and easy to handle context: This category addresses entanglements in the tax system side of things, at level 1, and must be disentangled by tax specialists – the disentanglement is based on legal expertise and can be seen as the making of a missing technical/regulatory tile. In this case the tax authorities try to find out how the taxpayer fit to their representational categories and which of these categories s/he matches.
4. Complicated tax rules and complicated context: This category is a knot where the tax problem is inseparable from the social problem, cf. the example of the woman on social welfare who needed to sell property to finance her water and sewage bills but then could lose her right to social welfare if the sale was categorized as income. Like in category 2 the tax authorities work with making a match between a citizen and the formal-technical categories (is the women a social welfare client or a worker?). The difference here is that the person-representation relation is intertwined with a socio-technical entanglement on the taxpayer side. The knot can probably not be disentangled, at least not during the phone call, as it involves the intertwining of two levels of entanglements as it presents itself to the taxpayer: the representation of the taxpayer as a worker or a social welfare client after performing the act of selling property (which is neither social welfare nor work) is deeply intertwined with her economy and social rights (e.g. right to social welfare) in the short and long term.

Building on our previous categories table 2 indicates the different types of entanglements and hence the ways to disentangling them:

Table 2. Entanglement types and disentangling strategies

Tax rules Contexts	easy	complicated
easy	Imbrication, "missing a tile" – TICC teach taxpayers	Imbrication for taxpayer, entanglement on the TICC side
complicated	Entanglement on taxpayer side, TICC disentangles to imbrication often providing missing "tiles" for taxpayers	Inseparable interdependencies between level 1 and level 2 entanglements

The literature discusses sociomateriality with a focus on the entangled nature of material/technical and human agency. This focus is fruitful in a theoretical discussion of social or technological change in that it gives a role for all kinds of agencies and influences. When explaining social change [12, 13] or the development of scientific theory [15] we cannot separate human from material agency.

However, the mundane practices of supporting citizens' autonomy trying to get callers to understand the issues and choices as well as the possibilities for action seem to be best described as acts of disentangling. Disentangling an entanglement into an imbrication makes visible the scope of possible actions for changing an unfavorable condition. This would, however, require some analytic capabilities not granted to everyone.

TICC offers their callers exactly this: by analyzing the situation as described by the caller and giving advice about what to do they disentangle the sociomaterial knot. In order to act autonomously one has to know where to start acting and which acts to choose.

Into Threads and Tiles

Orlikowski [13] concludes that "all practices… are always configured by some specific sociomateriality" and that "we must study the dynamic and multiple sociomaterial (re)configurations as these are performed in practice" [13:137]. Furthermore, "a perspective that renounces the categorical presumption of separateness is likely to offer a more useful conceptual lens with which to think about the temporally emergent sociomaterial realities that form and perform contemporary organizations" [13:137]. At the same time, she acknowledges that technological specificities can give various influences to the social: "different technological capabilities […] will have particular effects" [13:137].

In order to address "the different technological capabilities" within a sociomaterial perspective we argue that we need to talk about the analytically separable constituents of the entanglement. Discussing the constituents will enable us to identify which constituents can be influenced or changed so that the sociomaterial assemblage as a whole changes in a wanted direction. Confronted with the emerging outcome of a sociomaterial assemblage it can be difficult to see the openings for change or improvements. However, to be able to act out a need for change is an important aspect of autonomy.

The notion of disentangling refers to the process of analyzing a sociomaterial entanglement into its constituents. Disentangling makes it possible to see through the entanglement and get a grip on the possibilities for action by sorting out the "tiles" of the imbrication or the "threads" of the knot. We can compare disentangling with reverse engineering of the outcome of an assemblage, aiming to identify the source of the problem and try to opt for some other outcome. In this way human agency can arrange material agency so that a more wanted outcome is possible.

7   Autonomy

We argue that it is important for human autonomy to be able to act in complicated situations where autonomy is challenged. The sociomaterial assemblage of tax needs to be opened up for detailed scrutiny in order for the taxpayer to understand the material agency of some of its constituents. If a tax issue does not work well or the tax context changes, all taxpayers will need to know about legal, economical or technical details in order to assess what is beneficial for oneself and act upon this knowledge. Knowing to some degree how the entanglement of law and technology works will make it possible to analytically separate human and material agency, and thereby change the view of the technology from an entanglement to an imbrication. This will open up for an understanding of if and how a dire situation can be changed, helping a user away from seeing the situation as "so overwhelmingly difficult as to seem impossible" [23:29][4] to a more empowered position.

Both getting things done for you by others and being able to do things yourself can be seen as autonomy, based on different interpretations. In many ordinary tax questions the autonomy of the taxpayers can be increased by teaching them to help themselves. This will give them a better basis for the yearly tax cycle with tax card, tax return form and tax assessment. However, if the taxpayer experiences difficulties in understanding the tax rules and calculations or in using the online services, s/he will be better off by getting the services carried out by the tax advisor on the phone. The caller needs the help of the tax advisor for disentangling as well as for carrying out some of the actions.

Seeing sociomaterial assemblages as inseparable, unsolvable entanglements can lead the citizen to give up, and not make any move towards disentangling. The case could seem to leave no openings and be too complicated to handle for the caller. This leaves less space for action and change. It can reduce the autonomy: the situation can stay less satisfying or the citizen will not experience any learning that can increase the possibilities for doing better next time. If you see a problem as an entanglement, your only options are to accept or not accept: There is no space in between – for negotiation and improvement.

By disentangling the tax questions together with the callers the advisors help reducing the complexity of the tax issue: They "translate" the problem from an entanglement to an imbrication, where steps can be taken to address or even solve the

---

[4] Rose and Jones (2005) refer to technology. We think that it also fits tax as an example of a sociomaterial entanglement.

issue. Seen as an imbrication, as something that can be analytically separated into human actions and legal/formal/technical issues, a space for action is opened. Seeing the problem as an imbrication opens up for compromises, action and change. Being able to govern oneself – to address one's problems and changing an unfavorable situation – is essential for the autonomous citizen.

8   Conclusions

In this paper we have used empirical data from the Tax Information Call Center (TICC) to discuss how a public service can support citizens' autonomy. Our basis for the paper has been empirical: We have analyzed empirical data on the practical use of a public service as to understanding how and what are experienced as difficult. We have also worked theoretically with concepts that can be used for talking about the intertwining of social, technical, formal (tax rules), and organizational (organization of work in the Tax Agency and TICC) elements of a situation: the notion of sociomaterial entanglement. Sociomaterial entanglement has been used to point to the inseparability of the social and the technical (and material) in our lives.

Although we share this view, we have suggested a concept for disentangling that will help us to act and change a difficult situation. We find it important to be able to disentangle into the constituents of the entanglement of the difficult situation: only then will we open a space for negotiation, choice, action and change – and for autonomy. We have put emphasis on explaining the disentangling and have introduced the notion of imbrication to characterize entanglements that are possible to analytically separate into the social and the technical and by indicating a process of addressing the elements of the imbrication (the "tiles") one by one in a sequence. The paper discusses how the tax advisors help the taxpayers to help themselves by changing entanglements into imbrications, as a means towards more autonomy.

Acknowledgments. We would like to thank Arild Jansen and Ina Wagner for valuable comments to previous versions of this paper, and Ola Henfridsson and the other participants in working group 1 of the Oslo PhD-Days. We will also thank our colleagues in the Design group for several interesting discussions about sociomateriality.

References

1. Van der Velden, M., Bratteteig, T., Finken, S., Mörtberg, C.: Autonomy and Automation in an Information Society for All. In: IRIS 32 Information Systems Research Seminar in Scandinavia, Molde University College, Norway (2009)
2. Oxford Concise Dictionary 10th edn. Oxford university Press, New York (1999)
3. Simon, H.: Bounded Rationality and Organizational Learning. Organization Science 2, 125–134 (1991)
4. Kahneman, D.: A Perspective on Judgment and Choice. Mapping Bounded Rationality. American Psychologist 58, 697–720 (2003)

5. Bowers, J.: The work to make a network work: studying CSCW in action. In: Proceedings of CSCW Conference, pp. 287–298. ACM, Chapel Hill (1994)
6. Mörtberg, C., Elovaara, P.: Attaching People and Technology: Between E and Government. In: Booth, S., Goodman, S., Kirkup, G. (eds.) Gender Issues in Learning and Working with Information Technology: Social Constructs and Cultural Contexts, pp. 83–98. Information Science Reference, Hershey (2010)
7. Ekelin, A.: The Work to Make eParticipation Work. PhD dissertation, Blekinge Technical University, Karlskrona (2007)
8. Axelsson, K., Melin, U., Lindgren, I.: Exploring the importance of citizen participation and involvement in e-government projects: Transforming Government. People, Process and Policy 4, 299–321 (2010)
9. Borchorst, N.G., Bødker, S.: You probably shouldn't give them too much information" – Supporting Citizen-Government Collaboration. In: Bødker, S., et al. (eds.) Proceedings of ECSCW 2011, pp. 173–192. Springer, London (2011)
10. Sassen, S.: Towards a sociology of Information Technology. Current Sociology 50, 363–388 (2002)
11. Leonardi, P.M.: When Flexible Routines Meet Flexible Technologies: Affordance, Constraints, and the Imbrication of Human and Material Agencies. MIS Quarterly 35, 147–167 (2011)
12. Orlikowski, W.J.: Sociomaterial practices: Exploring technology at work. Organization Studies 28, 1435–1448 (2007)
13. Orlikowski, W.J.: The sociomateriality of organisational life: considering technology in management research. Cambridge Journal of Economics 34, 125–141 (2010)
14. Orlikowski, W.J., Scott, S.V.: Sociomateriality: challenging the separation of technology, work and organization. The Academy of Management Annals 2, 433–474 (2008)
15. Suchman, L.: Human-Machine Reconfigurations: Plans and Situated Actions, 2nd edn. Cambridge University Press, New York (2007)
16. Bjerknes, G., Ehn, P., Kyng, M. (eds.): Computers and Democracy – a Scandinavian Challenge. Avebury, Aldershot (1987)
17. Verne, G.: Between the Citizens and the Web Pages is the Classification. In: Leino, T. (ed.) In: Proceedings of IRIS 2011, Turku, Finland, TUCS Lecture Notes No 15 (2011)
18. Glaser, B., Strauss, A.: The Discovery of Grounded Theory: Strategies for Qualitative Research. Aldine Transaction, Chicago (1967)
19. Verne, G.: What's in a category? Telephone log as a record of citizen's concerns. Working paper, Department of Informatics, University of Oslo (2012)
20. Pickering, A.: The mangle of practice: Time agency and science. University of Chicago Press, Chicago (1995)
21. Barad, K.: Meeting the Universe Halfway: Quantum Physics and the Entanglement of Matter and Meaning. Duke University Press, Durham (2009)
22. Star, S.L., Ruhleder, K.: Steps Toward an Ecology of Infrastructure: Design and Access for Large Information Spaces. Information Systems Research 7, 111–133 (1996)
23. Rose, J., Jones, M.: The Double Dance of Agency: A Socio- Theoretic Account of How Machines and Humans Interact. Systems, Signs & Actions 1, 19–37 (2005)

Materializing Organizational Information Security

Dan Harnesk and John Lindström

Luleå University of Technology, Department of Computer Science,
Electrical and Space Engineering and Department of Engineering Sciences and Mathematics,
971 87 Luleå, Sweden
{dan.harnesk,john.lindstrom}@ltu.se

Abstract. In the context of situated elderly care this paper discusses the intertwined relationship between organizational security objectives, technology, and employees' security behavior. We use findings from a single case study to aid in our understanding of how managers sought to create a secure work environment by introducing behavioral security technology, and how employees appreciated the new security software in everyday routines. Theoretically the case study is informed by sociomateriality in that it employs the notion of technological affordances of behavioral security technology. Findings show that security technology material is an integral part of security management and security in use, and that both the technical actor and human actors contributed to cultivation of the information security practice in the elderly care center.

1 Introduction

Today, behavioral security technologies are being widely developed and deployed to provide greater security to users and warrant security managers reliable control and audit mechanisms within the information security management practice [1]. Currently, however, this attention rarely mirrors affordances of behavioral security technologies and how they significantly can contribute to the shaping of the information security practice within organizations. A majority of research has centered on the study of employees' security policy compliance [2, 3], 'managers intention to adopt anti-malware software'[4], 'behavior during security implementation' [5], 'employees knowledge of the installed security base' [6] Similarly, effective information security management is primarily seen as result of the organizations ability to manage and counteract threats to organizational information assets [7, 15]. Giving attention to the affordances of technology entails a shift in modes of analysis towards co-evolution of technological material and social agency [8]. To this end, technological affordances have been used to describe how information technology induces change in organizational processes [8-12]. For example, as Holmström and Robey [13] have showed, technological inscriptions are sources to radical organizational transformation. Interestingly, while researchers agree that security technologies are of outmost importance in the set of interconnected security safeguards designed to control security behavior [14-16], we find no studies focusing on how technological affordances

C. Keller et al. (Eds.): SCIS 2012, LNBIP 124, pp. 76–94, 2012.

matter for organizational information security. In other words how does security management and employees security behavior become materialized?

In order to develop a better understanding of the intertwined relationship between organizational security objectives, technology, and users' security behavior this paper draws on the body of sociomaterial research [8, 9,17]. Scholars have produced a significant body of knowledge on sociomaterial entanglement, which suggests that technology and humans are entangled through different objects in the surrounding whole. Examples of such objects are: infrastructure, configurations, routines associations, etc. that are enacted in the sociomaterial practice. To chart and contrast security managers and employees views on the introduction of behavioral security software into the security system infrastructure, we study how protection need and expectations from technology gets materialized through affordances of the security technology.

In order to develop our argument, the paper is structured as follows. First, we present the mainstream perspectives in information security to give a picture how this vein in research has kept security management and employees separated from each other. Second, we provide the constitution of behavioral security technology to develop an understanding of how its material features function. Third, we develop and discuss the conceptual framework that guides data collection and analysis in this study. Fourth, we discuss the methodological considerations of this study and illustrate the process of implementing behavioral security software into the case organization's system infrastructure. Finally, we present discussion and conclusion where we summarize the study.

1.1   Existing Views of Information Security

The information security literature includes rich and varied descriptions of design methods for information security, efficiency of technical security controls, socio-organizational challenges for security management, and organizational maturity towards information security [15, 18-20]. Despite detailed and clarifying research results, the discipline has been criticized for its inability to recognize the difficulty of adequately capturing and defining the security concept [15]. One example is the separation between the formal and informal aspects of security configurations and neglecting uncertainties during the systems introduction phase [21]. This is recognized in the literature as a potential source of different security behaviors, as employees' intention to obey to given security frameworks largely depend on their motivation to comply with the frameworks [3]. To this end Myyry et al. [3] suggest that organizations implement education programs to ensure that people internalize information security policies. Although the effectiveness of such programs have been criticized to deliver weak content [22], Puhakainen and Siponen [2] argue that compliance can be achieved if users systematically utilize cognitive processing of information they receive through training activities. Interestingly, despite possible impact from training programs Stanton et al. [23] illustrated that improvement in these areas is associated with a greater likelihood of writing down one's password, which indicates lack of security awareness [24]. This is just one example of users developing certain use patterns while seeking to comply with security instructions. Such dimensions have been identified in the literature and contain different assumptions and terminology to describe the discrepancy between emerging security patterns and security responsibility [25]. Because security patterns and responsible actions are not isolated occurrences but progress in a tight relationship between what is anticipated by security managers and enacted by users, von Solms [26] stressed the importance of cultivating information security practice throughout the company.

Clearly there is a risk of failing in the institutionalization of security if security in use is misaligned with organizational security objectives. As noted by Hsu [5:149], institutionalization of security management practices can be strengthened if organizations understand how different groups perceive IS security. Whereas aspects of the institutionalization of security practices have received attention over the years, e.g. [26-27] the material features of security technology has typically been conceptualized as a risk phenomenon [28], and commonly suggested solutions to deal with risk are different types of security controls [29].

Furthermore, behavioral information security research suggests that security management can secure work environments if effective 'fear communication' [30] and 'persuasion' [31] is used for changing employees' attitudes and motivations to comply with given information security objectives. However, it can be argued that such management style does not warrant secure user behavior since users vary in terms of motivation and ability to perform information systems attributes [5]. This is one obvious reason to the lack of sustainable change that all-inclusive doctrines, such as training programs, bring to the employees [22]. With a few exceptions, e.g. [32, 33] the information security literature is currently dominated by investigations that prescribe different accounts of management support to ensure the success of information security and its implementation process. Typically user compliance [34] and risk analysis [19] have guided the framing of security in use throughout a great variance of organizational settings. Although these accounts have proven valuable in research they are criticized for reducing security in use to a management practice [5]. Moreover, it is argued, for instance, that security technology is not productivity-enhancing because it is not intended so, and therefore factors such as ease-of-use and enjoyment are not applicable [4].

Other research has directed its focus on motivations to use security artefacts and argued that employees employ compliant behavior if security recommendations meet their efficacy levels [6]. In a study of fear appeals on end-user compliance, Johnston and Warkentin [30] conceptualize and test a model for predicting how users will respond to fear-inducing communications. These studies lead us to an understanding that material features of security technology can contribute to an understanding in moving beyond the traditional approach that defines security use and the user as a consequence of intentional security management practice. Our objective is to develop better understanding of what appropriate security practices contain and how that lead, via delegation and inscription, to expectations about information security that the material is/is not capable of constituting.

1.2   Behavioral Security Technology

With a focus on materializing information security, we think of behavioral security technology as material that constitutes human behavior as well as how it gets constituted by humans [9]. The way that this entanglement becomes visible is through the process of executing the features of the technology that holds defined assumptions of its user. These assumptions are built up from biometrically collecting, storing, and continuously analyzing data about employees [35]. The typical biometric authentication process consists of the following:

- Enrolment, which measures a subject for the first time, extracts features from the measurement, creates a biometric profile containing the measurement-based features and stores the profile in a database.
- Identification is a process in which a biometric sample is compared with all of the biometric templates, or a subset based on search algorithms, in the database in order to find a matching template and thus identify the person who provided the biometric sample.
- Verification is a process in which a biometric sample is compared with a particular, previously generated biometric template, stored in a database or on an ID card, in order to verify the correctness of the user's 'claimed identity'.

Behavioral security technology has one major advantage compared to traditional subject-object security approaches in that it supports automated authentication, which overcomes the user related problem of disrupted information flow in work processes [36]. At the same time it permits effective monitoring and control of user behavioral patterns [37], by producing performance statistics. However, behavioral security technology is not the silver bullet in security as it can be compromised by, for example, an inadequate matching process of stored templates and samples taken during user authentication [1]. This has been addressed in the literature as a permanence problem because it could involve multiple biometric enrolments for different situations, which would pose a major inconvenience to the users [38]. Within the frame of biometric authentication process described above more detailed feature descriptions are available in the literature (Table 1).

Table 1. Features for personal recognition [39]

Universality	Each person should have the characteristic
Distinctiveness	Any two persons should be sufficiently different in terms of the characteristic
Permanence	The characteristic should be sufficiently invariant (with respect to the matching criterion) over a period of time
Collectability	The characteristic can be measured quantitatively
Performance	Refers to the achievable recognition accuracy and speed, the resources required to achieve the desired recognition accuracy and speed, as well as the operational and environmental factors that affect the accuracy and speed
Acceptability	Indicates the extent to which people are willing to accept the use of a particular biometric identifier (characteristic) in their daily lives
Circumvention	Reflects how easily the system can be fooled using fraudulent methods

A number of positive and negative effects of behavioral security technology have been highlighted in research that has implication for the understanding of information security management. In general, organizations motivate security introductions by referring to security effectiveness, reliability, and cost-effectiveness [40]. Regarding implementation of behavioral technology, Chandra and Calderon in [1] argue that the direct costs are immediate, tangible, and measurable; the benefits are qualitative, longer term, and difficult to estimate monetarily. One reason for the difficulty to assess benefits can be found in the material features of the technology. Performance of behavioral security technology is pertinent to the structure of identification and verification, which makes the two operations incomparable. Essentially, this is due to differences in performance measures, which in the identification system concerns the ability to identify a biometric owner's signature, whereas in the verification system performance is measured by characterized by two error statistics: false-reject rate (proportion of impostors admitted in the systems) and false-alarm rate, proportion of authentic users not admitted in the system [37]. These features can be adjusted to fit desired levels of sophistication of any organizations security system as one can override the error rates given the protection need at any given time. Overall, a biometric system should meet the specified recognition accuracy, speed, and resource requirements, be harmless to the users, be accepted by the intended population, and be sufficiently robust to various fraudulent methods and attacks to the system [39].

The biometric security system in our study, hereafter called BehavioSec builds on a process oriented data collection, and is transparent and non-intrusive to the users. Thus, the users do not notice or get affected by it while working at the computer. It is based on behavioral biometrics, and the security method used in this case is keystroke dynamics. As each user has a unique way of typing on a keyboard or keypad, a unique pattern is generated that can be associated with a particular user [36]. BehavioSec extracts quantitative information from the interactions between a user and a keyboard and use this to, after the logon to the operating system, continuously authenticate the user until log off. In our case, BehavioSec was also configured to send notifications to the administrator if an operating system user account was shared between users in any application or information system.

Behavioral security software is thus relevant to managers' intention to create changes in security behavior among employees because of its material features. As noted above, these features allow security systems to collect, store, and continuously analyze data about the state of security behaviors across application boundaries in an organization [36, 39]. Similarly, behavioral security software features create ease-of-use expectations among employees with technology operating in the background as users navigate through the application landscape [41]. Given the emphasis on features of security technology, the next section explains why the concept of technological affordances is relevant for our study of implementation of behavioral security technology.

2   Theoretical Background

Our reasoning in this paper follows the research, which suggests that humans delegate action to a technical actor that constitutes other actors (also humans) as part of sociomaterial practices [17]. Sociomateriality is about the constitutive entanglement that describes the relation between the technical and the social, which can be used for understanding how technology and humans encounter each other in different use situations [9]. From what such encounter produces we can as argued by Introna and Hayes [9] design new routines and new material that allows new actions. Criticism against this view argues that designing and implementing artefacts while hoping for patterns of action is a mistake because material artefacts will determine patterns of action [42]. The way to avoid this, according to materialists is to treat the technical and the human ontology as inseparable. While the material matters, new routines and patterns are afforded by the very interpretations that human actors have for technology use, which, in turn, are the sources to (un)intended outcome described in the concept of entanglement [17]. We want to argue that our case study is an example of entanglement in that intentionality to resolve unwanted security behavior by implementing a behavioral security platform renders a security practice that builds on technological affordances. We believe the premise for such entanglement falls back on the inter-subjective experience from encountering information technology in different contextual situations. To this end, behavioral security technology has been suggested as momentous approach to integrated organizational security management as it is not only an access control technology, but more so a process oriented artefact [41]. This emerging process with features that shapes shifting interpretations that hinge on the ways the technology defines information security also become defined by humans as they encounter it in different use situations, cf. [9]. In particular, behavior oriented research in information security emphasizes the increasing complexity of the information systems landscape organizational actors must navigate to manage intertwined activities in organizational departments and processes [5]. While traditional approaches to changed security behavior presupposes continuous and integrated information security training and communication efforts [2], material features of behavioral security technology are embedded in the security processes so that security monitoring and user identification becomes inextricably intertwined. Hence, this intertwined constitution implies a kind of continuous management and use experience that goes beyond the traditional security approach [43].

Specifically, the sociomaterial perspective asks how technology co-shape perception of the world by mediating human intentions and technology features [11]. Yet another view of the relation between humans and technology is entanglement; defined as the "constitutive role of technology in everyday life." Orlikowski in [12:1435], This constitution presumes that there are no independently existing entities with inherent characteristics, Orlikowski posit while referring to [44]. The central argument is insisting on speaking of the social and the material in the same register, and of not reverting to a limiting dualism that treats them as separate phenomena [45]. The fundamental assumption is that material differences between IT systems afford different outcome in different contextual settings [10]. Leonardi and Barley [8:161] thus make the point that "Materiality matters for theories of technology and organizing because the material properties of artifacts are precisely those tangible resources that provide people with the ability to do old things in new ways and to do things they could not do before."

Interestingly, the features of behavioral security technology offer precisely such opportunities as they are embedded in the practices of information security and establish a connection between actual user behavior and the intentions with any chosen security management routine. A practical example of this is how materiality seamlessly operates while inscribing run-time statistics of (mis)use to security logs, as well as delegating user identification by replacing alphanumeric passwords with biometric counterparts [37]. This praxiological view aligns mostly with what [10] and [8] refer to as a fruitful arena to examine how material and increasingly embedded features afforded by IT re-organize the social and the technical elements at a certain point of conception. The material features of security technology based on behavioral factors differ from the traditional subject-object based approach, which in essence is a transaction system [29]. While a transaction approach merely transmits user credentials for further authentication, i.e. mediates information processing, the behavioral security approach entangles user behavior through new opportunities for security management to automatically collect, analyze, and monitor user behavior.

3   Conceptual Framework

In this paper we draw on some of the ideas in sociomaterial research that focus on affordances of information technology that have not yet appeared in information security research. A central aspect is that even though sociomaterial research advocates that changes in the surroundings of technology should be read through the artefact itself [46], the introduction of technology derives from intentionalities in organizations and it also creates expectations among users [9]. Essentially this means that there are always some underlying problematic situations that need attention and in many cases problems are being solved by implementing new functionalities in old configurations. For example, Introna and Hayes [9] discuss the problem with plagiarism in a student context and explains how information technology produces intentionalities that constitute some students as plagiarists and others as not. Introna and Hayes case study is an example of the importance for one type of social agency (universities) to have plausible detection systems to make visible what is unwanted behavior. The students are recipients of education but utilize university resources and therefore they are part of the relational material such resources deploy, e.g. learning systems. Consequently, capacities for action need to be studied as relational, distributed and enacted through particular instantiations of information technology [45].

As a starting point for our analysis, we develop a conceptual framework (Figure 1) of information security practice technology dimensions, which not only renders what is visible, but also what is accepted in the security practice as a whole. The dimensions are action, intention and expectation and we believe they operate in the same way in the management domain as they do in the user domain – it is the content of these dimensions that differ when they encounter the material features of the behavioral information security technology. The conceptual framework is based on a thorough literature review of the existing literature in mainstream information security e.g [15, 18-20] and recent literature in sociomaterial research relevant for understanding the impact of materiality on management and use.

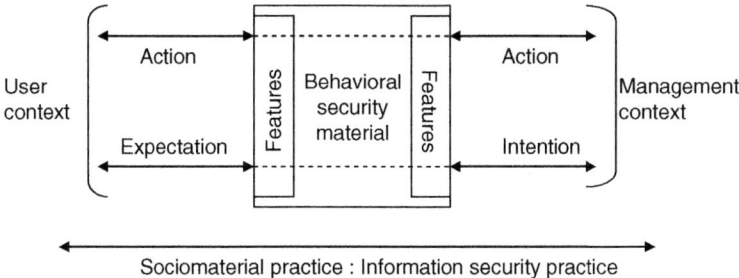

Fig. 1. Conceptual framework

- *Action.* Although behavioral security features are discrete technical states they contribute to the process of constituting appropriate security management and user behavior. This process evolves as technology delegates action opportunities to security managers and users even though it occasions different types of action. For security managers a typical action would be to reinforce the power of security polices by communicating risk of security breaches [2]. For users, action means something else. Typically it refers what they can do with information security technology to complete their work tasks. Sometimes this lead to opportunistic user behavior as users for example might share passwords with other employees [46]. Viewed from the point of conception where the technology operates; action is about features that can be delegated to managers and users. To security management, technology delegates for example the feature collectability to maintain durable knowledge of computer use. To users, technology delegates distinctiveness to ensure that each and every user can be identified and verified. In this array of delegation, human actors similarly over and over inscribe the constitution of technological operations into the security practice, cf. [9].

- *Intention.* Intentionality is what lies at heart for security management when considering protection mechanisms in the system landscape of an organization. The well-acknowledged view of protection as 'activity to respond to possible threats and select among coping alternatives to facilitate adaptive intentions or behaviors' [47] means that, with enrolment of user characteristics, stored in a database of individual biometric measures, delegation to control the security environment is assigned to security managers. This type of delegation could, for example make audit of policy compliance less bothersome. On the user side intention is somewhat more complex yet important because users may act unintentionally and counterproductively to intentions residing in technology. A typical example is sharing of passwords, which can be seen as avoiding the feature of authentication [46] that lies within the identification system. As Introna and Hayes [9:109] continue, "they are bound to enact (or be enacted within) inappropriate interpretive frames that may lead to consequences not intended by any of the actors as such."

- *Expectation*. Bhattacherjee and Premkumar [49] argue that users of information technology form an initial pre-usage expectation (belief) about a product, experience its usage over time, and then form post-usage perceptions of the product. This has been previously conceptualized as a process of sensemaking e.g. [49], and means that humans form assumptions and develop knowledge of information technology, which subsequently define action towards it [9]. One important expectation that security managers have is that user should comply with security frameworks but perhaps more importantly they consider technology a safeguard and that it can help in avoiding negative outcome from computer abuse [50]. In this regard, behavioral security technology is a promising construct because of features such as permanence and performance, which allow managers to maintain high security level over longer periods of time. For users that encounter these safeguards on daily basis expectations may take another turn. For example, issues regarding continuous use and opportunity to induce change in work processes may be of strong interest even though technology efficiently enables and support work flow activities. An important criteria is then that technologies are not stabilized in design but embedded into on-going open-ended use situation, and that they allow reinterpreting and modifying technology over time [45, 51].

The conceptual framework constitutes a relevant view of the information security practice as an instantiation of sociomaterial practices. The objective is to use it in the course if interviewing and analyzing to chart and contrast material affordances in the context of managerial issues and different interpretations of security that exist in organizational information security processes. Essentially we emphasize the existing and strong relationship between the material, and the social that [8] and [9] consider vital for our understanding of the social dynamics of technology and our understanding of the social dynamics of its use.

4   Research Method and Case Description

This study adopts a case study epistemology [52] because we are interested in individual cases of technology use rather than looking across instances to make generalized claims [45]. The case was previously presented in published work with explicit focus on information security management [46]. However, it can be reinterpreted to illustrate how features of behavioral security software materialize organizational need for protection and users expectation from encounter the technology.

The design of our case inclined conceptual discussions of the particular context and its constitutive actors, which we developed into a cognitive map to identify its working parts. Beside the material as such, it was obvious to us that our case's working parts contained different levels of relatedness to the subject matter. This means that some of the respondents concern themselves with the issues of responsibility and security management, while others experience security on day-to-day basis as users of information security controls. Therefore, the characteristics of proximity involve a wide range of security related components, such as the legal framework for information handling in the elderly care context over to privacy keeping issues for the care receivers.

The case site was an elderly care center in the municipality of [location blinded] with approximately 75,000 inhabitants in 2009. The municipality's social department promoted the introduction of a new security application to this facility with the aim of resolving the misaligned security behavior among daily users that they experienced. In some of these cases of computer resource misuse actions, such as warnings and notice of dismissal, were taken.

The main problem that the introduction BehavioSec resolved was the detection of any unauthorized disclosure and sharing of user credentials. The on-going situation at the elderly care center was that co-workers shared their user-id, either intentionally or unintentionally, which opened up the possibility of misusing computers and confidential information regarding care receivers. It also meant that the managers responsible to uphold the compliance of the legal framework had problems with the traccability of information entered into the information systems, as well as those who accessed the information system. In order to address this problem, we design our research as shown in figure 2.

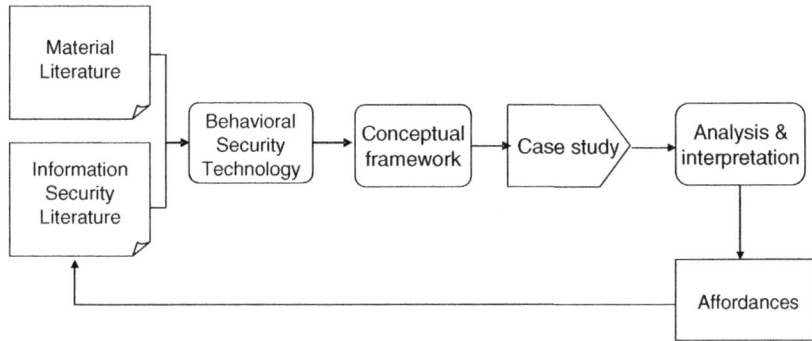

Fig. 2. Research design

5   Data Collection and Analysis

Miles and Huberman [53] explain that qualitative researchers usually work with small samples of people, and that the samples are purposive, rather than random. The data collection strategy we utilized was within case sampling [53], which accounts for a nested case structure implying that our case consisted of different activities, processes, events, locations, and role partners, all in relation to the material features of the implemented behavioral security software. We interviewed three representatives at the management level in the social department at the municipality office, IT service unit at municipality head office, and the nursing home. These people were chosen due to their relatedness of subject matter, i.e., the decision to introduce the security software in the infrastructure of security systems at the municipality. We also conducted interviews with four representatives from the nursing staff to obtain a clear understanding of the daily usage experiences from the security software. Our data collection method was in-person interviews. We scheduled our interviews within a period of

1.5 months in 2009. Interviews were audio-recorded and transcribed. Below are some examples of questions asked to security managers and employees:

- (Managers) How does the organization believe that work tasks will be correct and successfully performed with BehavioSec?
- (Managers) Are there any prescriptions in the organization of what secure behavior is?
- (Employees) Do you believe using the security software would improve performance in managing elderly care information?
- (Employees) Do you consider your expectations from using BehavioSec were confirmed?

Data analysis coding strategy followed on the conceptual framework constituents: *action, intention* and *expectation* with a focus on how organizational actors made sense of BehavioSec and how these constituents made actors intertwined in the emerging relationship between organizational security objectives, technology, and users.

6   Results and Findings

6.1   Illustrating the Protection Need

As stated by security managers, the overall goal at management levels was to assure secure behavior while using the department's computer resources. Complying with legal and regulatory frameworks is of outmost importance in organizations of this type. To ensure that, great efforts are put in communicating the protection need to employees within the organization, especially as the organization have experience of computer misuse by employees. The initiators of the security introduction, the IT manager at the social department and the IT manager at the IT service unit in the organization, stressed that the privacy regulation in elderly care necessitated a change in security behavior.

In the municipality organization, the initiators considered potential security problems/threats to be well known in user groups. Accordingly, the users were kept informed of privacy issues, and users also must sign a confidentiality agreement when employed. While involved managers contend that awareness for privacy matters was high in the organization, still, there is always a risk of computer abuse, due to the reluctance of fulfilling logout procedures, which enables others to using computers with other people's user credentials. The monitoring of security at the IT service unit reveals 40 people may utilize one computer during a day for reporting completed work tasks. This was typically accomplished during lunch breaks and at the end of the workdays. Monitoring before BehavioSec involved checking log files, which were available from the municipalities IT department, and crosschecking the logs for abuse.

With the introduction of the BehavioSec platform the security management intended to substantially improve protective measures for patient records. For example, while intention to use the new technology to collect and in run-time be able to analyze behavioral data; one expectation from the technology was increased security aware-ness among the work staff. Interestingly, the latter was more or less taken for granted due to an understanding that the software was self-instructive when being used. How-ever, we find that BehavioSec substantially improved the monitoring activity by in-ducing an automated process. The elderly care organization, however, required some general efforts from users to achieve a successful use of BehavioSec.

One important aspect we found was the three managers' uniformed view that the organization has suffered from maladaptive security behavior. However, they also illustrated separate views in preparing for the security software introduction. This in turn, affected the ability to communicate the further instructions to work groups. While the initiators of the security software introduction used a push approach when persuading the work group to participate in the project, we could identify that there were no interactions between management levels and employees after the decision for the introduction was made. It was anticipated that the identification and verification features of the BehavioSec security platform would be sufficient enough to render a change in security behavior.

6.2   Illustrating the Use Context

The employees anticipated substantial impact from BehavioSec on work performance, productivity, and effectiveness as they performed quite many administrative tasks dur-ing a workday. The employees were obliged to record electronically but since they had too few computers available this is done both on paper and electronically. In total the elderly care center maintained 2 workstations except the one on the manager's office, which was constantly occupied. Accordingly, the log on procedure on computers and applications was very time consuming, and staff solved this with sharing user creden-tials. We could identify that the employees partly see this as a problem with slow sup-port from the IT service unit's helpdesk, and partly having too few available computers. Given the expectations of the new system together with non-existing training activities, we describe the encounter using the general terms adaptation and acceptance.

6.3   Starting to Adapt

Adaptation concerns how users perceive usefulness of technology and how it trans-lates into work processes and hence security behavior [15]. Prior to the introduction of BehavioSec, all employees complained about the significant number of computer related problems affecting the use of care applications. With the introduction of Be-havioSec, the security system remained invisible in the sense that employees were not intruded by system properties and it was agreed that the usefulness of security procedures indeed had increased after the introduction. Once enrolled, the employees confirmed that their experience of the system was better than expected prior to the introduction. Two of the employees even expected that the general service level of the new system would increase after some time of use. We could identify that this was due to high expectations among these employees that the system would, more or less, entail changed and improved work processes. While managers uniformly distributed the responsibility to prepare for enacting the new security system, employees initially expected completely other benefits from the system, which the technology could not deliver upon.

6.4   Acceptance

Acceptance concerns satisfaction with new technology and how it can be subject to continuous use after introduction [54]. Considering the overall computer situation in the elderly care center (40 people on two computers), as explained by the user group, there were clear signs of potential mal-adaptive security behavior. For example, when having trouble with passwords employees were expected to call local support for further assistance. However, this was not efficient according to the work staff because of long response times to get a new password from the support function.

The employees intended to continue using the security software, rather than use any alternative means, such as having colleagues' entering healthcare information in the security software on their behalf. BehavioSec thus constituted new action patterns among employees. However, we could observe that the employees would have been more obliging for the initial introduction motives if they actively could have affected the work processes as such, in relation to training in how to best exploit BehavioSec.

Looking at these two sides of the system introduction we identified that the initiation of BehavioSec was rather well communicated between the different managers. The communication to employees was more ad-hoc oriented and unstructured, which meant that the importance of the introduction became blurred, since work staff had no, or low, knowledge of the actual motives. However, for employees work life became easier as the single sign on authentication procedure in BehavioSec resulted in seamless identification and less intrusive security controls. Table 2 summarizes the change in security management practice and the perceptions among employees affected by the new way of enacting security applications.

Table 2. Key features enhancing aspects of the information security practice

	Before BehavioSec	*After BehavioSec*	*Affordances*
Information security management practice	Legal/regulatory requirements about confidentiality and privacy not fulfilled	Clearer view and higher level of legal/regulatory fulfillment	Transparency
	Cross checking log files	The software triggers action by notifications	Continuous monitoring
	Low awareness levels of security among employees	Improved security awareness among employees	Awareness
Users' perception of information security	Security limits work efficiency	Increased efficiency	Non-intrusiveness
	Partial single sign-on	Automatic single sign-on to additional applications	Seamlessness
	Non-satisfactory level of computer availability/service level	Improved service level on available resources.	Acceptability

7   Discussion

This paper discusses the intertwined relationship between organizational security objectives, technology, and employees' security behavior. We applied the concept of technological affordances to investigate the introduction of a behavioral information security platform into an organization's IS infrastructure. We draw on recently developed insights in material research arguing for the strong relationship between agency, the material, and the social [8], which are implicated in all manner of engagements in work practices [11].

Protection need is a predominant mode in the security literature and has for decades favored techno-centric approaches as more beneficial than softer approaches because they are more tangible and contains quantifiable measures of security breaches. Recent behavioral security studies suggest that, for example, perceived vulnerability significantly influence managers intention to adopt security software [4], and employee's adherence to security policies [47]. Although these studies are designed differently and giving different support to its hypothesis, they both show that intentionality to follow a spokesman's advice for protection is important. In Lee and Larsen's case this was achieved through vendor support, and in Pahnila et al.:s research, spokesmen such as the security staff should communicate the importance of compliance. This is supported by [2] who suggest that improved security behavior among employees is the result of effective security education.

Regarding the need for protection in organizations our findings are consistent with earlier security research results. However, the findings also differ because where earlier research stressed the need for external programs, such as, awareness campaigns, the initiators at the elderly care center trust the security platform's ability to render improved security behavior. To this end the security features identification and verification play a particular role because the security system operations are dependent on adaptive response from employees to build up comparable data sets. In so doing the technology constitutes a specific pathway for humans to adopt in the routines of security management. This pathway for instance entangles the technical feature circumvention with human intention to act elusive. In particular, if employees intent to lure the security system by sharing passwords it cannot succeed because employees are now bound to enact security the way BehavioSec delegates action opportunities. Essentially, employees cannot circumvent BehavioSec because of its feature distinctiveness, which is entwined with the uniqueness of each and every employee.

One consequence, however, is that the understanding of protection motivation seem to stretch as far as the managers own individual responsibilities reach. The arguments for protection motivation became more objective when statements were made higher in the organizational hierarchy, whereas the manager close to daily work tasks and security operations had to cope with her uncertainty about detailed motives for the new system. Ultimately the security managers presupposed the material features as means to externalize the protection need into the use context. Behavioral security technology is thus capable of defining actions because its features become enacted in a relational setting that is constructive to human actors [45].

In terms of expectations the security literature is far more fragmented and uncharted than research on protection need. Valuable insights can be found in critical, institutional, and social learning security research. Stahl et al. [15] for instance, suggest that the status of information security management is determined by how users for instance perceive access regulations. Hsu in [5:148] adopts an institutional view on security misalignment in which people behave in a certain way towards the introduction of new organizational practices because of existing "undesirable attitudes toward IS security". Hsu [5] suggests that a frame analysis would help IS security professionals and company managers to identify whether any staff members have undesirable attitudes toward IS security, and activate an early intervention strategy accordingly. Warkentin et al. [6] argue that there is little existing insight into how the social elements of an organizational setting, also called external cues, influence employee compliance outcomes.

Our study shows that the material features of behavioral security software materialize intentions and expectations of IS security and makes them visible and creates acceptance for the need to secure information systems. As the reason for sharing passwords between employees is rooted in the miserable situation of access to computer resources, the affordances of BehavioSec formed the attitude that the new system would enhance work productivity, and accordingly employees want the technology to behave in that manner. As the employees sought for ways to achieve that, the less intrusive enrolment procedures constituted enhanced work productivity. Although employees understand the concept of access control, they expect BehavioSec to provide new ways of performing daily work tasks. This has never been the ambition with the introduction of BehavioSec, but reveals that communication about protection actually can form unintended expectations depending on different views of the materials promising effects. Hence, the result from intentions and expectations found in our case is a mixture of social cues [6] and technological affordances [8]. Highlighting entanglement between technology and human agency means in this regard that performance of BehavioSec resulted in improved security policy compliance. We suggest that this can be understood as an attainment aspect, which for security managers is an important goal. The employees on the other hand attained for example less maintenance of passwords.

Drawing on the sociomaterial literature, our study suggests that the success of security behavior can be better understood when analyzed systematically by taking into consideration the entanglement perspective. In particular, technological affordances is one approach to achieve what [5] calls an intervention strategy to understand undesirable attitudes toward IS security. Instead of looking at security as a black-box the affordance view suggests that the social and the material are fundamentally co-constitutive [8, 9, 17]. In our case the assumptions of protection need and expectation of the new technology is embedded in the features provided by BehavioSec. This does not mean that we can claim materiality as the single handed factor for creating changes in the workplace, to use the words of Leonardi and Barley in [8]. However, the material features are entangled to every relevant entity of the security management practice and therefore sets the stage for a durable unity of institutionalized commitment to organizational information security.

8   Conclusions

In this study, we draw on the sociomaterial literature to develop a better understanding of how behavioral information security technology materializes organizational information security. In this regard we followed a case study research strategy to describe an organizations motive to implement a new type of security formula into employees every day work tasks. We read action, intention and expectation through material affordances that the selected security technology display as being a central actor in the information security practise as Orlikowski [45] advice when conducting sociomaterial research. Our single case study is limited in that it presents only a snapshot picture of the reality within one organization. More extensive research is needed and longitudinal and comparative approaches to co-evolution of technology and humans are required to develop better knowledge of security technology materials [8]. However, our research approach made it possible to understand, how behavioral security technology afford a number of qualities that have impact on the overall information security practice. Our approach thus suggests a possible pathway to cope with the challenge of how to change employees' security behavior, while at the same time improving management of information systems security.

Future research along this vein may challenge the traditional understanding of security technologies as controlling artifacts only. Indeed, we see that our research is promising for organizations that actively consider information security a potential productivity enabler. The reason for this is the affordances that behavioral security technology offers to integrate security management and security in use within organizations value/activity chains. In this regard, we believe it is important to study how behavioral security technologies for instance can strengthen alignment between business processes and IT services at any level within and between organizations.

References

1. Chandra, A., Calderon, T.: Challenges and constraints to the diffusion of biometrics in information systems. Communications of the ACM 48, 101–106 (2005)
2. Puhakainen, P., Siponen, M.: Improving employees' compliance through information systems security training: An action research study. MIS Quarterly 34, 767–793 (2010)
3. Myyry, L., Siponen, M., Pahnila, S., Vartiainen, T., Vance, A.: What levels of moral reasoning and values explain adherence to information security rules: An empirical study. European Journal of Information Systems 18, 126–139 (2009)
4. Lee, Y., Larsen, K.R.: Threat or coping appraisal: determinants of SMB executives/' decision to adopt anti-malware software. European Journal of Information Systems 18, 177–187 (2009)
5. Hsu, C.W.: Frame misalignment: interpreting the implementation of information systems security certification in an organization. European Journal of Information Systems 18, 140–150 (2009)
6. Warkentin, M., Johnston, A.C., Shropshire, J.: The influence of the informal social learning environment on information privacy policy compliance efficacy and intention. European Journal of Information Systems 20, 267–284 (2011)

7. Wade, H.B., Linda, W.: Is information security under control?: Investigating quality in information security management. IEEE Security & Privacy 5, 36–44 (2007)
8. Leonardi, P.M., Barley, S.R.: Materiality and change: Challenges to building better theory about technology and organizing. Information and Organization 18, 159–176 (2008)
9. Introna, L.D., Hayes, N.: On sociomaterial imbrications: What plagiarism detection systems reveal and why it matters. Information and Organization 21, 107–122 (2011)
10. Jonsson, K., Holmström, J., Lyytinen, K.: Turn to the material: Remote diagnostic systems and new forms of boundary spanning. Information and Organization 19(2009), 233–252 (2009)
11. Scolaí, P.: Materialising materiality. In: Proceedings of the Twenty Ninth International Conference on Information Systems, Paris, pp. 1–10 (2008)
12. Orlikowski, W.J.: Sociomaterial practices: Exploring technology at work. Organization Studies 28, 1435–1448 (2007)
13. Holmström, J., Robey, D.: Inscribing organizational change with information technology. In: Czarniawska, B., Hernes, T. (eds.) Actor-network Theory and Organising. Copenhagen Business School Press, Copenhagen (2005)
14. Choobineh, J., Dhillon, G., Grimalla, M., Rees, J.: Management of information security: challenges and research directions. Communications of the Association for Information Systems 20, 958–971 (2007)
15. Stahl, B.C., Shaw, M., Doherty, N.F.: Information systems security management: A critical research agenda. In: Association of Information Systems SIGSEC Workshop on Information Security and Privacy (WISP 2008), Paris (2008)
16. Woodhouse, S.: Information Security: End User Behavior and Corporate Culture. In: Proceedings of the Seventh Conference on Computer and Information Technology, pp. 767–772. IEEE (2007)
17. Orlikowski, W.J.: Sociomaterial practices: Exploring technology at work. Organization Studies 28, 1435–1448 (2007)
18. Siponen, M.: Analysis of modern IS security development approaches: Towards the next generation of social and adaptable ISS methods. Information and Organization 15, 339–375 (2005)
19. Dhillon, G., Backhouse, J.: Current directions in IS security research: Towards socio-organizational perspectives. Information Systems Journal 11, 127–153 (2001)
20. Baskerville, R.: Risk analysis: An interpretive feasibility tool in justifying information systems security. European Journal of Information Systems 1, 121–130 (1991)
21. Dhillon, G.: Princples of information security: Text and cases. John Wiley & Sons, New Jersey (2007)
22. Lacey, D.: Understanding and transforming organizational security culture. Information Management & Computer Security 18, 4–13 (2010)
23. Stanton, J.M., Mastrangelo, P.R., Stam, K.R., Jolton, J.: Behavioral information security: Two end user survey studies of motivation and security practices. In: Proceedings of the Tenth America's Conference on Information Systems, New York (2004)
24. Dinev, T., Hu, Q.: The centrality of awareness in the formation of user behavioral intention toward protective information technologies. Journal of the Association for Information Systems 8 (2007)
25. Backhouse, J., Dhillon, G.: Structures of responsibilities and security of information systems. European Journal of Information Systems 5, 2–10 (1996)
26. von Solms, B.: Information security - The third wave? Computers & Security 19, 615–620 (2000)

27. Silva, L., Backhouse, J.: The circuits-of-power framework for studying power in institutionalization of information systems. Journal of the Association for Information Systems 4, 294–336 (2003)
28. Whitman, M.E., Mattord, H.: Principles of information security. Course Technology, Boston (2005)
29. Bishop, M.: Computer security: Art and science. Addison-Wesley, Boston (2003)
30. Johnston, A.C., Warkentin, M.: Fear appeals and information security behaviors: An empirical study. MIS Quarterly 34, 549–565 (2010)
31. Siponen, M.: A conceptual foundation for organizational information security awareness. Information Management & Computer Security 8, 31–41 (2000)
32. Dhillon, G., Torkzadeh, G.: Value-focused assessment of information system security in organizations. Information Systems Journal 16, 293–314 (2006)
33. Hedström, K., Dhillon, G., Karlsson, F.: Using Actor Network Theory to Understand Information Security Management. In: Rannenberg, K., Varadharajan, V., Weber, C. (eds.) SEC 2010. IFIP AICT, vol. 330, pp. 43–54. Springer, Heidelberg (2010)
34. Siponen, M., Willison, R.: Information security management standards: Problems and solutions. Information & Management 46, 267–270 (2009)
35. Elgarah, W., Falaleeva, N.: Adoption of biometric technology: Information privacy in TAM. In: Proceedings of AMCIS The Americas Conference on Information Systems. Paper 222 (2005)
36. Matyas, S.M., Stapleton, J.: A biometric standard for information management and security. Journal of Computer Security 19, 428–441 (2000)
37. Phillips, P.J., Martin, A., Wilson, C.L., Przybocki, M.: An introduction evaluating biometric systems. Computer 33, 56–63 (2000)
38. Boatwright, M., Luo, X.: What do we know about biometrics authentication? In: Proceedings of the 4th Annual Conference on Information Security Curriculum Development. ACM, Kennesaw (2007)
39. Jain, A.K., Ross, A., Prabhakar, S.: An introduction to biometric recognition. IEEE Transactions on Circuits and Systems for Video Technology 14, 4–20 (2004)
40. Lease, D.R.: Factors influencing the adoption of biometric security technologies by decision-making information technology and security managers. Dissertation 179, Capella University (2005)
41. Gamboa, H., Fred, A.: A behavioural biometric system based on human computer interaction. SPIE (2004)
42. Pentland, B.T., Feldman, M.S.: Designing routines: On the folly of designing arti facts, while hoping for patterns of action. Information and Organization 18, 235–250 (2008)
43. Kong, J., Zerfos, P., Luo, H., Lu, S., Zhang, L.: Providing robust and ubiquitous security support for mobile ad hoc networks. In: The Ninth IEEE ICNP, Riverside, USA, pp. 251–260 (2001)
44. Barad, K.: Posthumanist performativity: Toward an understanding of how matter comes to matter. Signs 28, 801–831 (2003)
45. Orlikowski, W.J.: The sociomateriality of organisational life: considering technology in management research. Cambridge Journal of Economics 34, 125–141 (2010)
46. Harnesk, D., Lindström, J.: Shaping security behavior through discipline and agility: Implications for information security management. Information Management & Computer Security 19 (2011)

47. Pahnila, S., Siponen, M., Mahmood, A.: Employées Adherence to Information Security Policies: An Empirical Study. In: Venter, H., Eloff, M., Labuschagne, L., Eloff, J., von Solms, R. (eds.) New Approaches for Security, Privacy and Trust in Complex Environments. IFIP, vol. 232, pp. 133–144. Springer, Boston (2007)
48. Bhattacherjee, A., Premkumar, G.: Understanding changes in belief and attitude toward information technology usage: A theoretical model and longitudinal test. MIS Quarterly 28, 229–254 (2004)
49. Orlikowski, W.J., Gash, D.C.: Technological frames: Making sense of information technology in organizations. ACM Transactions of Information Systems 2, 174–207 (1994)
50. Straub, D.W., Welke, R.J.: Coping with systems risk: Security planning models for management decision making. MIS Quarterly 22, 441–469 (1998)
51. Cordella, A.: Information infrastructure in action. London School of Economics and Political Sciences, Department of Information Systems (2006)
52. Yin, R.: Case study research. Sage Publications, Thousand Oaks (1994)
53. Miles, M.B., Huberman, M.A.: Qualitative data analysis. Sage Publications, Thousand Oaks (1994)
54. Chattacherjee, A.: Understanding information systems continuance: An expectation-confirmation Model. MIS Quarterly 5, 351–370 (2001)

What If Design Is Something Else: The Challenges of Dealing with Interdependencies

Margunn Aanestad

Department of Informatics, University of Oslo, P.O. Box 1080, N-0316 Oslo, Norway
margunn@ifi.uio.no

Abstract. The interactive society is also the interdependent society, and this poses challenges to the IS field's conceptualization of what design entails. ICTs are intimately intertwined with work practices, institutions and with other technological systems, and the resulting assemblage exhibits a complexity that challenges design interventions. Relevant conceptualizations from the IS field should be further developed to help us come to grips with the challenges. The nature of design is explored through two empirical vignettes. Both vignettes illustrate design "in the large", involving more participants, different objectives and multiple types of tasks relative to classical instances of software or systems design. The interdependencies' implications for design are examined, and a conceptual decomposition of interdependencies is proposed. The three-dimensional decomposition into spatial extent, functional coverage and temporal duration can potentially be used for a more proactive approach to intended and unintended interdependencies during design "in the large".

1   The Interdependent Society

Connectivity and interactivity are salient aspects of the current ICT landscape in the Western world, and this has dramatically impacted several aspects of our personal and collective lives. For instance, mobile technologies have changed how social relations are mediated and coordinated. Moreover, due to the interactive nature of these technologies, they are not primarily stand-alone tools or applications used by individuals. They have spurred the emergence of entirely new products, markets and business relations, as well as stimulated new production models, such as user-driven innovations in the digital ecologies around the iOS and Android platforms. However, the technological infrastructure that allows connectivity and interactive flexibility also imply couplings and interdependencies. Connectivity and interactivity come with immense benefits, but also with a price related to vulnerability and risk when large-scale systems fail to function. For both the IS community and the larger society it is crucial to understand this double-sided nature of the interactive society better.

Here I want to pursue the theme of interdependencies and link it to a discussion of the object of research within the IS field. I will argue that we should not only consider standalone information systems, but should conceptualize our research objects in ways that encompass their interactive and interdependent nature. Designing the interactive society means designing the interconnected and interdependent society.

C. Keller et al. (Eds.): SCIS 2012, LNBIP 124, pp. 95–108, 2012.

We need to question how we think about design in this context, and I will present an argument that aims to expand the scope of the definition of design in both a temporal and a spatial sense.

This premise implies that the paper do not align itself with the ongoing discourse where the IS field is positioned as one of the design-oriented disciplines, together with e.g. engineering, arts and architecture. For instance, the Design Science approach is an applied and pragmatic research paradigm, emphasizing how the IS field should be geared towards practical problem solving. In addition, the formulation of Design Science seeks to induce scientific rigour into the IS field, and seeks to produce generalizable, highly useful and fundamental knowledge about appropriate design principles for specified problems. A limitation of this stream is that it focuses its attention just on the design of software artefacts: "Design in information systems is both an interactive process (set of activities) and a resulting product (artifact) – a verb and a noun [...] Very simply stated, design in information systems deals with building software artifacts which solve a human problem" [1]. The narrow focus on the IT artefact have been challenged by recent research contributions that argues that IT artefacts evolve in interaction with an organizational context [2, 3], advocating an integration of Action Research and Design Research approaches. Here is presented a somewhat more encompassing conceptualization of the technology artefact as an "ensemble artefact", i.e. as bundles of software and/or hardware that have both material and organizational features, and that are dynamic and emergent. A central motivation behind the Action-Design Research approach is to overcome the separation that Design Research poses between design (building) and use (evaluation). Still, the aim is to generate prescriptive design knowledge in the form of generic design principles. Both the problem and the solution are generalizable, through being framed as an instance of a class of problems and a class of solutions to the particular problem.

This approach is valuable because it acknowledges the interplay between design and emergence in the development of information systems. That there is no simple relationship between designers' initial intentions and the resulting outcomes has been known for long in the IS field (see e.g. [4]). To expand the focus from the software artefact to the "ensemble artefact" brings us one step closer to more appropriate conceptualizations of the complex reality. However, in this paper we will argue that we need to go further in order to start to conceptualize the challenges posed to designers by the interdependent society.

In order to illuminate this we present empirical material generated within two different healthcare organizations. These cases show different facets of interconnectedness and interdependency, and our analytic focus will be to identify the implications of this for design activities. We discuss design activities in a broad sense and within an extended scope, both spatially and temporally. In the next section we present existing conceptualizations and discuss their relevance and limitations. We then present the empirical material, reflecting on what design may entail. The emphasis is on how design involves other participants, tasks and object than the traditional conceptualizations cover. To better understand how to deal with interdependencies, they are decomposed into three dimensions.

2   Relevant Conceptualizations

The IS field has for long recognized that systems development in practice show limited compliance with formal, prescriptive methodologies, and often occur "in the wild" [5], [6]. This is often seen in the context of end-user tailoring, customization and further development of the systems portfolio in an organizational context. One stream of research that has explicitly challenged the belief in orderly and rationalistic design processes is studies of information infrastructures. The case collection published in 2000 with the indicative title "From Control to Drift" [7] contains numerous case stories about how intentional design plans become thwarted. One of the major reasons is the conservative power of what is called the installed base. The installed base is a given in all situations of change, and it will impact and sometimes thwart design initiatives. In such a situation, pragmatic, evolutionary and iterative approaches seem appropriate. This stream of research proposes 'cultivation' rather than 'construction' as a guiding metaphor for the interventions, building on [8]. Cultivation of the installed base point to the mixture of deliberate design effects and emergent, unexpected or unintended effects. However, not only does the installed base pose challenges. Also the degree of interconnectedness and integration between systems and components of the socio-technical assemblage lead to the emergence of unexpected outcomes. These issues of integration and interdependencies and their effects on IS, are explicitly discussed in another collection of cases [9]. In addition a collection of studies from the public sector [10], describes the digitization as a process of establishing a composite architecture, not only of technologies, but of institutional architectures and administrative processes. The existing institutionalized frameworks are being reconfigured, with intended or unintended outcomes.

Thus this stream of research acknowledges that deliberate action generate side-effects, and unintended consequences. Its conceptualization of what "design" entails thus encompass a notion of deliberate and intentional interventions mixed with emergence. The interest centers on the evolutionary dynamics, i.e. on understanding how these complex systems evolve. Similar insights are represented also in the broader, emerging streams in IS that focus on more complex research objects such as digital ecosystems and/or platform ecologies [11, 12, 13, 14].

While relevant conceptualizations do exist, we also believe that there is ample scope for researchers to push further, in order to understand what design for an interdependent society can and should be. While the notion of 'cultivation of the installed base' is a useful metaphor, it should be complemented with more specific descriptions of concrete strategies. We could also benefit from a clearer, more nuanced conceptualization of 'installed base'. Rather than a notion that cover (and black-box) all that is pre-existing in a situation, we need to come to grasp with which elements of the installed base impact the design initiatives in which way. In the following, we will seek to focus on achieving more granular and nuanced conceptualization of how interdependencies impact design initiatives.

3   Dealing with Interdependencies

In this section we will present two empirical vignettes that illustrate some aspects of what it implies to deal with interdependencies. The two vignettes describe different types of interdependencies. The first vignette is set in a large specialized hospital, which is a teaching hospital with a high degree of specialization and research activities. The vignette describes the IT department's struggle over more than 15 years to offer the hospital's clinical staff access to multiple relevant information systems, first within a single hospital context and then, following an organizational merger, across multiple hospitals. The second vignette is from a considerable smaller hospital in size, but it is also the country' largest within its specialized domain of rehabilitation. The vignette describes a process where new tools were introduced in the collaboration between a hospital and its external partners, and we offer a few glimpses from the subsequent process of redesign of the service provision in order to achieve continuity of care between multiple partners.

3.1   Research Approach

The material presented here was generated through longitudinal contact and involvement with the two organizations. The IT department in the large specialized hospital in the first vignette has been a research partner for more than a decade. An intensive study was carried out by four researchers between 2001 and 2005, when the major changes of digitization occurred. The fieldwork consisted of practical participation in projects as well as observations of health personnel's work, and interviews with users and IT staff. The study for the second vignette was carried out during 2007-2011, also here with participation in practical projects, observations and interviews. Both accounts below are highly abstracted summaries that do not reflect the richness of the empirical material collected in the studies (which is also reported in other publications); however, the detailed studies were necessary for the interpretation of the events that are accounted for here.

3.2   Vignette 1: Organizational Management of IS Portfolio

The hospital's first information systems had been administrative mainframe systems for tasks related to personnel, payroll, accounting, as well as a patient administrative system, which was used also by secretarial staff in the various clinics. In 1995 several projects to develop and implement other clinical IS were initiated. The hospital now wanted to implement both a number of laboratory systems, radiological information systems and image archives (RIS and PACS) and an electronic patient record system (EPR). The EPR system was to be developed by a national consortium of the largest specialist hospitals together with the national branch of a large, international software and hardware vendor. The EPR was at this time envisioned as the central information system for the clinician. It should offer complete information for every patient across the organization, and it should replace the previous paper-based, non-standardized, local archives that each department had maintained. An integration of these local archives into one central archive, together with standardization of documentation routines and forms were conducted prior to the digitization of the record. At the time, there was also a handful computerized local systems. These had often been developed in-house or purchased by individual doctors or departments, to suit their needs for collecting more specific information on certain patients or diseases, both for treatment and for later quality assurance and/or research purposes. The initial idea was to incorporate this functionality into the EPR system to avoid double data entry.

The EPR system developed in the national project was supposed to be finalized by 1999 [15]. However, due to various factors the project struggled to deliver according to plan, and was terminated in 2004 with a less-than agreed-on functionality of the software. Earlier versions of the system had been piloted since 1996 in a few departments, offering extensive local customization. Wider roll-out was planned to occur after the hospital had moved into new facilities in October 1998. The move was postponed several times, and did not occur until May 2000. This delay not only necessitated spending time and resources on the Y2K issue instead of just leaving the old IT systems behind, but it also delayed the broader EPR implementation. The implementation across the whole hospital occurred during 2002, with the current release covering just about 30-40 % of the intended functionality. At the time when the EPR system was widely implemented, the number of smaller clinical systems had grown from a handful to over 160, and a replacement or even an integration of them all with the EPR would be infeasible. The IT department decided instead to develop a portal solution that would provide a "visual integration" (presentation layer integration) of the various underlying information systems. This was developed in-house by the IT department who had highly competent staff and enjoyed a high level of autonomy. However, from January 1st 2002 a health sector reform had changed the ownership structure for the hospitals, which were now governed by regional health trusts. Within these trusts there were strong drivers for streamlining and standardizing applications across the region, and in order to avoid being stopped in developing the portal solution, the development team created an independent company and left the hospital organization.

Still much of the information within the hospital only existed on paper, and even the digital documents had to be printed and archived in the paper record to create one legally valid, complete record. The new facilities had been built with a relatively small space allocated for the archive, in the expectation that the EPR system would already be installed. Soon the archive was full, and in 2003 a scanning project was initiated to try to cope with the situation. Incoming letters, printed results from various equipment or systems, and other documents were scanned and stored as images in the patient's file in the EPR system. While this was initially planned as a 6 months project, it ran for over two years, since digitizing the documents implied a significant degree of workflow and organizational redesign. The official switch from a paper-based to a digital patient record did not happen until March 2006.

The external company that developed the portal also looked towards other markets in their commercial strategy, leaving the original customers in this hospital somewhat marginalized. In 2009 a merger between four large hospitals was announced, and a tender process initiated by the regional health trust for a new portal solution for the new, merged organization. In December 2009 an international vendor was selected instead of the existing portal vendor (the local company). The implementation schedule was tight, with the first large deliverable due 6 months after the decision. Multiple delays occurred during 2010, and to few people's surprise, in May 2011 the media disclosed that the project was terminated, having achieved little result from the 20 million euro spent thus far. The previous portal solution was still in use among the earlier users, and ad hoc measures had to be taken to offer access to the systems of the merged organization for all its members who needed it. What the regional health trust sees as the way forward is currently not clear.

Summary of Vignette No. 1

This account is by necessity brief and superficial, as we only can summarize a few events and processes during this period. Despite this, the vignette hopefully illustrates the diverse set of issue that the IT department has had to deal with in the period in order to offer its clients the suite of well-working information systems that they needed. This goes far beyond producing a software artefact, or even an ensemble artefact. It also went beyond the need to define and implement enterprise architecture to govern the diverse systems portfolio. The IT-department had to deal with a lot of other issues than technology. This required a multi-modal strategy and ability to navigate in a political context. The number of actors that they had to interrelate with was large, and the actors did not only belong to their own organization. They had to maneuver in relation to users who requested solutions, to vendors that did not deliver according to plan, and to authorities that did not endorse their development activities. Practically, their plans were influenced by other actors, both inside and outside the organization. This implied that they had to turn quickly to exploit opportunities and avoid threats. The work was continuous on a long time scale, incorporating multiple more targeted projects, and saw a mixture of planned initiatives and emergent responses.

The existing portfolio of information systems in the hospital strongly impacted the scope for change and action. Each step in a change process had to have a non-disruptive effect on the organization's functioning, both with respect to information systems and work practices. Thus, we see a 'muddling through' strategy rather than a straight-forward implementation of a vision or strategy. The "design work" here; i.e. the deliberate efforts of implementing the goals, includes practical and creative action not only within a development or implementation frame, but within a management frame that involved other action modalities.

3.3   Vignette 2: Creating Interconnected Service Provision

Here we describe an attempt by a specialist rehabilitation hospital with a nation-wide catchment population to establish novel, ICT-enabled communication forms with its external collaborators. The hospital's patient categories included victims of accidents, violence and debilitating long-term diseases; conditions that demanded cross-disciplinary and long-term care. After some weeks or months of hospitalization the patients were usually transferred to a care setting that was administered by the patient's home municipality. A suitable care solution needed to be established before the patient was discharged from the hospital. If the patient would live in her or his home, partial re-building of the home could be necessary. These aspects required contact with the receiving municipality well in advance of discharge. Also there were considerable need for extensive transfer of knowledge and practical skills along with patient transfer. The carers in the municipality would need to learn to know the patient and what the condition entailed. There might be special needs for diet, supporting equipment and tools, as well as an exercise regime designed by the hospital's physiotherapists.

Such needs for communication with the hospital's external partners had been the impetus behind the hospital's experimentation with telemedicine in the form of videoconference meetings. Through previous project activities, traditional videoconferencing equipment had been installed in various studios (meeting rooms) at the hospital. After some years with relatively small-scale experimentation of telemedicine usage in various projects, an institutionalization project was started in 2008. The explicit aim of this project was to establish use of telemedicine as a routine service across the whole hospital. This meant that several new user groups, both health personnel and patient groups, would become involved. Previously, the common mode of cooperation was based on either physical travel or on limited communication via telephone and paper reports.

The new form of service delivery changed several aspects of the task. Instead of one-to-one conversations (e.g. hospital physiotherapist to municipal physiotherapist) the telemediated meetings became a larger forum where the whole teams met, and discussed matters in a way that allowed for different outcomes, e.g. instant rather than sequential and thus prolonged decision-making processes. Also the patient could be more involved if the health condition allowed it. In addition, the hospital staff could offer sustained support to the care teams after the patient had been transferred to the home municipality. Regular videoconferencing meetings allowed transfer of knowledge and skill that supported the care team (who were not specialists) to perform more than what they would otherwise do. Also pre-hospitalization meeting were held. This could be related to repeated stays at the hospitals after some time had elapsed, for a re-assessment of rehabilitation potential and a redesign of the training program. It was also used for selection of patients that would be suitable for (in the sense of being able to benefit from) group treatment. This allowed the minimization of travels for such a personal assessment, which could be very cumbersome and expensive since a wheelchair needs special handling on airplanes. It also helped to adjust expectations on both sides for the planned hospital visit.

During the project the project leaders realized that the diversity in the hospital was too large to just copy some work patterns across the whole hospital. Different departments in the hospital catered for patient groups with different problems, and consequently the collaboration needs differed a lot. For instance, while some departments catered for patients who would stay for several months at the hospital, other departments had organized their activities as outpatient clinics or daycare. This could be for standardized assessments of e.g. work ability, suitability for getting a driver's license or need for special support in the employment or school situation. These departments had less need for communication with external partners, and they also had less time available to organize a videoconference meeting. A process of trials and experimentation in the various departments allowed them to get experience with the suitability, requirements and limits of the technology.

A large part of this job was to embed these technology-mediated models for improved collaboration into the organizational routines. This required dedicated work to spread the changes and make them 'stick' in the organization. The project leaders achieved this through asking the project participants to rewrite the local procedures for patient discharge (or other relevant procedures) in the internal quality handbook. An active policy of pushing information through various channels was complemented by a comprehensive training programme, with both scheduled, on-demand and repeat training in a studio and in web courses. However, the organization did not have any funds for these activities, and the employees needed to juggle their schedules and find time and space to participate in project meetings, as well as to plan and set up the patient-related video conferences. The project leaders defined shared procedures and resources for the whole hospital, such as an Outlook-based solution for studio booking, shared facilities for video production (recording and editing), and joint production of information materials. A technical support team was created, with a dedicated hotline telephone number. The support team established catalogues over local VC studios in the different municipalities, defined routines for pre-testing in order to detect out-dated equipment and incompatible software, problems with microphones or cameras etc. Also routines were established for exchanging contact information between technical personnel to conduct the practical work of setting up the videoconference sessions.

Because more than health personnel started to participate in the meetings, for instance social workers, employers, or teachers, the need for patient consent to information sharing arose. Had the meeting involved only health personnel from different institutions, implicit patient consent would have been assumed, but now also other actors were present, and this required explicit consent. Thus the project had to create a suitable form for this, include in the procedures information on how to obtain consent, scan and where in the EPR to put the document. Also on other issues, the whole organization rather than the project had to take a stand. "We are disturbing a lot of nests" said the project leader to indicate that they were touching upon many issues external to the project. The project participants also started to investigate for which groups and under which conditions these new services would be reimbursed. In general, there were some flexibility within organization to cover costs, but if novel services should be deployed on a grand scale; the issue of reimbursement was significant. The project leader contacted the national health authorities to have them clarify the existing financial regulations, since these dealt primarily with doctor-centered consultations and did not encompass these new models of collaboration, where a medical doctor was not necessarily in charge of the interaction. The organization decided on procedures that would release a certain type of reimbursement, while others were discontinued due to resource constraints.

Not all communication partners were healthcare institutions, some were schools or social security offices, or it could be the patient in his or her home; where access to the healthcare-specific broadband communication network had to be negotiated. Initially in the project, many municipal care teams did not have easy access to a studio. However, the project leader approached central technical persons within the welfare sector, which was undergoing a large reform and invested in videoconferencing studios for the required training of its employees. A formal agreement made between the hospital and the welfare sector organization made the local studios available for local healthcare personnel free of charge. The use of videoconference for this kind of meetings increased throughout the hospital, and the project received much attention for the organization-wide usage pattern it had succeeded in establishing

Brief Summary of Vignette 2
What is being designed here, and what were the design activities? The project leaders had very clear visions for what could be achieved, and they did to a large degree succeed in realizing the vision of institutionalizing new models for service provision. In order to achieve this, their activities were ongoing throughout the period, dealt with many different entities, and worked through different modalities. Except from developing a room booking application in Outlook, the project did not involve any software development, but quite a lot of technical work with respect to LAN administration, external network access, selection of cameras, microphones, loudspeakers, projectors etc. The redesign of care relations required learning by every participant, as actually trying out what worked and not was crucial. It was also evident that many issues that were encountered needed to be handled by the whole organization rather than by the project alone. While some issues had to do with individual health workers (e.g. improve the technical skills), other dealt with coordination of work on a work group level (agreement on routines), other with the whole organizations (support solutions, standards), other with the individual collaborators (type of service), and still others with the whole (national) health system (reimbursement, legal regulation). To clarify the reimbursement rules required 'political work', as did the deal with the welfare sector on free-of-charge studios. To mobilize the staff through examples, training and information required also that the project leaders devised feasible and creative strategies. Partly, the work of the project leaders may be called change management, but there was also a large component of explorative design of new services, not only a pre-specified change of the organization.

4   Designing the Interdependent Society

So, what implications are there to draw from these vignettes about the nature of design in the "interactive society"? If we extend the design perspective (what we intended to do with the vignettes), we see that change processes frequently extend beyond single projects, and encompass more than just one organization. The work of "designers" is then often ongoing throughout longer time periods, need to deal with many different types of issues and entities, and has to be implemented through different modalities. Thus design "in the large" points to a different phenomenon than if we had limited design to mean software design (or systems design and implementation) within a project in a given organization. Both the participants, tasks and object of design activities change.

There are **participants** both from within and from outside the organization; they may belong to institutions that have formal power to influence the processes, or they may be users which are crucial to enroll into the project. Design necessitates navigation in a field where these actors have different and possibly conflicting interests. Negotiations of goals, clarification, coordination, strategic moves and counter-moves are all examples of what "design in the large" may involve.

The **object** of design is often changing, as it is based on an elusive vision about a future state. The object gets realized through dynamic and complex configurations and reconfigurations of socio-technical assemblages, which may change the expectations and wishes along the way. Moreover, the object is composite; many small parts need to be realized. For instance, for new models of collaboration to work, the equipment must work the health personnel on both sides need familiarity and skills on how to conduct videoconferences, and the legal and financial regulations must allow the encounter. All of these preconditions represent different sub-objects and necessitate different types of activities. It is crucial to be able to coordinate the work on all of the elements, the sub-objects, to create a trajectory that bridges between the future vision and the existing reality. A goal description is not enough; it must be complemented with a transition strategy, where each intermediate step is non-disruptive.

The concrete **tasks** in these activities are multiple. If we follow [16], we may differentiate between three different types of activities that relate to different temporal scales of design. First, there is "enactment of technology" in the concrete "here-and-now" context. At every step in the change process there must be a working solution, a practical fit with existing work practices and interoperability with pre-existing systems. On the next temporal scale, there emerges a need to adjust or recreate the work organization. And finally, there is work that is oriented towards achieving institutionalization and sustainability of the solution. All of these activities then happen in a context that may intervene; where budget cuts can put a project on hold for some time, and where technical setbacks may thwart an initiative.

4.1   Zooming in on the Role of Interdependencies

Design "in the large" points to a different phenomenon than if we had limited design to mean software or information systems design. Above I claimed that both the participants, the tasks and the objects of design activities would change. Whether, and how these changes are related to interdependencies and couplings, is another question, to which we now turn.

The interdependencies in the large, socio-technical assemblage called "healthcare" are many. Thus any change attempt is difficult to conduct well, since the outcomes are difficult to predict. The interdependencies are also enormously difficult to chart. I believe, however, that we can start to differentiate between a number of dimensions of these interdependencies. In the following a three-dimensional decomposition, inspired by [17] will be presented (see figure 1). The purpose of this model is that it may help us to think more proactively about design challenges in a context where interdependencies seem to preclude traditional approaches to change the status quo.

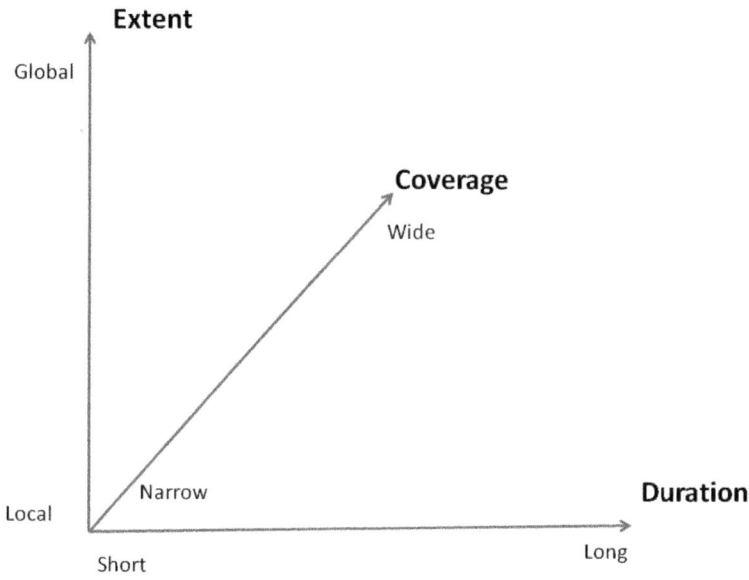

Fig. 1. Three dimensions of interdependencies

First, the interdependencies have different spatial extent. Some involve only local stakeholders, such as individuals, work groups, departments or the entire organization. Other involve external stakeholders where the "designer", however much management support has been secured within the organization, do not have any formal mandate to instruct actors beyond its borders. The importance of this dimension has to do with the fact that it is linked to decision-making. When the decision-making rights are distributed beyond the design context, the traditional command-and-control strategies need to be exchanged with strategies that engage in negotiations and mobilization, based on a recognition of the political nature of the task. The struggles of the IT-department in vignette no. 1 illustrates the negative impact of competitive interests between different actors belonging to different levels in the hierarchy, where some sought standardization and the others sought working solutions. Many resources were spent in the various moves and counter-moves among the parties. In vignette no. 2, we also saw the need to extend beyond the organizational context, and create alliances both with the communication partners and with external actors (e.g. the welfare sector). Here the negotiations were successful, leading to the establishment of a robust infrastructure for the new service. In general, interdependencies within a local context are easier to detect and deal with, while interdependencies that extend beyond the designer's decision-making power sphere are more challenging. A general advice when planning change initiatives would be to match the ambitions to the power and resources available. This means that the extent of interdependencies introduced should be assessed relative to the potential power to mandate and/or negotiate solutions.

Second, the interdependencies are of different types, i.e. they involve different types of actors or components. Some interdependencies are related to system-to-system integration, involving primarily technical issues. Other are related to how a new IT system is integrated with work practices, where a number of different types of socio-technical links may become relevant. Some interdependencies may have to do with the technical details of communication tools. Other involve a number of issues required to establish different care models, such as equipment, routines, competencies, regulations, finances etc. Predicting which interdependencies that will arise is challenging, and also to know what outcomes to expect. In general, this prediction becomes more difficult the more the interacting components are different. When the interacting components belong to different domains (e.g. technical and legal) their interaction may be unexpected until it suddenly emerges as a problem. In general, the wider the scope of the initiative, the greater the heterogeneity of components and the more challenging it gets to detect and deal with the interdependencies. They may also require different approaches and modalities of action to be resolved.

Thirdly, the temporal character of the interdependencies differs significantly. Some emerge as "here and now" problems, other become relevant only in the perspective of years, decades or centuries. On the whole, design is never-ending but occurs in "the long now" [16]. Designers therefore need to deal with and balance decisions within the short, medium and long time frame. The elusive and emergent nature of design work may be due to the need to detect, understand and sort out these interdependencies. The unexpected consequences of design decisions may emerge long after the decision; they may have propagated far away from source and have created unexpected effects.

5   Concluding Remarks

The paper has proposed to understand design within an extended scope, both spatially and temporally, in order to address the challenges posed by interconnections and linkages. In the evolution of the large and complex assemblages of information systems, organizations, and regulatory measures that underlie the interactive society, deliberate design is interwoven with emergence. Design interventions are not the only driving force for change. The durability, the spatial extent and systemic nature of the information infrastructures generate couplings and interdependencies, and design in this context resembles the task of managing these interdependencies. Design is thus ongoing, with little distinct end-points (if it ever ends). It is not limited to a project's timeframe, nor is it bounded by the project's extent. A "designer" needs to deal with vastly different types of problems and employ a heterogeneous set of modalities of action. The three-dimensional decomposition of the role of interdependencies offered above may help towards managing and navigating in relation to interdependencies.

This extended view on what design entails is perhaps compatible with Boland's reading [18] of Simon's classical work, "The Sciences of the Artificial" [19]. Boland emphasizes how Simon saw design as a management activity, as well as how design activities, problem structuring and representations were linked. The representations we select will shape how we perceive the problem as well as how we design the intervention. To be appropriately matched with the reality, our conceptualizations of design need to encompass also the challenges that emerge from the durability, spatial extent and systemic nature of the information infrastructures that constitute the interactive society. Herbert Simon emphasized how the manager is a designer in the sense of a formgiver. The core responsibility of the manager-as-designer is thus not to fathom the truth but to "act responsibly in the world".

We may not be able to produce general design principles for such "design in the large" in the same way as the Design Science stream proposes. Rather we should aim to generate better heuristics for this work of management, cultivation and navigation. We need to continue to collect stories from case studies that illuminate design "in the large", so that researchers and students within the IS field are exposed to a number of real world cases. Perhaps researchers need to cultivate a somewhat 'journalistic' sensitivity towards identifying and examining interesting cases? In parallel with collecting and sharing empirical cases, the work of producing, testing, discarding or building on theoretical conceptualizations needs to continue. The experiential learning emerging from this exposure to multiple cases, coupled with proper analytic work would foster a complementary skill set to the skill set which is generated by teaching rigorous methodologies and approaches. Such skills would contribute to a more proactive approach towards intended and unintended interdependencies in design activities.

References

1. Hevner, A., Chatterjee, S. (eds.): Design Research in Information Systems: Theory and Practice. Springer, New York (2010)
2. Purao, S., Rossi, M., Sein, M.K.: On Integrating Action Research and Design Research. In: Hevner, A., Chatterjee, S. (eds.) Design Research in Information Systems: Theory and Practice, pp. 179–194. Springer, New York (2010)
3. Sein, M., Henfridsson, O., Purao, S., Rossi, M.: Action Design Research. MIS Quarterly 35, 37–56 (2010)
4. Curtis, B., Krasner, H., Iscoe, N.: A Field Study of The Software Design Process for Large Systems. Communications of the ACM 31, 1268–1287 (1998)
5. Dittrich, Y., Eriksén, S., et al.: PD in the Wild: Evolving Practices of Design in Use. In: PDC 2002, Malmö, Sweden (2002)
6. Aanestad, M., Henriksen, D., Pors, J.K.: Systems Development in the Wild: User-Led Exploration and Transformation of Organizing Visions. In: Proceedings from IFIP WG. 8.2, Manchester, UK, vol. 143, pp. 615–630 (2004)

7. Ciborra, C., Braa, K., Cordella, A., Dahlbom, B., Failla, A., Hanseth, O., Hespø, V., Ljungberg, J., Monteiro, E., Simon, K.A. (eds.): From Control to Drift - The Dynamics of Corporate Information Infrastructures. Oxford University Press, Oxford (2000)
8. Dahlbom, B., Jahnlert, L.E.: Computer Future, mimeo. Department of Informatics, University of Gothenburg, Sweden (1996)
9. Hanseth, O., Ciborra, C.U. (eds.): Risk, Complexity and ICT. Edward Elgar Publishing, Cheltenham (2007)
10. Contini, F., Lanzara, G.F. (eds.): ICT and Innovation in the Public Sector. European Studies in the Making of E-Government. Palgrave Macmillan, Basingstoke (2008)
11. Tiwana, A., Konsynski, B., Bush, A.A.: Research Commentary: Platform Evolution: Coevolution of Platform Architecture, Governance, and Environmental Dynamics. Information Systems Research 21, 675–687 (2010)
12. Yoo, Y., Henfridsson, O., Lyytinen, K.: Research Commentary: The New Organizing Logic of Digital Innovation: An Agenda for Information Systems Research. Information Systems Research 21, 724–735 (2010)
13. Tilson, D., Lyytinen, K., Sørensen, C.: Research Commentary: Digital Infrastructures: The Missing IS Research Agenda. Information Systems Research 21, 748–759 (2010)
14. El Sawy, O.A., Malhotra, A., Park, Y., Pavlou, P.: Research Commentary: Seeking the Configuration of Digital Ecodynamics: It Takes Three to Tango. Information Systems Research 21, 835–848 (2010)
15. Ellingsen, G., Monteiro, E.: Big is Beautiful: Electronic Patient Records in Large Norwegian Hospitals 1980s – 2001. Methods of Information in Medicine 42, 366–370 (2003)
16. Ribes, D., Finholt, T.A.: The Long Now of Technology Infrastructures: Articulating Tensions in Development. Journal of the Association of Information Systems 10, 375–398 (2009)
17. Jensen, T.B., Aanestad, M.: National initiatives to build healthcare information infrastructures. In: Proceedings of MCIS 2010 Mediterranean Conference on Information Systems. Paper 43 (2010)
18. Boland, R.J.: Design in the Punctuation of Management Action. In: Boland, R. (ed.) Managing as Designing: Creating a Vocabulary for Management Education and Research. Frontiers of Management Workshop, Weatherhead School of Management (2002)
19. Simon, H.: The Sciences of the Artificial. MIT Press, Cambridge (2006)

Constructing a Design Framework
for Performance Dashboards

Heikki Lempinen

Aalto University School of Economics, Runeberginkatu 14-16, 00100 Helsinki, Finland
heikki.lempinen@aalto.fi

Abstract. The purpose of this paper is to outline a framework for designing *performance dashboards*, a type of information system used for performance measurement in organizations. Initial briefing in a case company indicated that a framework is needed due to the complexity and spread of the issues related to designing such systems. However, existing literature does not offer a proper tool for this purpose. Instead, earlier literature concentrates either on measurement design or information systems design and does not illustrate the interplay between them very thoroughly. Hence, drawing from a synthesis between performance measurement and information systems literature, a framework for dashboard design was constructed and then refined with the case company in an iterative manner. Action design research method was used to produce a set of principles for design and development of the system. Furthermore, by depicting links between the suggested design principles, the final framework for dashboard design is presented. Practical relevance of the suggested design framework is illustrated in the case context.

Keywords: performance measurement, dashboards, business intelligence, action design research, executive information systems, information systems development, information systems design theory, visualization.

1   Introduction

A performance dashboard enables organizations to effectively measure, monitor, and manage business performance [1]. Dashboards visualize organizational key performance indicators (KPIs) and utilize different performance measurement models to identify and implement measures for all levels in the organization. Technologically, dashboards are multilayered applications built on business intelligence (BI) and data integration infrastructure. Dashboards are gaining popularity both in private and public sectors and being implemented by organizations worldwide. Due to the growing interest of practitioners, plethora of practitioner-oriented literature on dashboards exists [e.g. 1, 47, 48], while earlier literature published in academic outlets is relatively scarce. Some initiatives have been made to explain what dashboards are [2], how they apply to certain organizational contexts and industries [3, 4] and what drives their adoption [5].

C. Keller et al. (Eds.): SCIS 2012, LNBIP 124, pp. 109–130, 2012.
© Springer-Verlag Berlin Heidelberg 2012

Performance dashboard research stems from performance measurement (PM) and information systems (IS) literature. While there is a rich stream of research in both areas, a holistic framework for designing performance dashboards that is both relevant and does not compromise on academic rigor is missing. Performance measurement literature mostly concentrates on identifying right measures and KPIs [6], but tend to overlook the complexity of implementing the chosen measures from the information systems perspective. On the other hand, IS literature rarely addresses the process of identifying relevant measures very carefully [7]. In order to make a measurement model work, understanding of IT systems is required, and in order to create an IT system that supports decision making and analysis in the right way, one needs to understand how to measure performance.

These challenges in performance dashboard design are manifested in the case organization, Finnish web design and marketing agency Activeark Ltd. The company has grown substantially during its ten first years and during this fast growth, the company management realized that decisions are ever more difficult to be based on a "gut feel". Due to this, the company started to take interest in data-driven management and decision making. Their previous attempt to build an integrated system for performance measurement and reporting failed after the company management realized that they had no clear understanding of what they wanted to measure and how they would actually put the measurement into effect. The case company struggled particularly with finding reliable data for measuring the utilization of internal resources and project performance. These challenges, combined with the lack of a proper framework for addressing the issues, acted as a trigger for the research project.

The problems experienced by the case company are commonplace in many organizations as they grow and diverge. As performance dashboards run on electronic data that needs to be complete and easy to process, populating the dashboard with data is anything but trivial [5]. The precursors of modern BI-based dashboards, executive information systems (EIS), faced problems because the data required was not often readily available; considerable human effort was needed to acquire, analyze, and then enter the data into the system [1]. It is believed that today's data warehouses make data sourcing much less of an issue than it was in the 1980s and 1990s, however, [8], but at the same time, data sources are getting broader and more versatile. Organizations are faced with enormous quantities of data from many sources; "big data" from the internet and information sharing between organizations being increasingly important sources.

This study follows the IS design science paradigm in attempt to illustrate how to develop performance dashboards. Information systems design science approach focuses on designing and building innovative IT artifacts [9], by aiming to answer "how to?" questions [10]. The overriding goal of this research project is to construct a framework for dashboard design rather than the resulting system itself. The practical value of this study is in the guidance for designing such a system in the case company. Action design research methodology (ADR) [11] is used as the research method. As oppose to the traditional stage-gate design research methods that emphasize a technological view of the IT artifact, ADR recognizes that the artifact emerges from interaction with the organizational context. Thereby, ADR is found as a suitable research method for closing the gap between organizational measurement and IT in dashboard design. Learning from the case project is documented as general design principles and a framework to apply in similar conditions outside the case organization, as well.

2   Performance Dashboards

2.1   Performance Measurement and IS

Performance measurement systems are IS that transform performance data into assessments of organizational and individual performance [12]. Even so, performance measurement systems seem to receive little attention in information systems literature [13]. Very few studies discuss the interplay between performance measurement and information system literature as thoroughly and explicitly as Marchand and Raymond [14], who synthesize the two as performance measurement information systems (PMIS), as illustrated in Figure 1.

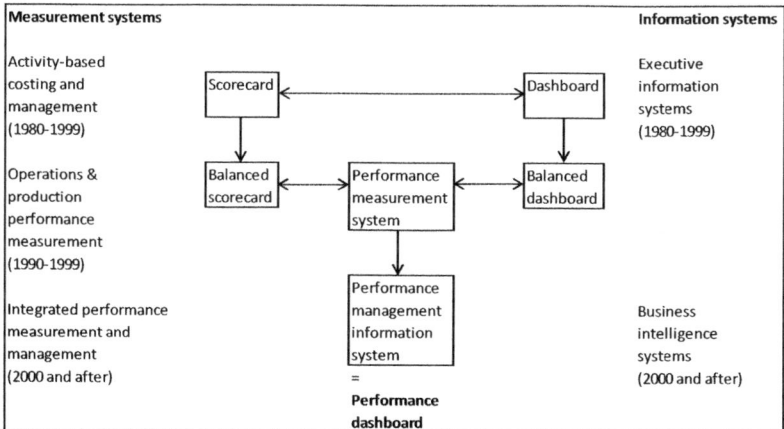

Fig. 1. Evolution of measurement systems and information systems (adapted from Marchand and Raymond 2008)

Research in measurement systems has produced several measurement models [see 6, 15 for reviews] and discussed the design, implementation and use of these models from several perspectives [e.g. 15, 16]. The most well-known and widely used performance measurement framework is the Balanced Scorecard (BSC), originally introduced by Kaplan & Norton in 1992 [17], and in several papers and books after that. Today's measurement systems literature is increasingly integrated with "performance management", and deal with issues including setting strategic goals and objectives, establishing initiatives and plans to achieve those goals, monitoring actual performance against the goals, and taking corrective action [18].

On the information systems side, executive information systems (EIS) were studied from several perspectives particularly during 1980s and 1990s. Executive information systems (EIS) are computer-based information systems that support decision making of executives [19]. EIS can be seen as a subcategory of decision support systems (DSS). A "dashboard" metaphor has been used for describing EIS interfaces, while in this paper a "performance dashboard" has a broader meaning. Information systems literature has dealt with a variety of EIS issues including adoption [e.g. 19, 20], and design [7, 21]. Currently, information systems literature in this area is mostly situated in the business intelligence (BI) domain, as BI provides the IT infrastructure and applications required to implement business performance management [22]. The performance dashboard, an instantiation of PMIS, stems from a "marriage" between performance management and BI [1].

As the visible part of a dashboard system is its user interface, many definitions focus on its visual features. For example, Few [23] defines a dashboard as a "visual display of the most important information needed to achieve one or more objectives; consolidated and arranged on a single screen so the information can be monitored at a glance". However, some authors accentuate that performance dashboards are essentially performance management systems [1] including two necessary features: performance measures and the supporting infrastructure [24]. The existence of measures in a PMS comes without explaining. The supporting infrastructure can vary from very simplistic manual methods of recording data to sophisticated information systems whereas the supporting procedures include data acquisition, collation, sorting, analysis, interpretation, and dissemination [24]. Yigitbasioglu and Velcu [2], define a dashboard as "a visual and interactive performance management tool that displays on a single screen the most important information to achieve one or several individual and/or organizational objectives, allowing the user to identify, explore, and communicate problem areas that need corrective action".

In this paper, a performance dashboard is defined as *an interactive performance management tool consisting of a measurement system and an information system, and supported by the models and processes for information gathering, processing, distribution, and visualization.*

2.2   Designing and Developing Performance Dashboards

Walls et al. [21] used the term "information systems design theory" ISDT to refer to solutions for specialized classes of IS design problems, such as DSS and EIS. ISDT is a prescriptive theory integrating normative and descriptive theories into design paths intended to produce more effective information systems [25]. The role of ISDT is two-fold; it is based in theory, and it provides guidance to practitioners. The benefit of an ISDT is that it reduces developers' uncertainty by restricting the range of allowable system features and development activities to a more manageable set, thereby increasing the reliability of development and the likelihood of success. In addition, ISDT stimulates research by suggesting testable research hypothesis [26].

In performance measurement design, questions generally relate to what to measure and how to structure the performance measurement system [6]. This is what performance measurement literature has been mostly dealing with over the last decades and has suggested numerous models and techniques to achieve this. IT, on the other hand, plays a more significant role in designing how to deal with processes including data creation, data collection, data analysis, and information distribution in performance measurement [6]. EIS design studies [21, 27] generally address these issues.

Some development steps have been presented even for performance dashboards but they are either targeted at a practitioner audience [1, 47, 48] or tend to be rather non-specific [5]. Generally speaking, the issue of dashboard design has been left essentially unaddressed in scientific studies [2].

According to Walls et al. [21], an IS design theory is a package of three interrelated elements: a set of user requirements derived from kernel theory, a set of principles governing the design of a system, and a set of principles regarded effective for guiding the development process. By addressing all three elements, an IS design theory can provide a "complete package of guidance for designers facing particular sets of circumstances" [26]. In order to provide a complete package of guidance for performance dashboard designers, a design framework is constructed in the present study. The design framework consists of a set of principles for governing system design, as well as a set of principles for guiding the development process. The design principles are concerned equally with performance measurement and information systems design. Following the approach by Walls et al. [21], a kernel theory and user requirements for performance dashboards are presented as basis for developing the design principles. The kernel theory and user requirements constitute a "theory-ingrained artifact" that is discussed in detail in the next section.

3   Research Approach and Theoretical Grounding

3.1   ADR

The method chosen to carry out this study is action design research (ADR) introduced by Sein et al. [11]. It is an action research (AR)-based method for conducting IS design research (DR). DR seeks to develop prescriptive design knowledge, sometimes referred to as design principles [21], through building and evaluating innovative IT artifacts intended to solve an identified class of problems [9, 28]. AR is grounded in practical action, aimed at solving an immediate problem situation while carefully informing theory [29].

The dominant DR thinking takes a technological view of the IT artifact while ADR, by incorporating action, posits that the artifact emerges from interaction with the organizational context. In ADR, the research problem is derived from practice and the theory-ingrained artifact is then developed iteratively together with the case organization. As the organizational needs are essential in the development of systems for performance measurement, ADR is deemed a suitable method for investigating how to design and develop performance dashboards.

The ADR process starts from problem formulation, which includes determining the initial scope, deciding the roles and scope for practitioner participation, and formulating the initial research questions [11]. Critical issues in this stage are securing the long-term commitment of the organization and formulating the identified problem as an instance of a class of problems. Problem formulation in the case context and its expansion to a class of problems is discussed in more detail in the section 3.2. Roles and scope of the practitioner participation is discussed in section 4.1.

In the next stage, the IT artifact is developed through several cycles of building, intervention, and evaluation (BIE) with the case organization. The main difference to previous stage-gate DR methods is that evaluation of the IT artifact is interwoven with building of the artifact. This stage draws on three principles: reciprocal shaping, mutually influential roles, and authentic and concurrent evaluation [11]. Reflection and learning continues throughout the ADR process, emphasizing that the ensemble artifact reflects not only the preliminary design but is shaped by organizational use, perspectives and participants. Section 4.2. outlines the cyclic BIE process in the case setting and describes how the design was shaped throughout the process with practitioner involvement.

Finally, in spite of the situated nature of ADR, learning from the project is further developed into general solution concepts for a class of similar problems. This stage aims therefore to formalize learning through design principles derived from the design research outcomes. Principles for performance dashboard design are drawn together in section 5.

3.2   Problem Formulation

The case organization, a Finnish web design and marketing agency Activeark Ltd, has undoubtedly been a success story in its first ten years. When it was founded in 2003, the company had three employees and an office space in a basement in Helsinki, Finland. Since those days, the company's business has grown in scale and scope. Currently, the company employs around 80 people in their offices in Helsinki, London and Mumbai. The financial numbers have developed accordingly – the annual turnover reached 8 million euro in 2011. Activeark produces web sites and digital marketing campaigns for their customers on project basis. Although the projects usually yield concrete outputs such as websites, Activeark is essentially a service company since their production leans, to a large extent, on human resources. Customer projects are carried out by a team of web designers, coders, project management and sales personnel. In order to coordinate the big picture, the company has implemented a matrix structure in which project teams complement traditional business functions.

The fast growth in the case organization led to problems with maintaining visibility and control of different functions and business units. There had been several initiatives to plan and implement metrics for different business areas, but there was no holistic measurement framework in use nor was there a clear agreement of the key metrics for the company and its units. Company management was aware that they had data that could be better utilized in performance measurement but the problem was that this data was stored in several information systems and people were using the data in different ways. This resulted in inconsistent and incomparable performance reporting. Efforts had been made to achieve a common system for performance measurement and internal reporting, but much of it was still based on manual, highly time consuming, and error-prone procedures. Due to this, the information was already out-of-date when it was delivered to the user. Furthermore, performance reports were distributed in static sheets and hence the users could not easily make further analysis from the information. A specific challenge related to unreliable information about how the company utilized their human resources and hence managed production. The staff was obliged to input their working hours to a project management system every week based on which the management could then analyze, for example, how efficiently they had completed customer projects. The problem was that all employees did not use the system regularly. Table 1 outlines the problems in the current systems and processes.

Table 1. Problems with current performance measurement

Problem	System in use
Key measures not agreed upon	Inconsistent performance evaluation
Data scattered in several systems	Poor overall visibility to performance Decentralized analysis
Unreliable data collection procedures	Poor data quality, particularly regarding utilization of human resources
Manual reporting	Time consuming and prone to errors Static and not up-to-date

The problems experienced by the case company are doubtless common in many organizations as they grow and diverge, and as internal and external organizational environments change. Companies need to be more responsive to rapidly changing customer and market needs and co-ordinate a whole network of supply chain partners, whilst reducing costs [6]. Managers need up-to-date performance figures on production, quality, markets, customers, etc. through which they can achieve overall performance targets by proactively controlling several processes [6]. Identifying the right KPIs for an organization, in other words answering the question "what to measure?", is far from being trouble-free in complex circumstances like these, as observed also in the case setting. Furthermore, in many cases, performance measurement today is not sensitive enough to changes in the internal and external environment of the organization [6].

The case organization experienced severe problems with scattered data and unreliable data collection procedures. These problems are commonplace in many organizations as data expands in scale and scope. More often than not the information needed is spread around several sources and in various different formats. "From where and how to find data?" is an increasingly important question in performance measurement, and a critical challenge in performance dashboard design in particular, as these systems run on electronic data that needs to be complete and easy to process [5].

Many companies are using information technology to provide performance measurement to the users online. However, few performance measurement systems have an integrated management information systems infrastructure [6]. Lack of IS support results in cumbersome and time-consuming data collection, sorting, maintenance and reporting [14]. Manual reporting should be replaced by a more efficient way of gathering and analyzing relevant data, and finding and effective way of distributing this information to users. The challenge of "how to deliver performance information to the users?" is enduring and also present in the case organization.

Based on the problems experienced by the case organization and reflecting them upon other organizations facing similar circumstances, three general challenges in performance dashboard design are formulated. These design challenges represent the areas of organizational and technological issues and choices that an organizations need to consider when designing the systems.

In conclusion, the design challenges for performance dashboards are:

1. What to measure?
2. Where and how to capture data?
3. How to deliver performance information to the users?

3.3   Theory-Ingrained Artifact

The kernel theory, which underlies an IS design theory, may be an academic theory (such as organizational psychology) or a practitioner theory-in-use [26]. Following the approach by Markus et al. [26], and Ngai et al. [25] the characteristics of performance measurement and decision making in today's organizations are analyzed as the kernel theory. Then, user requirements for a system that supports these processes (performance dashboard) are derived from the kernel theory. Building on this knowledge, learning through building, intervention and evaluation (BIE) with the case organization is articulated into IS design and development principles in sections 4. and 5.

Kernel theory. Overall, the rationale for developing performance measurement and the related information systems in organizations today arise from an increasing need to improve both the efficiency and effectiveness of decision making. The traditional view is that DSS primarily attempts to improve the effectiveness of decision-making (accuracy, timeliness, quality) rather than its efficiency (cost of making the decision, including the charges for computer time) [30]. However, as observed in the problem formulation stage, there is also an increasing pressure to improve the efficiency of decision making in situations in which performance measurement is not properly supported by IS. These pressures can be explained by some special characteristics of today's organizational decision making, as described next.

C#1: Decision makers suffer from information overload as the volume, velocity, and variety of data is growing rapidly. Organizations face enormous quantities of data from various sources, easily cumulating to terabytes and even petabytes of information. *Furthermore, data is o*ften time-sensitive, and should be used as it is streaming in to the organization in order to maximize its value. Data also extends beyond structured data, including unstructured data of all varieties: text, audio, video, click streams, log files and more [31].

C#2: Excessive information may lead to disregard of information and to decision inaccuracy. Information processing theory posits that decision makers can only process a fraction of the available information which has implications to how performance measures are used [32]. Ittner & Larcker [33] found evidence that corporate managers routinely discount or ignore non-financial measures. While the notion that other than non-financial measures are also needed in management dates as far back as to the 1950s [34], there is no consensus what the other dimensions are and in fact the evidence that there should be a "balance" in the measures is far from conclusive [24]. Most authors do tend to agree that a contingency approach is most suited, meaning that there is no universal best way to manage and hence the measures should reflect the strategy of the organization in order to steer it towards a desired direction.

C#3: Performance information is complex and challenges human cognition. Decision makers process information by structuring problem spaces and searching those spaces until a goal is achieved [2]. The space search is limited by the human attention span. Information visualization can potentially amplify human cognition as it helps to digest complex information more efficiently [2]. Visualization is effective when perceived data quantities and relationships between data reflect the actual data. Visualization is efficient if the maximum amount of data is perceived in a minimum amount of time [2].

C#4: Decision making takes place in semi-structured and unstructured situations, and it is therefore difficult to predefine in detail what the decision makers need [30]. Complex decision making problems are increasingly emergent and unexpected.

C#5: Decision makers include individuals from all levels in the organization, not only executives. It must be also noted that the users' information needs in these kinds of decision making situations are heterogeneous and change over time.

User Requirements. Requirements determination aims at defining what a specific system should be like and what it should be able to do. Based on an extensive literature review, Marx et al. classify the most cited EIS requirements into four categories: the scope of information, system functions, user interface, and information management [7]. As performance dashboards represent a new generation of DSS, and share many characteristics with EIS, the categories presented by Marx et al. [7] are discussed next in the performance dashboard context. Requirements that constitute these categories should be satisfied in the system design.

Information scoping: The system should provide relevant information to the user. The dashboard terminology in the organizational context originates from the vehicle dashboard, which reports the few metrics that the driver needs to know [2]. Considerations in this category include whether to include financial vs. non-financial data, internal vs. external data, task-related vs. individual data, and so forth [7]. This set of requirements corresponds to characteristic C#2.

Information management: DSS in general should be able to handle large amount of data [30]. Dashboards, as other BI-based analysis and decision making tools, are built on data warehousing technologies [35]. In addition to the quantity, also the correctness and quality of data should be ensured [7]. Timeliness of information is another requirement for performance dashboards; "third-generation" data management and decision support rely on real-time data [35]. This category corresponds to C#1.

Functions: The system should facilitate effective decision making through functions that fit the user need. It should offer a single screen view to all relevant information but with the possibility to drill-down to detail [2]. Other relevant functional requirements include: simulations, trend and sensitivity analyses, exception reporting and alerts, hierarchical information aggregation, and mobile access [7]. Instead of static reporting, flexible "ad-hoc" analysis capabilities should be promoted to support semi-structured and un-structured decision making, as described in C#4.

User interface: The system should have graphical orientation. Graphical orientation in DSS is believed to give decision makers a better understanding of the true situation in a given market place [30]. Today's decision support systems can help managers make attractive, informative graphical presentations by producing line drawing, pie chart, trend line and more [30]. A dashboard conveys information through visualization, referring to the use of interactive visual representations of abstract, non-physically based data to amplify cognition [2]. The system should offer information accessibility for different user groups in order to provide support to individuals at all levels in the organization. Furthermore, considering the different skill levels of the users, the system should be easy to use [7]. These requirements correspond to characteristics C#3 and C#5.

4   Performance Dashboard Design in the Case Organization

4.1   Setting up the Project

To overcome the problems with the current performance measurement, Activeark decided to initiate a performance dashboard project. The goal was to build a system that would offer them a balanced view to relevant information on a single screen. This would enable more informed, timely decision making, streamline processes and cut slack from reporting. While the purpose of the company's project was to build the system itself, the goal of the research project was to construct a framework for designing such a system, since one that would address all these issues properly, did not exist.

The study was conducted over a six-month period between August 2011 and January 2012 by being involved in the case company's performance dashboard project. An ADR team was established to coordinate the project and the related research effort. The ADR team consisted of a researcher and the CFO of the company, who was also assigned project owner. Other project stakeholders in the company included the executive team (lead by the CEO), responsible managers for each KPI (COO, Resource manager, CAO, Head of HR), users of the system, and the IT department. These groups are in part overlapping but treated as separate because of the different roles through which the people contributed to the project.

For the purpose of coordination, the project was set to be conducted in three consecutive phases after planning and initiation. This division was made based on the three general design challenges. The different groups, their roles, and their involvement in different project phases are listed in Table 2. Types of encounters with the different groups and data collection methods are listed. In addition to the data collected from the encounters with the stakeholder groups, the ADR team had access to the source systems and current performance measurement/reporting systems at all times during the project.

Table 2. Stakeholders

Group	#encounters with the ADR team	Type of encounter /data collection methods	Role/ competence area	Involvement in project phase
ADR team	8	Brainstorming sessions, unstructured interviews, e-mail	Project management, design methods and tools	1, 2, 3
Executive team	3	Planning sessions, follow-up meetings	Overall business strategy + related KPIs, authority to make decisions	1, 2
Responsible managers for each KPI (users)	4	Semi-structured interviews, performance measure record sheet	Detailed understanding of KPIs, user needs	1, 2, 3
IT department	2	Unstructured interviews	Source systems, integrations	2, 3
IT vendor	3	Planning sessions, negotiations	Dashboard software	2, 3

4.2 Building, Intervention, and Evaluation

The design challenges were addressed in three project phases as illustrated in Fig 2.

In the first project phase, the goal was to develop a general measurement scheme for the company by identifying Key Performance Indicators (KPIs) through a systematic method. In the second phase, the goal was to investigate in detail how the KPIs would be put into operation. In the third phase, issues related to formulating requirements and choosing a suitable IT system for collecting, analyzing and visualizing the information. The process was kept flexible so that previous and future choices could be reflected and refined iteratively during each of the phases.

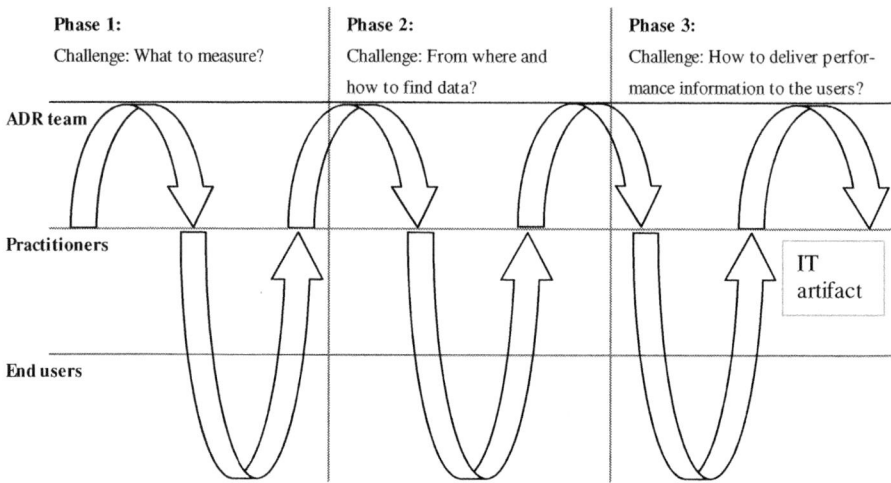

Fig. 2. ADR process

In addition to determining the design challenges and outlining the ADR process, the purpose of this study is to come up with a set of design principles for the design product and process by looking more in-depth into the design challenges and related issues through the case example. Next, we shall go through all of the three in more detail and reflect them upon the four classes of dashboard requirements.

Phase 1: What to measure? In the first project phase, the goal was to identify what the company should measure and build a general framework for performance management. From the IS perspective, this phase deals mostly with the "information scoping" requirement. However, advice in IS literature to address these issues is quite weak. Instead, performance measurement literature concentrates heavily on measure design and selection by dealing with what organizations should measure and how to structure performance measurement systems [24]. Several models and frameworks for categorizing measures and KPIs have been presented, including the Performance measurement matrix [36], the Performance pyramid [37], the Balanced Scorecard (BSC) [17], and the Performance Prism [38]. The purpose of these models is to identify areas where measurement is needed, and design metrics and key performance indicators (KPIs) for those areas (a metric becomes an indicator when it is set against a target value). BSC is the most widely used, and has also proved to yield good results as a measurement framework for dashboard systems [4].

The measurement frameworks gained criticism in the 1990s because they alone do not tell a company what to measure [39]. To complement these models and frameworks, several performance measurement design processes have been presented in earlier literature. The purpose of these processes is to show how to actually implement the measurement frameworks to practice and integrate performance measurement into the management of business. For example, design processes for the balanced scorecard include "Putting the BSC to work" [40], and "The performance model" [41] (see Bourne et al. [39] for an extensive review on different PM design processes).

At Activeark, the company management had initial ideas of some relevant KPIs, yet there was no consensus about the entire set of measures or a proper scheme for implementing them. As a first step, the ADR team, together with the executive team, formulated a preliminary set of KPIs for the company. The four dimensions of the Balanced Scorecard [17]; financial, internal business process, customer, and learning and growth, were used as the grouping principle, and the process presented by Kaplan and Norton [40] was used to derive the KPIs from company strategy. The BSC was chosen especially because the company wanted to see the trade-offs between different business aspects (profit vs. customer satisfaction, employee satisfaction vs. productivity).

The starting point for KPI formulation was company values (pro-activity, humble attitude, customer service, quality, innovation, and results focus) and the strategies to achieve them. The ADR team met with the executive team to brainstorm and choose appropriate measures. The company had well-thought existing KPIs in some areas which could be utilized as-is. For example, the "internal business process" dimension of the BSC was covered by the company's existing "profitability framework", a three-KPI scheme for monitoring the utilization of internal resources and project performance. The goal was to develop a maximum of 10 KPIs altogether, but in the end the company came up with 14. To keep the number of KPIs appropriate, it should be carefully examined which metrics allow the company to make informed decisions and are thereby essential, and which are just nice to have. Importantly, in order to ensure management commitment to each KPI, the company also assigned owners for each KPI. Having a responsible person for each KPI would also help in the next phase when the KPIs are investigated in more detail.

Based on the first project phase, and in order to address the design challenge "what to measure?", two design principles are formulated (followed by comments and related issues observed in the case project):

P1: Define a general performance measurement framework
- use one of the several available models and frameworks and/or utilize an existing set of measures
- selection criteria: information scoping
- output: suitable categorization of KPIs, not necessarily "balanced"

P2: Follow a structured process for selecting key measures
- several processes presented in literature
- limit the number of KPIs by sparing only those that are essential
- assign an owner for each measure

Phase 2: How to find data and from where? Data capture processes are set to identify sources of data and the processes used for data generation [24]. These processes are increasingly important as data sources expand in scale and scope, and as performance management systems set ever-tightening demands for the data. In this phase, feasibility of suggested metrics and KPIs is evaluated in more detail by determining whether they can actually be measured with the data to which the organization has access. It may also involve initiating new procedures, so that information currently not recorded is captured and it may involve completely new initiatives, such as setting up a regular customer or employee survey [16].

This phase contributes to several of the IS system requirements. It is concerned with particularly with information management issues, but also looks into the scoping of information in more detail. It is also necessary to make some preparatory work for system functions at this phase.

The performance measurement record sheet [42] was used to analyze each individual measure. It is a tool for investigating the relevant aspects of each performance measure or KPI in detail and documenting this knowledge in a structured format. It aims to clarify the purpose of the measure, set targets and formulas, and decide how often the information needs to be updated. An essential purpose of the record sheet is to identify the data sources for each measure. It is also used for identifying the people involved in generating the data and articulating the data generation process.

For the purposes of performance dashboard design, a new information element, "level of analysis", was added to the sheet to indicate the drill-down capabilities of each KPI (according to the CEO, the drill-down feature was the single most important function in the dashboard system because it allowed them to identify the root causes of problems). The ADR team interviewed the managers responsible for each KPI individually. The interview data was documented on separate performance measurement record sheets. The record sheet turned out to be a very useful tool for analyzing how the KPIs would be put into operation and offered a good overall view of the KPIs.

During the interviews, some of the source systems (e.g. project management system and accounting system) were investigated in more detail. The ADR team noticed that there were some inconsistencies in the meaning and definition of certain data elements. For example, the company used the terms "billable hours" and "invoiceable hours" to indicate the amount of project work conducted. In the end, these two information elements turned out to mean different things. Also, some of the KPIs were readjusted because the executive team though that the KPI in its initial form would be updated too infrequently. After all, one of the key problems in the existing performance measurement was that it was static. Finally, after a wider revision of the KPIs with the company COO, two new KPIs, "sales pipeline" and "project pipeline", were added to the list for better support of forecasting sales, business planning and managing resources.

The source of data for each KPI was perhaps the most crucial aspect to investigate at this point as data was stored and updated in several source systems. These included systems for project management, accounting, HR, and finance. In order to address issues related to the quality and completeness of data, it was very important to look into the data generation processes in more detail. Although documented in electronic systems, much of the data is still generated manually. For example, the employees use a project management system to allocate their hours to different customer projects and other work. The human element brings considerable uncertainty to the data and thereby creates a lot of pressure to ensure that the employees input their hours in the system every week. The same goes for project managers who are asked to input, for example, the amount of offers they have made during the month for sales forecasting purposes. This clearly highlighted the importance of data generation processes in addition to the technological issues and the source system itself. As an implication, company management has to find ways for supporting these processes to ensure completeness and quality of data.

The following design principles can be drawn from the second project phase in order to address the design challenge "from where and how to find data?":

P3: Analyze systematically how each measure should be put into operation
- Performance measure record sheet [42], or similar tool recommended
- Critical questions: Is data available for measurement and where to find it? Is there other data that could be utilized for PM?
- Revise the metrics: were some KPIs forgotten or neglected in the first phase? How frequently is the measure updated, is there a need for re-adjustment?
- Investigate the hierarchical structure of data through a "drill-down capability" sheet

P4: Ensure completeness and quality of data
- Processes: investigate how data has been generated so far. How to improve these processes if necessary and how to handle possible new ones?
- Ensure that data is in standard format and clearly defined. Facilitate consensus regarding the meaning of each data element

Phase 3: How to deliver performance information to the users? In this phase, systems and procedures are put in place to collect and process data that enable measurements to be made regularly [16]. These information provision processes [24] deal with how the measures can be linked to databases and information systems, and how the measurement framework can be communicated throughout the organization [40]. Design issues in this phase relate to finding the most suitable way of linking the dashboard system into source systems and designing an effective dashboard display [1]. This corresponds to the EIS requirements of information management, functions, and user interface.

Performance dashboards, along with other BI-based tools are usually built on a data warehousing solutions. Furthermore, extract, transform, and load (ETL) processes are put in place to gather the data and transform it to usable format. Processes of distributing this information to the users are then essentially carried out through a user interface. Yigitbasioglu and Velcu [2] divide dashboard interface design features into functional and visual. Functional features are features that relate indirectly to visualization but describe what the dashboard can do. These include drill-down tables, drillable charts, hierarchical information aggregation, simulations, trends, and sensitivity analysis [7]. Visual feature design, in turn, is concerned with e.g. how the use of colors affects decision-making performance. Although the use of colors may improve the process of visualization, excessive use of colors can have an adverse effect on decision making by distracting the user [2]. This problem can be potentially reduced by maximizing the "data-ink ratio", which measures the proportion of ink used to represent data to the total ink used to print the graph [2]. Furthermore, a good balance between visual complexity and information utility is required. Visual complexity can be defined as "the degree of difficulty in providing a verbal description of an image" [43].

Based on the analysis made during phases 1 and 2 Activeark started to negotiate with a software vendor for IT system delivery. The company could efficiently communicate their needs to the vendor through completed record sheets in the kick-off meetings. The case company has a relatively light IT infrastructure, and it was not economically viable to build a separate data warehouse for storing data. Instead, an alternative solution was found. Today's software market offers dashboard systems that utilize associative technology, meaning that it can gather data from multiple sources without having to store the data in intermediate storages. As the source systems were not too complex, and discussions with the company IT department showed that integrating the dashboard directly to the source systems was possible, it was considered a suitable solution. Also, the implementation would be quicker and less expensive this way. Flexibility with regard to possible future changes in the underlying IT systems is a further benefit in using this type of technology.

As for the functional features, the drill-down capability was seen as the most important from the users' point of view. It would enable pinpointing causes for possible problems and deviations in measurement. The user interface should enable flexible information filtering and ad-hoc analysis capabilities. The final design of the functional features was left undecided, though, because needs would emerge when the system is in use. This would of course require flexibility from the software. Visually, the goal was to design the user interface so that it showed all relevant information at a glance, but at the same time, was not too crowded. In addition to the indicator scores, the company especially wanted to illustrate trends, i.e. how performance develops over time. The company had already constructed a "mock-up" version of the dashboard interface earlier, which could be directly utilized as a starting point for designing the system's visual display.

The premise of performance dashboards, as oppose to EIS, is that they can be accessed at all levels in the organization. However, the questions regarding who should have access to the dashboard turned out to be not that straight-forward. According to the HR manager, all employees were not interested in the performance information to begin with. Instead, they felt that performance measurement is de motivating and they were anxious about "being lead with numbers". Hence, after careful consideration, the company decided to give access to the executive team and business unit leaders at this point. All employees could be given (limited) access to the system in the future.

Based on this, the company formulated initial specifications for the system together with the software vendor who then made an offer to Activeark regarding the delivery. Currently, the company is moving to the implementation phase of the system.

The following design principles are formulated based on the third project phase to give guidance in dealing with the final design challenge "How to deliver performance information to the users?":

P5: Design for efficient integration to source systems
- choose a system that is most suited for the IT infrastructure of the organization (data warehousing vs. associative technology)
- use the record sheet to show necessary integrations to the software supplier

P6: Design for a an effective user interface
- Provide functional features that fit the task, revise in use
- Visualization: single-screen view to all relevant information preferred, should be kept simple. Aim at a good balance between visual complexity and information utility.
- Frugal use of colors recommended, maximize data-ink ratio.
- use the record sheet to communicate user needs to the software supplier

Table 3. A design framework for performance dashboards

Design challenge	What to measure?	Where and how to capture data?	How to deliver performance information to the users?
Design principles (product related)	P1: Define a general performance measurement framework	P3: Analyze systematically how each measure should be put into operation	P5: Design for efficient integration to source systems
	P2: Follow a structured process for selecting key measures	P4: Ensure completeness and quality of data	P6: Design for a an effective user interface
Emerging principles (process related)	P7: Use an iterative, agile development process		
	P8: Use a modular approach in system design		
	P9: Facilitate interaction between the interest groups and individuals		
	P10: Ensure user involvement at each phase		

5   Conclusions

Design can be seen as both a product and a process [21]. The design *product* is the set of requirements and necessary design characteristics that should guide IT artifact construction. The design *process* is composed of the steps and procedures taken to develop the artifact. In addition to the principles presented in the previous section that directly relate to the design product (performance dashboard), some further observations were made regarding the design process. It was recognized early that the systems development lifecycle, or "waterfall" model, does not work well for decision support applications. Instead, an iterative or evolutionary design was recommended [44]. Such an approach is particularly suitable in design situations involving complex or vaguely defined user requirements [26]. Furthermore, a DSS should be developed using a modular approach. With this approach, separate functions of the DSS are placed in separate module allowing efficient testing and implement of systems. It also allows various modules to be used for multiple purposes in different systems [30]. Users of the system should be involved at each phase in order to ensure their commitment and that the system satisfies their needs. Furthermore, the case project showed that in order to succeed, interaction between all stakeholders should be facilitated throughout the process. Based on these observations, four more design principles were formulated (P7, P8, P9, P10). Due to space limitations, these principles are not discussed in detail in this paper. Instead, they are presented as emerging principles that need to be investigated further in future studies.

6   Theoretical and Managerial Implications

Several methods both for designing performance measures and for developing IS systems for decision support have been presented before. However, performance measurement design methods tend to forget IT, and at the same time the information systems development (ISD) methods are many times overly IT-driven. The case project shows that both viewpoints should be equally present when designing performance dashboards and performance management information systems in general. Furthermore, earlier literature seems to overlook the complexity of data capture. Generally speaking, the amount and complexity of data that organizations are facing is increasing rapidly and finding suitable data for performance dashboards is anything but trivial. The case project highlights challenges of data capture in service organizations where business processes are not automated and data generation relies solely on human effort. With regard to design, not only the source of data is important but also the processes for generating the data should be carefully examined in the performance dashboard context.

The academic contribution in this study draws from the synthesis built between performance measurement and information systems in designing performance dashboards. Following the approach by Walls et al. [21], elements of ISDT are discussed in the performance dashboard context. By discussing the characteristics of today's organizational decision making, a kernel theory and user requirements for performance dashboards are presented. This contributes to theoretical knowledge on this new type of DSS used for performance measurement. Based on the theory-ingrained artifact, a framework for performance dashboard design is suggested. The framework comprises of a balanced set of organizational (measurement) and technological (IT) design principles that govern the design of system features and four emerging design principles for guiding the development process.

As a managerial implication, the case study shows that the framework is useful in addressing key practical issues in performance dashboard design. Furthermore, it gives structure to the design process through the modular development process with three design challenges. The design framework should be useful for companies outside the case context as well, since it utilizes well-established tools to solve the design challenges (e.g. BSC, or other performance measurement framework). In other words, separate elements used within the design framework are based in theory and already validated in practice to an extent. The novelty of the present approach comes from providing a comprehensive framework for understanding how modern-day information systems for performance measurement should be designed and developed.

As for limitations, although it is acknowledged that design continues throughout the lifecycle of the system, this paper focuses on the design issues during system building. Use and review phases are left out from the scope of this paper. Although learning from these phases eventually affects system design, the most influential design decisions are made essentially during design and implementation. Furthermore, the suggested design framework should be validated through further empirical studies in the future. Particularly the emerging design principles need further validation.

A deeper investigation of data issues offers another interesting avenue for future research in this area. The amount of data that organizations have is growing exponentially, and although data sourcing can sometimes be problematic, new data can also help to measure things that would not have been possible to measure before. These changes have an effect on all of the grand challenges in performance dashboard design. They influence what an organization should and is able to measure, where and how data is captured, and how the information is finally provided to the users. Another interesting future research topic is whether data capture processes can be successfully built on "decentralized" databases, like in the case context. The common view is that BI-based analysis tools and DSS require a centralized data warehouse [45]. However, Van Alstyne et al. [46] posit that due to data ownership issues, having a centralized data base might not be even desirable. A key reason for the importance of ownership in this regard is self-interest: owners have a greater interest in system success than non-owners. Theoretically this could be explained by incomplete contracts approach from economics. Van Alstyne et al. [46] gives an illustrative example: "Just as rental cars are driven less carefully than cars driven by their owners, databases that are not owned by their users are maintained less conscientiously than databases used by their owners.". Hence, locally autonomous databases could be a more effective way to organize data capture, particularly in situations where information sharing between organizations or groups is the primary source of data, such as in inter-organizational settings.

References

1. Eckerson, W.W.: Performance Dashboards: Measuring, Monitoring, and Managing Your Business. New Jersey. John Wiley & Sons, Inc., Hoboken (2010)
2. Yigitbasioglu, O.M., Velcu, O.: A review of dashboards in performance management: Implications for design and research. Int. J. Account. Inf. Syst. 13, 41–59 (2012)

3. Cleverley, W.O.: Financial Dashboard Reporting for the Hospital Industry. J. Heal. Car. Fin. 27, 30–40 (2001)
4. Briggs, L.: BI case study: Balanced scorecard system keeps university health system in the pink. Bus. Int. J. 15, 28–30 (2010)
5. Pauwels, K., Ambler, T., Clark, B.H., LaPointe, P., Reibstein, D., Skiera, B., Wierenga, B., Wiesel, T.: Dashboards as a Service: Why, What, How, and What Research is Needed? J. Serv. Res. 12, 175–189 (2009)
6. Nudurupati, S.S., Bititci, U.S., Kumar, V., Chan, F.: State of the art literature review on performance measurement. Comp. & Ind. Eng. 60, 279–290 (2011)
7. Marx, F., Mayer, J., Winter, R.: Six principles for redesigning executive information systems - findings of a survey and evaluation of a prototype. ACM Trans. Manag. Inf. Syst. 2 (2011)
8. Wixom, B.H., Watson, H.J.: The BI-based organization. Int. J. Bus. Intell. Res. 1, 13–28 (2010)
9. Hevner, A.R., March, S.T., Park, J., Ram, S.: Design science in information systems research. MIS Quart. 28, 75–105 (2004)
10. Gregor, S.: The nature of theory in information systems. MIS Quart. 30, 611–642 (2006)
11. Sein, M.K., Henfridsson, O., Purao, S., Rossi, M., Lindgren, R.: Action design research. MIS Quart. 35, 37–56 (2011)
12. Burney, L.L., Matherly, M.: Examining Performance Measurement from an Integrated Perspective. J. Inf. Syst. 21, 49–68 (2007)
13. Salleh, N.A.M., Jusoh, R., Isa, C.R.: Relationship between information systems sophistication and performance measurement. Ind. Manag. & Data Syst. 110, 993–1017 (2010)
14. Marchand, M., Raymond, L.: Researching performance measurement systems. Int. J. Oper. & Prod. Manag. 28, 663–686 (2008)
15. Neely, A., Mills, J., Platts, K., Richards, H., Gregory, M., Bourne, M., Kennerley, M.: Performance measurement system design: developing and testing a process-based approach. Int. J. Oper. & Prod. Manag. 20, 1119–1145 (2000)
16. Bourne, M., Mills, J., Wilcox, M., Neely, A., Platts, K.: Designing, implementing and updating performance measurement systems. Int. J. Oper. & Prod. Manag. 20, 754–771 (2000)
17. Kaplan, R.S., Norton, D.P.: The balanced scorecard - measures that drive performance. Harv. Bus. Rev. 71–79 (1992)
18. Turban, E., Aronson, J., Liang, T., Sharda, R.: Decision Support and Business Intelligence Systems. Prentice Hall, Upper Saddle River (2007)
19. Rai, A., Bajwa, D.S.: An empirical investigation into factors relating to the adoption of executive information systems: an analysis of EIS for collaboration and decision support. Decis. Sci. 28, 939–974 (1997)
20. Poon, P., Wagner, C.: Critical success factors revisited: success and failure cases of information systems for senior executives. Decis. Sup. Syst. 30, 393–418 (2001)
21. Walls, J.G., Widmeyer, G.R., El Sawy, O.A.: Building an Information System Design Theory for Vigilant EIS. Inf. Syst. Res. 36–59 (1992)
22. Ariyachandra, T.R., Frolick, M.N.: Critical Success Factors in Business Performance Management - Striving for Success. Inf. Syst. Manag. 25, 113–120 (2008)
23. Few, S.: Information dashboard design, the effective visual communication of data. O'Reilly Media Inc. (2006)

24. Franco-Santos, M., Kennerley, M., Micheli, P., Martinez, V., Mason, S., Marr, B., Gray, D., Neely, A.: Towards a Definition of a Business Performance Measurement System. Int. J. Oper. & Prod. Manag. 27, 784–801 (2007)
25. Ngai, E.W.T., Leung, T.K.P., Wong, Y.H., Lee, M.C.M., Chai, P.Y.F., Choi, Y.S.: Design and development of a context-aware decision support system for real-time accident handling in logistics. Decis. Sup. Syst. 52, 816–827 (2012)
26. Markus, M.L., Majchrzak, A., Gasser, L.: A design theory for systems that support emergent knowledge processes. MIS Quart. 26, 179–212 (2002)
27. Watson, H.J., Rainer Jr., R.K., Koh, C.E.: Executive Information Systems: A Framework for Development and a Survey of Current Practices. MIS Quart. 15, 13–30 (1991)
28. March, S.T., Smith, G.F.: Design and natural science research on information technology. Decis. Sup. Syst. 15, 251–266 (1995)
29. Baskerville, R.L.: Investigating Information Systems with Action Research. Commun. AIS 2, 1–32 (1999)
30. Asemi, A., Safari, A., Zavareh, A.A.: The Role of Management Information System (MIS) and Decision Support System (DSS) for Manager's Decision Making Process. Int. J. Bus. and Manag. 6, 164–173 (2011)
31. Laney, D.: 3D Data Management: Controlling Data Volume, Velocity and Variety. Gartner (2001) (retrieved February 9, 2012)
32. Neumann, B.R., Roberts, M.L., Cauvin, E.: Financial and Nonfinancial Performance Measures. Cost Manag. 22, 5–14 (2008)
33. Ittner, C.D., Larcker, D.F.: Coming Up Short on Nonfinancial Performance Measurement. Harv. Bus. Rev. 81, 88–95 (2003)
34. Neely, A.: The Evolution of Performance Measurement Research: Developments in The Last Decade and a Research Agenda for the Next. Int. J. Oper. & Prod. Manag. 25, 1264–1277 (2005)
35. Watson, H.J., Wixom, B.H., Hoffer, J.A., Anderson-Lehman, R., Reynolds, A.M.: Real-Time Business Intelligence: Best Practices at Continental Airlines. Inf. Syst. Manag. 23, 7–18 (2006)
36. Keegan, D.P., Eiler, R.G., Jones, C.R.: Are Your Performance Measures Obsolete? Manag. Account. 45–50 (1989)
37. Lynch, R.L., Cross, K.F.: Measure Up - The Essential Guide to Measuring Business Performance, Mandarin, London (1991)
38. Neely, A., Adams, C., Crowe, P.: The performance prism in practice. Measur. Bus. Excell. 5, 6–13 (2001)
39. Bourne, M., Neely, A., Mills, J., Platts, K.: Implementing Performance Measurement Systems: a Literature Review. Int. J. Bus. Perf. Manag. 5, 1–24 (2003)
40. Kaplan, R.S., Norton, D.P.: Putting the balanced scorecard to work. Harv. Bus. Rev. 71, 134–142 (1993)
41. Kaplan, R.S., Norton, D.P.: Using the Balanced Scorecard as a Strategic Management System. Harv. Bus. Rev. 74, 75–85 (1996)
42. Neely, A., Richards, H., Mills, J., Platts, K., Bourne, M.: Designing performance measures: a structured approach. Int. J. Oper. & Prod. Manag. 17, 1131–1152 (1997)
43. Heaps, C., Handel, S.: Similarity and Features of Natural Textures. J. Exp. Psych.: Hum. Percept. Perf. 25, 299–320 (1999)
44. Sprague, R.H.: A Framework for the Development of Decision Support Systems. MIS Quart. 4, 1–26 (1980)

45. Watson, H.: Tutorial: Business Intelligence – Past, Present, and Future. Comm. AIS 25, 487–510 (2009)
46. Van Alstyne, M., Brynjolfsson, E., Madnick, S.: Why Not One Big Database? Principles for Data Ownership. Decis. Sup. Syst. 15, 267–284 (1995)
47. Rasmussen, N., Chen, C.Y., Bansal, M.: Business dashboards: a visual catalog for design and deployment. Wiley, Hoboken (2009)
48. Malik, S.: Enterprise dashboards: design and best practices for IT. Wiley, Hoboken (2005)

On Goodness of Models and Instantiations in Design Research: Some Potential Perspectives

Pertti Järvinen

University of Tampere, School of Information Sciences,
33014 University of Tampere, Finland
pj@cs.uta.fi

Abstract. In this paper, we discuss how to evaluate (models and instantiations), which criteria for goodness that are applicable within different research approaches. In the prevalent (positivist) research we are accustomed to ask whether a certain model truthfully describes an object under study, and how useful is a new IT artifact. But researchers can also take other perspectives than the prevalent one on the world, e.g., interpretive or critical. In addition to models, researchers can also evaluate a wider information system than the new IT artifact only. We restrict our consideration into design research, the models developed and the outcomes constructed. We must model the old system in the problem space and the new system in the solution space. We therefore collect and analyze various guidelines for modeling from different perspectives (positivist, interpretive and critical). Concerning design outcomes we pay attention to different stake holder groups and their different evaluation criteria.

Keywords: Perspectives, Positivist, Interpretive, Critical, Design research, Models, Instantiations.

1 Introduction

This Referring to the debate around the rigor and relevance of Information Systems (IS) research also Constantinides et al. [9] (as we) very recently paid attention to the ends of IS research. They "argue that any effort to understand the state of the Information Systems field has to view IS research as a series of normative choices and value judgments about the *ends of research* (cursive added) [9:1]. To assist a systematic questioning of the various ends of IS research, we propose a pragmatic framework that explores the choices IS researchers make around theories and methodologies, ethical methods of conduct, desirable outcomes, and the long-term impact of the research beyond a single site and topic area." They illustrate their framework by considering and questioning the explicit and implicit choices of topics, design and execution, and the representation of knowledge in experimental research — research often considered to be largely beyond value judgments and power relations.

In addition to those general reasons presented by Constantinides et al. [9] we selected the goodness of models and instantiations in design research as research topic for private reasons, i.e., as a supervisor of doctoral candidates coming from industry.

C. Keller et al. (Eds.): SCIS 2012, LNBIP 124, pp. 131–144, 2012.
© Springer-Verlag Berlin Heidelberg 2012

When they are studying their own work their topic is relevant and publishing in scientific journal will implicitly take care of rigor. What we as a supervisor must then do is to present them how the IS community evaluates the IS research. To this end, we like in this paper find out *how the IS community is guiding the IS research and/or which criteria are recommended to be used in IS studies.*

Instead of considering experimental research as Constantinides et al. [9] do, we shall concentrate design research, especially models and instatntiations in that context. We shall exclude constructs (cf. March and Smith [29]) from our consideration because we then should analyze three approaches: the variance, process and systems approaches [4]. The three approaches can be taken as super-eyeglasses and an object of study will then be seen either as variables and their relationships (variance), or events and their sequences (process) or wholes, parts and their interactions (systems), respectively. This would enlarge our consideration threefold.

Our second restriction is to exclude methods. Here we have two reasons. Firstly, according to van Aken [38] design knowledge concerns three designs: an object-design, a realization-design, and a process-design. Both the realization and process designs concern methods. Second, there are both descriptive and prescriptive methods. The descriptive methods describe how the problem was solved. The logic of a prescription is if you want to achieve Y in situation Z, then perform action X. Inclusion of methods into our consideration would increase our analysis many fold.

March and Smith [29:258] state that "research activities in design science are twofold: build and evaluate. Build refers to the construction of the artifact, demonstrating that such an artifact *can* be constructed. Evaluate refers to the development of criteria and the assessment of artifact performance against those criteria.

We *evaluate* artifacts to determine if we have made any progress. The basic question is, how well does it work? Recall that progress is achieved when a technology is replaced by more effective one. Evaluation requires the development of metrics and the measurement of artifacts according to those metrics. Metrics define what we are trying to accomplish. They are used to assess the performance of an artifact. Lack of metrics and failure to measure artifact performance according to established criteria results in an inability to effectively judge research efforts." If "an *instantiation* is the realization of an artifact in its environment" (March and Smith [29:258]) then, to our mind, the description above mainly concerns IT artifacts, not models in design research.

According to March and Smith [29:256], "a *model* is a set of propositions or statements expressing relationships among constructs. In design activities, models represent situations as problem and solution statements." Hence we shall in design research have two or three models: 1) a model of the initial state, 2) a model of the desired state and 3) the model of the finished, realized state. The two last ones can be identical, if the realization was successful, but the final state is often "less" or "more" than desired.

March and Smith [29] give some goodness criteria, e.g., their fidelity with real world phenomena, completeness, level of detail, robustness, and internal consistency for models and the efficiency and effectiveness of the artifact, and its impacts on the environment and its users for instantiations, but they do not tell from which stake holder group their criteria are given. We guess that some of those criteria are given from the group of researchers and some other mainly from the group of managers.

Concerning the design process and its outcomes, there are at least three stake holder groups: managers, designers and customers (cf. Reeves and Bednar [35]), and they have different perspectives on the artifact or innovation designed, and therefore different goodness criteria, too. But a researcher can also take one of the many possible world views or (scientific-philosophical) perspectives, e.g., the positivist, the interpretive or the critical (cf. W. Chua [7]). The Chua's three perspectives were used in some literature reviews (Orlikowski and Baroudi [34], Chen and Hirschheim [5] and Richardson and Robinson [36]), and Iivari ([21-22]) used them in his paradigmatic analyses of both contemporary schools of IS development and Information Systems as a design science. The world views have an influence on modeling of the initial states and maybe on the desired states, too. We shall show that the assumptions on human being and human society based on those three world views or perspectives are different and will lead to different goodness criteria. Concerning the new IT artifact we shall refer to Reeves and Bednar [35] who show that managers often emphasize value of output, designers stress on conformance of output to specifications and customers wish that the output meets and/or exceeds their expectations. We are not aware of any paper that has described all the perspectives in one and the same paper.

March and Smith [29] and Hevner et al. [20] were mainly interested in IT artifacts. But there are also other innovations than technical ones, for example, social innovations. A new information system is a socio-technical system, not only the IT artifact alone but also people who use that IT artifact. Hence the goodness evaluation of the IT artifact gives different results from the evaluation of the whole information system consisting both the IT artifact and users. Moreover, a development of a certain social innovation is not as easy as technical ones, and it requires a special attention.

The rest of this paper is structured as follows: In Section 2 we shall analyze models as the design research output and we shall propose some goodness criteria from the three different perspectives (positivist, interpretive and critical). In Section 3 we shall consider the different stake holder groups of the design process and output of an IT instantiation and propose some goodness criteria for them. We shall also analyze special characteristics of a social innovation and its development process. Finally we shall summarize the results of our analysis and assess their merits and limitations.

2   Goodness Criteria of Models from the Different Perspectives

A researcher can approach a reality by taking different assumptions on the world as a starting point. We shall here use three perspectives: The positivist, the interpretive and the critical that describe the world views implicitly or explicitly.

According to Chua [7:611], the *positivist* researcher assumes that "empirical reality is objective and external to the subject. Human beings are also characterized as passive objects; not seen as makers of social reality". Chua continues as follows: "People are analyzed as entities that may be passively described in objective ways (for example as information-processing mechanisms or as possessing certain leadership or budgetary styles)." [7:606]. Chua defines that "theory is separate from observations that may be used to verify or falsify a theory. Hypothetico-deductive account of scientific explanation accepted." March and Smith [29:261] say the similar as more detail: "Models are evaluated in terms of their fidelity with real world phenomena, completeness, level of detail, robustness, and internal consistency." We choose those into our table below. We supplement Table 1 with the criteria presented by Straub et al. [37] and mainly intended to the construct level: content validity, construct validity, reliability, manipulation validity, and statistical conclusion validity. Straub et al. [37] concentrate on validity and refer to Nunnally [33:383] that "the purpose of validation is to give researchers, their peers, and society as a whole a high degree of confidence that positivist methods being selected are useful in the quest for scientific truth.". Straub et al. [37] give recommendations how to proceed in validation and checking: 1) Instrument is likely measuring the right content; 2) Constructs are likely real and reliable; 3) Rival hypotheses are ruled out, and 4) Mathematical relationships between the constructs are assured within certain degrees of confidence.

Table 1. Some criteria for positivist research

Model level
Fidelity with real world phenomena,
Completeness,
Level of detail,
Robustness
Internal consistency
Manipulation validity
Statistical conclusion validity
Construct level
Content validity
Construct validity
Reliability

We understand that verification of a certain theory in the sense of Chua means that the theory shows "fidelity with real world phenomena". Such criteria as completeness and level of detail mentioned by March and Smith measure how closely the theory is describing the object under study. Robustness and internal consistency refer to some internal properties of the theory. Two criteria proposed by Straub et al. [37], manipulation validity (a measure of the extent to which treatments have been perceived by the subjects of an experiment) and statistical conclusion validity (Type of validity that addresses whether appropriate statistics were used in calculations that were performed to draw conclusions about the population of interest) concern a actual reality and its measurements not the planned reality in the future and they are intended to verification of a certain theory in the sense of Chua. Three other criteria proposed by Straub et al. [37] (content validity, construct validity and reliability) concern validation of the instruments that are used to gather data on which findings and interpretations are based.

Concerning three types of models in design research (1) a model of the initial state, 2) a model of the desired state and 3) the model of the finished, realized state) from the positivist perspective, we can say that all the three models can be described. The initial and finished states refer to actual reality, but the desired state to potential reality. The latter brings two important remarks. First, an exceptional assumption is that there is consensus concerning the desired state. Second, a certain steady state concerning people must be assumed, although people can learn and forget, and Chua's assumptions on people are not hence quite realistic.

According to Chua [7:615], the *interpretivist* researcher assumes that "social reality is emergent, subjectively created, and objectified through human interaction". Chua also gives some criteria for models: "Scientific explanations of human intention sought. Their adequacy is assessed via the criteria of logical consistency, subjective interpretation, and agreement with actors' common-sense interpretation."

Klein and Myers [27:72] proposed seven principles for interpretive field research (see Table 2).

Table 2. Summary of principles for interpretive field research

1. The Fundamental Principle of the Hermeneutic Circle
This principle suggests that all human understanding is achieved by iterating between considering the interdependent meaning of parts and the whole that they form. This principle of human understanding is fundamental to all the other principles.
2. The Principle of Contextualization
Requires critical reflection of the social and historical background of the research setting, so that the intended audience can see how the current situation under investigation emerged.
3. The Principle of Interaction between the Researchers and the Subjects
Requires critical reflection on how the research materials (or "data") were socially constructed through the interaction between the researchers and participants.
4. The Principle of Abstraction and Generalization
Requires relating the ideographic details revealed by the data interpretation through the application of principles one and two to theoretical, general concepts that describe the nature of human understanding and social action.
5. The Principle of Dialogical Reasoning
Requires sensitivity to possible contradictions between the theoretical preconceptions guiding the research design and actual findings ("the story which the data tell") with subsequent cycles of revision.
6. The Principle of Multiple Interpretations
Requires sensitivity to possible differences in interpretations among the participants as are typically expressed in multiple narratives or stories of the same sequence of events under study. Similar to multiple witness accounts even if all tell it as they saw it.
7. The Principle of Suspicion
Requires sensitivity to possible "biases" and systematic "distortions" in the narratives collected from the participants.

Klein and Myers suggest that the principle of the hermeneutic circle is the overarching principle upon which the other six principles expand. For instance, a researcher's deciding on what relevant context(s) should be explored (principle two) depends upon the following: how the researcher "creates data" in interaction with the subjects (principle three); the theory or concepts to which the researcher will be abstracting and generalizing (principle four); the researcher's own intellectual history (principle five); the different versions of "the story" the research unearths (principle six); and the aspects of the "reality presented" that he or she questions critically (principle seven).

Chua's criterion logical consistency refers to the internal properties of the theory and Principle 7 is mostly supporting this Chua's view. Principle 3 is given with the same purpose as Chua's two other criteria (subjective interpretation, and agreement with actors' common-sense interpretation). The other principles 1, 2, 4, 5 and 6 are intended to guide the research process from the interpretive perspective.

Concerning three types of models in design research (1) a model of the initial state, 2) a model of the desired state and 3) the model of the finished, realized state) from the interpretive perspective, we can say that all the three models can be described but it takes time. The reason for the long time requirement is based on the Chua's assumptions on subjective interpretation, and agreement with actors' common-sense interpretation. All the participants and the researcher must have the common views on both the initial, desired and finished states and developing those views requires negotiations and discussions and it takes time.

According to Chua [7:622], the *critical* researcher assumes that "human beings have inner potentialities which are alienated (prevented from full emergence) through restrictive mechanisms. Objects can only be understood through a study of their historical development and change within the totality of relations." Chua continues that "criteria for judging [critical] theories are temporal and context-bound" [7:622].

Myers and Klein prepared an important paper with six principles of critical research (see Table 3). The authors cautiously express that their proposals are only applicable to when using one of the three critical streams or theories (Bourdieu [1-3], Foucault [10-13], Habermas [14-18].

When Chua claims that human beings have inner potentialities, Myers and Klein in their Principle 4 emphasize individual emancipation. In Principle 5 Myers and Klein refer to current forms of domination and Chua writes about restrictive mechanisms. Already Principle 3 speaks about revealing and challenging prevailing beliefs and social practices. Principles 1 and 2 guide the research process, and Principle 6 in a nice way underlines improvements in social theories.

Concerning three types of models in design research (1) a model of the initial state, 2) a model of the desired state and 3) the model of the finished, realized state) from the critical perspective, we can find many difficulties. Depending on different interested parties they can have different views on what is bad and what is good in the initial state. Describing the model of the initial state can hence be difficult or impossible. But finding the desired state is even much more difficult, because the different groups prefer different things. Mumford [31] in her historical consideration of socio-technical design found that a humanistic set of principles aimed at increasing

Table 3. A proposed set of principles for critical research (Myers and Klein [32:25])

The Element of Critique
1. The principle of using core concepts from critical social theorists
This principle suggests that critical researchers should organize their data collection and analysis around core concepts and ideas from one or more critical theorists.
2. The principle of taking a value position
Critical theorists advocate values such as open democracy, equal opportunity, or discursive ethics. These values drive or provide the basis for principles 4 through 6.
3. The principle of revealing and challenging prevailing beliefs and social practices
This principle suggests that critical researchers should identify important beliefs and social practices and challenge them with potentially conflicting arguments and evidence.
The Element of Transformation
4. The principle of individual emancipation
All critical social theory is oriented toward facilitating the realization of human needs and potential, critical self reflection, and associated self-transformation.
5. The principle of improvements in society
This principle suggests that improvements in society are possible. The goal is not just to reveal the current forms of domination, but to *suggest* how unwarranted uses of power might be overcome (although the critical theorist should not assume any special position of authority). Most critical theorists assume that social improvements are possible, although to very differing degrees.
6. The principle of improvements in social theories
All critical theorists believe that our theories are fallible and that improvements in social theories are possible. Critical researchers entertain the possibility of competing truth claims arising from alternative theoretical categories, which can guide critical researchers in their analyses and interventions.

human knowledge while improving practice in work situations. Evolution of socio-technical design in the 1960s and 1970s evidencing improved working practices and joint agreements between workers and management are contrasted with the much harsher economic climate of the 1980s and 1990s. We here also refer to the next section and especially to the Iveroth's [24] method to solve resistance of change.

3   Some Stakeholder Groups and Their Goodness Criteria on IT Instantiations

In this section we first present some universal criteria and guidelines of an IT instantiation. Concerning IT artifact and its design there are many interested parties that emphasize different aspects. Hence we shall consider different stake holder groups and their criteria. IT artifact rarely functions alone but some changes in user behavior are necessarily needed when a new IT system is implemented. The Iveroth [24] approach on introduction of a new information system is thereafter presented.

3.1   Universal Criteria and Guidelines

We use March and Smith's [29:258] definition: "An *instantiation* is the realization of an artifact in its environment" and consider an instantiation as product whose quality can be evaluated. They also defined some universal criteria for an IT artifact: the efficiency and effectiveness of the artifact, and its impacts on the environment and its users. Hevner et al. [20] followed the similar idea as Klein and Myers [27] and proposed the seven guidelines for design research.

The *guidelines* Hevner et al. [20:82] present below are adaptive and process-oriented. "Design science is inherently a problem solving process. ... Design-science research requires the creation of an innovative, purposeful artifact (Guideline 1) for a specified problem domain (Guideline 2). Because the artifact is *purposeful*, it must yield utility for the specified problem. Hence, thorough evaluation of the artifact is crucial (Guideline 3). Novelty is similarly crucial since the artifact must be *innovative*, solving heretofore unsolved problem or solving a known problem in a more effective or efficient manner (Guideline 4). In this way, design-science research is differentiated from the practice of design. The artifact itself must be rigorously defined, formally represented, coherent, and internally consistent (Guideline 5).The process by which it is created, and often the artifact itself, incorporates or enables a search process whereby a problem space is constructed and a mechanism posed or enacted to find an effective solution (Guideline 6). Finally, the results of the design-science research must be communicated effectively (Guideline 7) both to a technical audience (researchers who will extend them and practitioners who will implement them) and to a managerial audience (researchers who will study them in context and practitioners who will decide if they should be implemented within their organizations). Table 4 summarizes the seven guidelines."

We pay attention to Guideline 2 where it says that "the objective of design-science research is to develop technology-based solutions to important and relevant business problems". Hevner et al. consciously restrict their innovation into technology,

Table 4. Design-science research guidelines

Guideline	Description
Guideline 1: Design as an artifact	Design-science research must produce a viable artifact in the form of a construct, a model, a method, or an instantiation.
Guideline 2: Problem relevance	The objective of design-science research is to develop technology-based solutions to important and relevant business problems.
Guideline 3: Design evaluation	The utility, quality, and efficacy of a design artifact must be rigorously demonstrated via well-executed evaluation methods.
Guideline 4: Research contributions	Effective design-science research must provide clear and verifiable contributions in the areas of the design artifact, design foundations, and/or design methodologies.
Guideline 5: Research rigor	Design-science research relies upon the application of rigorous methods in both the construction and evaluation of the design artifact.
Guideline 6: Design as a search process	The search for an effective artifact requires utilizing available means to reach desired ends while satisfying laws in the problem environment.
Guideline 7: Communication of research	Design-science research must be presented effectively both to technology-oriented as well as management-oriented audiences.

especially IT technology and people using that IT artifact are excluded from their consideration. The evaluation of a design artifact then concerns the IT artifact only. We shall return to this view later in connection with Iveroth's [24] approach.

3.2   The Three Stakeholder Groups

According to Reeves and Bednar [35:427] "an essential building block for theory development about quality is an understanding of extant definitions and their origins. Different definitions of quality have been proposed at various times in response to the evolving and constantly changing demands of business. New definitions have not replaced old definitions; rather, all of the quality definitions continue to be used today." They found many definitions of quality, but the following ones were much distinguishing: Excellence, value, conformance to specifications and meeting and/or exceeding expectations. To clarify those four expressions we cite their strengths as Reeves and Bednar [35:437] presented them. The strengths of *excellence* are: Strong marketing and human resource benefits, universally recognizable - mark of uncompromising standards and high achievement. The strengths of *value* are: Concept of value incorporates multiple attributes, focuses attention on a firm's internal efficiency and external effectiveness, and allows for comparisons across disparate objects and experiences. The strengths of *conformance to specifications* are: Facilitates precise measurement, leads to increased efficiency, necessary for global strategy, should force disaggregation of consumer needs, and most parsimonious and appropriate definition for some customers. The strengths of *meeting and/or exceeding expectations* are: Evaluates from customer's perspective, applicable across industries, responsive to market changes, and all-encompassing definition.

Those characterizations given above will lead us to interpret that excellence is an overall measurement criterion that could correspond to our earlier proposal [26] called the *goal function* under which all kinds of different interests can be collected. The goal function is a goodness criterion of a new system. In addition, we think that the *managers* could emphasize value as a goodness criterion of a new system or artifact, *designers* would underline conformance of a new system to specifications, and *customers* might aim that a new system will meet and/or exceed their expectations. Hence there is no one criterion for a new IT artifact or the new information system, but different stake holder groups prefer different evaluation criteria.

3.3   The Iveroth [24] Approach

Hevner et al. [20:84] argue that "a combination of technology-based artifacts (e.g., system conceptualizations and representations, practices, technical capabilities, interfaces, etc.) organization-based artifacts (e.g., structures, compensation, reporting relationships, social systems, etc.), and people-based artifacts (e.g., training, consensus building, etc.) are necessary to address issues concerning the acceptance of information technology in organizations". Referring to Henderson and Venkatraman [19] Hevner et al. [20:78] state that "the effective transition of strategy into infrastructure requires extensive design activity on organizational design to create an effective organizational infrastructure and information systems design activity to create an effective information system infrastructure. These are interdependent design activities that are central to IS discipline." Although such tight connections exist between those two activities Hevner et al. limited their discussion of design science to activities of building the IS infrastructure within the business organization.

We can say that the range, the new IT artifact, taken by Hevner et al. [20] for accounting costs and benefits was too narrow (cf. Virkkunen [40]). Iveroth [24:136] crystallizes the reason as follows: "Research tells us that one of the major reasons for this is that managers treat IT as an isolated and mechanical tool that is and should be set aside and managed by the IT department. The underlying principle in this is that once the 'IT people' unleash the new technology, change spreads throughout the organization and employees simply and automatically adapt to the new circumstances. In short, managers often think that IT will take care of itself once it is implemented. What they tend to forget, however, is that IT is intimately interlinked with the organization and the way people go about their daily work. As a result, successful IT-enabled change implies managing both the IT itself *and* its social and organizational implications."

Iveroth [24:137] carefully summarized the success factors of the IT-enabled change projects that did not failed and tried "to find out how managers in practice lead global IT-enabled change, and what their activities and roles are in such work." (See Table 5) We agree with one of referees who writes that "many other IS researchers have done that as well". We picked up Iveroth's approach because, to our mind, Iveroth has collected many of the most promising ideas for change management and built the approach that seems to be efficient. Hence, Iveroth can be here considered as an example of many other similar approaches.

Table 5. The commonality framework for IT-enabled change (Iveroth [24:140]

Change Dimension	Change Activity	Role of Change Agent
Common Ground	Transactional activities such as the transfer of a change message between change agent and change recipient.	Messenger
Common Meaning	Translational activities aimed at overcoming interpretive differences between actors through learning and reflection.	Expert and Translator
Common Interest	Relational activities, both political and supportive nature. The political activities align interests by negotiations and informal relationships, and the supportive activities manage feelings and emotions, and motivate change recipients.	Negotiator and Coach
Common Behavior	Stabilizing activities—consisting of monitoring, communicating, and intervening actions—which secure long-term and recurrent behavior aligned to the new IT.	Observer and Intervener

We repeat that Table 5 shows activities for managers and change agents, and the activities proposed are taken from the managers' point of view. By looking at Table 5 and its activities we become to the following conclusions: a) The new IT system contains both technical and social components, b) Those two components behave differently – the technical one regularly but the social one unpredictably, c) The range for accounting the costs and benefits of the new IT system is now larger than in the case described by Hevner et al. [20], and d) the activities in Table 5 can be said to form a manager-driven social innovation.

In our approach to design research [25], in addition to the technical innovation, e.g., IT artifact, we have taken two other innovations based on two other resource types, social and informational innovations. Case Ericsson described by Iveroth [24] is a combined innovation consisting of both technical and social components.

Korpelainen et al. [28] found another social innovation when they studied a global company that purchased an ICT system, an internet-based meeting system, for training their customers. But customers had difficulties to connect with that system, and hence the system was given for internal use in the company. People in the company started to voluntarily use the system. Korpelainen et al. "show that the self-determined adoption of ICT systems has benefits like user motivation and satisfaction. Problems in such adoption relate to users' experiencing uncertainty regarding the organizational legitimization of the system and support for its use. Employees and organizations are likely to benefit from self-determined adoption because it promotes employees' motivation and initiative-taking. However, a shared understanding of self-determination and organizational support for it are required" [28:51]. Our reason to pick up the Korpelainen et al.'s finding is that it shows the distributed group of professionals voluntarily created a social innovation around a certain technical system originally intended to other purposes.

4   Discussion

Constantinides et al. [9] propose a pragmatic framework for ends of Information Systems research. This framework can be kept as the challenger of our results. The framework is presented in a tabular form consisting of 4 columns (logic, ethics, aesthetics, and the highest good) and 3 rows (before, during and after a study), and the ends are conditioned by power relations. Although the pragmatic framework seems to be very promising, one approach (experimental research) only is still analyzed and many others are lacking. Constantinides et al. [9] emphasize the truth only and they seem to forget utility and hence design research. In addition, our sets of criteria and guidelines contain at most the magical number seven [30] but the example table for the ends of experimental research shown by Constantinides et al. [9] contains 12 -15 entries. To this end, the pragmatic framework is not yet better than our collection of goodness criteria and guidelines.

In design research there are both the truth-seeking and utility-seeking studies. The former, e.g., models creating studies, can have different starting points, different world views and perspectives and hence different criteria. In the utility-seeking studies, there are different stake holder groups with different criteria, there are also different innovation types and different criteria, and the different ranges for accounting and hence different criteria. All the examples and references used show that they are already known but the scientific merit of this paper is that they are here collected into one presentation and structured in a new way.

Researchers can follow the criteria presented when they perform their research projects. In connection with our consideration of the world views we many times showed how problematic is that computers and data behave regularly but people unpredictably. Moreover, people construct social reality. Referees and editors can use the criteria collected when they evaluate the submitted papers. Evaluation can sometimes be problematic if the world view is only implicitly taken, not explicitly presented.

As we know our differentiation of the three types of models in design research (1. a model of the initial state, 2. a model of the desired state and 3. the model of the finished, realized state) is new, and their consideration in connection with the three world views (positivist, interpretive and critical) is also novel.

We know some limitations of our paper. We informed that an informational innovation can exist, but in the literature there are very few such innovations reported, perhaps Christiaanse and Venkatraman [8] where information asymmetry was utilized is one of those. In design research there are also other purposes than utility, like pleasure (van der Heijden [39]), and to artisticize and accompany (Iivari [22]). C. Chua et al. [6] found more stake holder types, e.g., supplier, investor, regulator, competitor etc., than Reeves and Bednar [35]. In addition to product also services where a customer can participate in creation process of service can be taken into account when criteria for new innovations are studied. In social innovations, e.g., for the competence development, such criteria can be proposed as our functionality, sensitivity and sociality (Illeris [23:438]. In the beginning we excluded both constructs and methods outside of our study, because they would increase many fold the volume of this study. All the limitations mentioned must be carefully studied in the future.

In connection with their validity considerations Straub et al. [37] ask: "How would one know which validation principles make sense, both on an individual basis and on the basis of the field as a whole? The social sciences tend to develop validation principles concurrent with the pursuit of research. ... Ironically, though, this question cannot be answered simply because scientific methods and techniques cannot themselves be used to validate the principles upon which they are based. Scientific principles for practice are only accepted as received wisdom by a field or profession through philosophical disputation (Nunnally [33]). Over time, they become accepted norms of conduct by the community of practice." The citation above well describes the role of criteria and guidelines presented. They are tentative proposals to give researchers, reviewers, donators, etc. for a while; some of them are accepted and some are improved by the community of practice and knowledge.

Acknowledgements. I am thankful for the referee's and Erkki Koponen's insightful comments and Foundation for Economic Education for financial support.

References

1. Bourdieu, P.: Outline of a Theory of Practice. Cambridge University Press, Cambridge (1977)
2. Bourdieu, P.: The Logic of Practice. Stanford University Press, Stanford (1990)
3. Bourdieu, P.: Concluding Remarks: For a Sociogenetic Understanding of Intellectual Works. In: Calhoun, C., LiPuma, E., Postone, M. (eds.) Bourdieu: Critical Perspectives, pp. 263–275. University of Chicago Press, Chicago (1993)
4. Burton-Jones, A., McLean, E.R., Monod, E.: On approaches to building theories: Process, variance and systems. Working paper, Sauder School of Business, UBC (2011)
5. Chen, W.S., Hirschheim, R.: A paradigmatic and methodological examination of information systems research from 1991 to 2001. Information Systems Journal 14, 197–235 (2004)
6. Chua, C.E.H., Khoo, H.M., Straub, D.W., Kadiyala, S.: The evolution of e-Commerce research: A stakeholder perspective. Journal of Electronic Commerce Research 6, 262–281 (2005)
7. Chua, W.F.: Radical developments in accounting thought. The Accounting Review LXI, 601–632 (1986)
8. Christiaanse, E., Venkatraman, N.: Beyond SABRE: An empirical test of expertise exploitation in electronic channels. MIS Quarterly 26, 15–38 (2002)
9. Constantinides, P., Chiasson, M.W., Introna, L.D.: The ends of Information Systems research: A pragmatic framework. MIS Quarterly 36, 1–19 (2012)
10. Foucault, M.: The Order of Things, Tavistock, London (1970)
11. Foucault, M.: The Archaeology of Knowledge, Tavistock, London (1972)
12. Foucault, M.: Discipline and Punish: The Birth of the Prison. Vintage Books, New York (1979)
13. Foucault, M.: Madness and Civilization: A History of Insanity in the Age of Reason. Routledge, London (1992)
14. Habermas, J.: Knowledge and Human Interests. Heinemann, London (1972)
15. Habermas, J.: The Theory of Communicative Action. Beacon Press, Boston (1984)
16. Habermas, J.: On the Logic of the Social Sciences. MIT Press, Cambridge (1988)
17. Habermas, J.: Justification and Application: Remarks on Discourse Ethics. Polity Press, Cambridge (1993)
18. Habermas, J., Lenhardt, C., Nicholsen, S.W.: Moral Consciousness and Communicative Action. MIT Press, Boston (1992)
19. Henderson, J.C., Venkatraman, N.: Strategic alignment: Leveraging information technology for transforming organizations. IBM Systems Journal 32, 4–16 (1993)
20. Hevner, A.R., March, S.T., Park, J., Ram, S.: Design science in information systems research. MIS Quarterly 28, 75–105 (2004)
21. Iivari, J.: A paradigmatic analysis of contemporary schools of IS development. European Journal of Information Systems 1, 249–272 (1991)
22. Iivari, J.: A paradigmatic analysis of Information Systems as a design science. Scandinavian Journal of Information Systems 19, 39–64 (2007)
23. Illeris, K.: A model of learning in working life. The Journal of Workplace Learning 16, 431–441 (2004)
24. Iveroth, E.: Inside Ericsson: A framework for the practice of leading global IT-enabled change. California Management Review 53, 136–153 (2010)
25. Järvinen, P.: On research methods, Opinpajan kirja, Tampere (2004)

26. Järvinen, P.: On reviewing results of design research. In: ECIS 2007 Proceedings. Paper 72 (2007), http://aisel.aisnet.org/ecis2007/72/
27. Klein, H.K., Myers, M.D.: A set of principles for conducting and evaluating interpretive field studies in information systems. MIS Quarterly 23, 67–94 (1999)
28. Korpelainen, E., Vartiainen, M., Kira, M.: Self-determined adoption of an ICT system in a work organization. The Journal of Organizational and End User Computing 20, 51–69 (2010)
29. March, S.T., Smith, G.F.: Design and natural science research on information technology. Decision Support Systems 15, 251–266 (1995)
30. Miller, G.A.: The magical number seven, plus or minus two: Some limits on our capacity for processing information. Psychological Review 63, 81–97 (1956)
31. Mumford, E.: The story of socio-technical design: Reflections on its successes, failures and potential. Information Systems Journal 16, 317–342 (2006)
32. Myers, M.D., Klein, H.K.: A Set of principles for conducting critical research in Information Systems. MIS Quarterly 35, 17–36 (2011)
33. Nunnally, J.C.: Psychometric Theory, 2nd edn. McGraw-Hill, New York (1978)
34. Orlikowski, W.J., Baroudi, J.J.: Studying information technology in organizations: Research approaches and assumptions. Information Systems Research 2(1), 1–28 (1991)
35. Reeves, C.A., Bednar, D.A.: Defining quality: Alternatives and implications. Academy of Management Review 19, 419–445 (1994)
36. Richardson, H., Robinson, B.: The mysterious case of the missing paradigm: A review of critical information systems research 1991-2001. Information Systems Journal 17, 251–270 (2007)
37. Straub, D., Boudreau, M.-C., Gefen, D.: Validation guidelines for IS positivist research. Communications of the Association for Information Systems 13, 380–427 (2004)
38. van Aken, J.E.: Management research based on the paradigm of the design sciences: The quest for field-tested and grounded technological rules. Journal of Management Studies 41, 219–246 (2004)
39. van der Heijden, H.: User acceptance of hedonic information systems. MIS Quarterly 28, 695–704 (2004)
40. Virkkunen, H.: Initial costs for product types and lots in manufacturing as a cause for decreasing unit costs and their treatment in cost accounting, Summary (Teollisuuden kertakustannukset - niiden degressio sekä käsittely kustannus-laskennassa) Helsinki research institute for business economics No 13 (Liike-taloustieteellisen Tutkimuslaitoksen julkaisuja 13) Helsinki (1951)

Information Systems Integration in the Food Industry

Jonas Hedman and Stefan Henningsson

Department of IT Management, Copenhagen Business School,
Howitzvej 60, 2000 Frederiksberg, Denmark
{jh.itm,sh.itm}@cbs.dk

Abstract. This paper presents a model explaining industry-wide information systems integration. Using a theoretical frame of value configuration analysis and information systems (IS) integration extent we find that the IS integration was inhibited by incompatible value integration. On the other hand product sensitivity, continuous production process and presence of "value chain captains" – powerful actors dominating the industry - led to higher levels of integration.

Keywords: Information systems integration, Value configuration analysis, Food industry.

1 Introduction

The purpose of this paper is to develop an explanation to the existence, and absence, of industry-wide information systems (IS) integration. The theoretical foundation is an extension of IS integration extent [17], which we combine with value configuration analysis [23]. With its foundation in production technology and work process interdependency [26] we believe that it will be especially suitable to explain why and how the actors integrate their IS. The interdependency frame enables us to identify potential information exchanges and value creation logic that explain industry integration.

IS integration is one of the IS domain's persistent problems that since the 1960's continuously has reappeared on the IS manager's agenda [1, 6]. Existing research has, in general, found a positive relationship between integration and organizational performance [4]. Studies reporting on business benefits associated with IS integration are numerous [5, 12]. Nevertheless, despite the importance of IS integration the field is sparsely developed. Theoretical development is needed in several directions in order to influence and improve practice. The IS integration concept itself is a limited explored. Conceptualizations of aspects such as integration extent, integration intensity, and integration type are still not developed and explored [16]. Exceptions include integration levels [2, 15] and integration architecture [16].

Apart from the development of the IS integration concept there is also a need to address IS integration on other analytical levels than the one of a single company or a two-part collaboration. Previous research addressing IS integration has focused on intra-organizational IS integration [3, 14] or inter-organizational systems, such as

C. Keller et al. (Eds.): SCIS 2012, LNBIP 124, pp. 145–160, 2012.

electronic data-interchange (EDI) [13, 17]. Less is, however, known about integration of processes that spans over industries and business networks [14]. The industry context introduces issues of inter-organizational collaboration among several actors, as well as an increased multitude of IS, organizational cultures and organizational objectives. Although the technical challenges of IS integration may be similar regardless of intra- or inter-organizational context, the organizational and managerial challenges in industry-wide IS integration needs special attention as they presents a different integration context [18].

2   Information Systems Integration

Integration of IS has showed that integration of business activities can improve both efficiency and effectiveness of business activities, but also lead to greater dependencies and decrease organizational flexibility. However, it has been acknowledged that dependent business activities exist also across organizational borders. Several studies address information integration between business activities of two different organizations [5, 12]. In this paper we take the study of inter-organizational information integration one step further. Studying two-part information integration has doubtlessly led to important knowledge contribution, but only recognizing the dependency of two parts is like only study integration of two activities of intra-organizational integration and not recognizing the advantages, disadvantages, and difficulties of integrating the whole organization. Much of the benefits created by intra-organizational are directly dependent on not only two activities becoming integrated, but on the orchestrating and harmonizing of all related activities. The same should logically be true for integration of industries, but the decision making business units have different requirements on the information-integration of the supply chain. Much of the benefits can only be derived if all activities are integrated, meaning that the integrated information flows should also be studied on an industry level.

Financial institutions can carry out real time electronic transactions with almost any other institution in the world [21]. In the automotive industry the use of EDI has led to decreased inventories and faster production cycles [9]. Other more fragmented industries such as construction seem to present IS integration that is only marginal in comparison [24]. The IS of industries are integrated to very different degrees, and the knowledge on why this is the case is limited [5].

There is a dearth of concepts for describing, explaining, categorizing and differentiating IS integration. Nevertheless, in the literature we find three differentiating dimension to describe IS integration: by IS type [27], by level of integration (IT-, IS-, and Business-level) [2, 3], and by integration extent [17]. In this paper we limit our study to the last category, even though it would doubtlessly be valuable if possible to relate IS type and level of integration to value configuration. However, as argued in previous research [16] that integration extent is one important concept that needs to be applied and tested in new contexts.

2.1   IS Integration Extent

IS integration refers in general terms to creation of some sort of linkage between two or more previously separated IS that originally were not intended to work together [16]. It can also be defined as the extent to which information through different communication networks can be shared and accessed for organizational use [5]. We broadly define IS integration in industry as the extent to which IS are used across the entire network. However, such a broad definition is not sufficient for the ability to collect data and say anything about to which extent an industry is integrated.

When it comes to integration extent there is a rough distinction between loose and tight integration [25]. Loose integration is related to the distribution of data through asynchronous communication and low mutual dependability of business processes. Tight integration refers to high level of business process dependence and sharing of information through homogenous infrastructures with synchronous communication. An alternative is to adopt the four proposed EDI usage measurement [17]: *volume*, *breadth*, *diversity*, and *depth*. This conceptualization was initially developed for two-part EDI. We are tentatively extending the use into the industry-wide application area and define the usage measurements as:

- *IS integration volume* represents the extent to which an industry's information processing is integrated. A measure of IS integration volume is useful since it illustrates an industry's progress towards integration of information processing.
- *IS integration breadth* represents the extent to which an industry has integrated IS along with its actors. The IS breadth gives an idea about whether industry try to get rid of bottlenecks in the information flow.
- *IS integration diversity* represents the extent to which an industry has integrated different types of business processes through IS. This measurement is connected to the different functionality an IS support.
- *IS integration depth* represents the extent to which an industry's business processes are supported by IS at different hierarchical levels. The IS depth lets us know if the industry uses IS as operational, tactical and strategic tool.

2.2   Value Configuration Analysis

The ways companies create value is similar across industries, but what activities distinguish companies is industry dependent [19]. Value configuration analysis aims at understanding what activities drives cost and value [23]. The value chain framework provides us with an approach that, in principle, de-composes a company into strategic important activities and analyses the activities impact on cost and differentiation [19]. The value chain analysis seems to be applicable and useful tool to understand how cost and value relates to IS integration. However, the value chain model has been criticized over the years. "*It is not only difficult to assign and analyze activities in terms of the five primary value chain categories, but the resulting chain often obscures rather than illuminates the essence of value creation* [23, p 414]". For instance, when applying value chain analysis in industries that are not based on transforming raw material into final products, e.g. software development firm, banks or telecom operator. Besides being difficult to apply, they also claimed that different technology lead to fundamentally different ways of creating value [23], e.g. in telecom value is co-produced in the actual linkage or the mediation of parties [20]. This is a different view than the classical industrial logic. Therefore is value configuration analysis proposed as a complement to value chain analysis. It draws upon three types of organizational interdependencies [26]:

- Pooled interdependency, meaning that each activity performed is interrelated and contributes to the final product.
- Sequential, the output of one activity is the input for next activity. It should be stressed that each activity is a prerequisite of the following activity.
- Reciprocal, the output of one activity is the input for another, which in turn, directly or via proxy, is the input for the first activity.

With these three types of interdependencies as basis, three sets of value configurations emerge, including the value chain, the value shop and the value network. The idea is that these value configuration display different patterns of interdependencies. The configurations may coexist within a company or within an industry with actors operating by different value creation logics.

The Value Chain assumes that conversion of raw material into final products creates value. In the process of converting inputs to final products long-linked technology is used. This is done through five primary activities: Inbound logistics, Operations, Outbound logistics, Marketing and sales, and Service [19]. The primary activities are mainly sequentially interdependent and managed through coordination. Meaning that the output of one activity is the input of the next. In addition there are four support activities of the value chain model: procurement, technology development, human resource management and firm infrastructure. The drivers of cost and value are scale, capacity utilization, linkages, interrelationships, vertical integration, location, timing, learning, policy decisions, and government regulations.

The Value Shop, such as consultancy, software development, medicine, and design, creates value by solving customer problems. The value shop uses intensive technology to solve customer problems [26] and drivers of differentiation are much more important than cost drivers [23]. Key processes are organized around identifying resources that matches the requirements of the problem. Value creation can be described as "moving from one state to a desired state". Value is created in the problem solving process between customer and provider. The activities are sequential and reciprocal interdependent. The primary activities of a value shop are: Problem-finding, Problem-solving, Choice, Execution, and Control and Evaluation. Learning is the most important driver of value.

The Value Network is the based on mediating technology [26]. This supports the process of creating links between customers who share a common interest. Mediating technology manages time and space for customers. Value creation is achieved by enabling linkage between actors, e.g. a telecom company how links phone calls between parties or a bank how creates links between depositors and borrowers. The relationship between network participants is often governed by a formal contract. Value increases with the number of participants. Value networks entail three distinct primary activities: Network promotion (marketing) and contract, Service, and Network infrastructure. The activities are often simultaneous and lead to strong reciprocal interdependency between them. Standards are the main principle to control and coordinate reciprocal activities. Cost and value is driven by scale.

3   Research Methodology

The research presented in this paper was carried out as a structured case study framework [8]. The structured case study approach includes guidelines for the process of developing knowledge and theory based on empirical data. This approach does not prescribe specific data collection techniques or ways of analyzing the data, but outlines a framework for how to develop knowledge and theory. The main steps are to develop an initial conceptual framework, to collect and analyze empirical evidence, and to reflect upon the result in order to induce knowledge.

To populate the theoretical framework we centred around four of the major products flows in the food industry: Milk, Pork, Peas, and Sugar. These four product flows are approached as embedded cases of the larger food industry case. The flows were selected partly due to their importance and since they present a variation in product characteristics. To achieve variation within the case, we started investigation with farmers producing output representing different technologies, market structure and governance structure: milk, meat, peas, and sugar beets. Milk and meat are produced through a continuous process, while the other two flows are based on batch production. Peas are very sensitive, while sugar beets are not sensitive at all. The latter since one of the core fundaments of the value configuration analysis is that how value is created is dependent on what business the company is into. A variation within the case was also considered to increase possibilities for valid theoretical generalization [10].

Data collection began with the first field visits. During the field visits we collected data through 27 semi-structured conversations guided by an interview guide. The visits lasted between 90 to 120 minutes. The interviews were taped and field notes were taken. After the field visit, the field notes were used to write a case story. The recordings were mainly used for supporting the field notes when writing up the case story. Interviewees were initially asked to explain and show the main activities of their organization. Whenever possible, we probed the farmer with questions about the role of IT in the activities The farmer's main activities, customers, suppliers, and collaborating organizations participating in the core activities were identified in order to complete the value configuration. Also the use of IS in the main activities was addressed. In addition public available documents, such as annual reports and web pages were used to enrich the picture and to triangulate findings [cf. 28]. The individual respondents were owners of the firms (farmers), chief information officers, or financial officers. For customers, suppliers, and collaborators the data collection was repeated until the most important actors, according to the respondents, were identified. In total we interviewed representatives from seven farmer units, four food processors, two grocery chains and two retailers. We also interviewed four organizations that influenced the IS integration among the actors in the southern Swedish food industry: one agriculture consulting company, one system integrator who had developed several of the integration solutions in the industry, the Swedish Agricultural Agency, and the Swedish Customs. Based on the data eleven rich case stories focusing on the primary actors of the industry of about 2000 word each were written. These were used as input for first round of analysis and reflection.

The first round of analysis and reflection was mainly done to capture the individual actors and the main forces shaping the IS integration. Since the focus of this paper is on the industry level and not the individual actors the case description and analysis in this paper is the study's second analytical phase, focused on the industry level and the integration of this. The industry level analysis followed a second empirical phase in which complementary data on the relations between identified actors were gathered. When gathering data special concern was given to the preliminary IS integration shaping factors and their explanation in the value configuration.

4   IS Integration in the Food Industry

The number of end consumers in the Swedish food industry is just above ten million consumers. Three large grocery chains, with a total market share of 72%, dominate the Swedish market. ICA and Axfood are privately owned, whereas Coop is a cooperative owned by the consumers.

There are several food producers in the area, such as Procordia Food AB, Findus Sverige AB, Skånemejerier, and Pågen AB. Skåne is the most important agricultural area of Sweden with some 8700 farmers. The main food products from Skåne are different types of crops, dairy products, rape seed oil, sugar beets, and meat. In addition to the companies directly involved in food production, there are several other actors in the food industry. These actors have a control and quality function, and the potential to influence the production and the end customers and their preferences, such as KRAV (certifier of organically produced food), European Union (EU) and its Common Agricultural Policy (CAP), National Food Administration, Consumers in Sweden, customs, service providers, and Agricultural Universities. In particular, CAP is influential, since it comprises a set of rules and mechanisms that regulate the production, trade and processing of agricultural products in the EU

4.1   Milk Flow

The milk production is largely automated and supported by milk robots and automatic feeding machines. The data collected by the milk robots (for example amount and quality) is linked trough an IS to the Diary Association, which makes analysis provides feedback, e.g. what to feed the cows.

The farmer sells its entire production to the dairy, and the price is based on quality (fat and protein) and quantity of the milk. When the milk is delivered to the dairy it is pumped into storage silos. The milk is checked for taste and quality upon arrival to the dairy. Thereafter the milk is cooled down and the cream is separated from the milk. Before the milk is packed it is homogenized. The origin of the packaged milk is kept track of by the dairy, which has about 900 dairy farmers delivering milk. Using an identification number it is possible to trace each package to a specific milk batch. The farmer use the shipment id to identify which cow delivered the milk and can thereby provide the full medical history of a specific cow. The dairy delivers its products to the local grocery stores or to central storage facilities of the large grocery chains. The end-consumers then buy the product from the local grocery.

To support the process between farmers and grocery stores the dairy uses two ISs. The ERP-system is used to handle logistics, purchasing, resource management, financial assets, maintenance, supply chain management and data warehousing. While the EDI/Link-XLM system is used to manage the electronic information flow (order, invoicing, and payment) to and from farmers and customers. The EDI/Link-XLM system is fully integrated with the ERP system.

The local grocery collects data through their sales terminal and customer loyalty card, but this data is not pushed down to the dairy or the farmer. The local groceries employ an automated inventory control system, which communicates the supply need to the dairy. End consumers have no automated information integration with any other actor than their local grocery. The data that is passed on from the local grocery to the retail chain is of transactional reporting on amounts sold and needed.

4.2   Sugar Flow

A web portal provided by the sugar mill supports the sugar production. The amount of sugar beets that the farmer is allowed to grow and deliver to the sugar mill is regulated in a contract between the parties. In order to control the flow of sugar beets to the sugar mill there are strict delivery plans that the farmer has to follow. Most of the information exchange between the farmer and the sugar mill is done through the portal. The information consists of invoices and dates for seed distribution. The information flow is more or less one-way, from sugar mill to the farmer.

The sugar mill has a regional monopoly an ERP-system to support its core activities, internally as well as externally. The modules used in the sugar beet information flow are: Agri, Sales & Distribution, and Logistics. The Sales & Distribution module is used to handle the information exchange between sugar producer and their customers, while the Logistics module aids the transportation of the processed product (feed and sugar). Agri is used to control the delivery of beets from farmers by creating delivery plans. The module is connected to the web portal www.sockerbetor.nu. The sugar producer aims to guide the farmer on how to best cultivate sugar beets by providing information, for example appropriate PH levels, protecting against erosion, balanced fertilization and numerous hints and tips on how to protect and salvage parasite infected crops and soil. After the sugar beets have been harvested and transported to the sugar mill's processing plants the raw sugar is extracted from the beets. For processed and packaged sugar the relation to the grocery store is similar to the relation between dairy and grocery store.

4.3   Pea Flow

The pea production is very controlled by the pea. The planning process has an 18-month time horizon, i.e. the foundation that is laid in March should produce a harvest in August the following year. To support this pea processor has developed a concept called LISA (Low Input Sustainable Agriculture), which aims to structure the process and minimize the weaknesses. The base in LISA is the selection of fields for growing peas by analyzing the soil in different fields, picking the most suitable fields and monitoring the development of the crops while looking for signs of harmful organisms. The subsequent harvest and processing of the peas is also a highly controlled and automated process. It is pea processor who controls the information gathering, and they more or less tells the farmer what and where to grow the peas. It is also the processor that does the actually harvesting. What can be said is that the farmer more or less only gives access to its field and make sure that the soil is prepared as it should be before the sowing is made.

The pea processor uses ERP-systems from both SAP (R3 for financials and administration) and Lawson (Movex for logistics and production). They supply the farmers with information about which fields are suitable for pea cultivation, when to plant seeds, how much and what kind of fertilizing. Information is extracted from databases, which are based on soil samples from the farmers' fields. This means that in many cases the processor knows more about a field than the farmer who owns it. In addition, the processor harvests the peas with their own machines. In the production at pea processor's plant, data about peas, such as quality and origin, is gathered enabling feedback to the farmer. Today the information flow is broken when the peas are packaged for consumers. There is no integration between the pea processor production system and the packaging system.

The relation between pea processor and the local grocery stores are similar to those for the milk and sugar producers. However, most of the pea production is frozen and exported abroad, mostly to Italy who is the worlds' largest consumer of peas. The peas are then sold on an open pea market to any willing buyer. However, using a printed code on the package peas can still be traced manually to a specific batch if necessary.

4.4   Pork Flow

The pork farmers are specialized on pig breeding and have one single costumer. Scan. The farmers make yearly agreements on production quotes. Pork quality is based on percentage of fat in the meat. Low percentage of fat increases the value, making slaughter easier. However, low fat percentage affects the taste in a negative way. To benchmark the individual farmer the slaughterhouse provides the farmers with access to a benchmarking system, namely PIGWIN. The farmers use PIGWIN to compare their own productivity with other breeders. They also use a web portal supplied by processor with information such as the quality of the animals they have delivered, and how much the processor are willing to pay for these. In addition, the pig farmers' informs the pork processor about how many animals they will deliver to the slaughter.

The food processor is one of the largest slaughterhouses in Sweden, owned by the breeders. The information flow starts with the communication between the farmer and the food processor. The farmer notifies the pork processor via the Internet, SMS or telephone, on how many and what kind of animal that he/she wants to deliver. The food processor uses several different systems to collect data about the animals, for example their weight, age and origin. All of the information from these systems is sent to the ERP system. The pork processor uses approximately 4-5 systems when interacting with the farmers for handling payment, butchering notifications and so on. They also use a CRM system when collecting the information from the farmers which is used to keep track of all of the 17 000 breeders. Swedish Meats has decreased their client list from over 10 000 customers when almost every super market was their customer, down to a customer basis consisting of 3 grocery chains and 100 industrial customers. Even though the system handles the whole process from the farmer to delivery, no detailed information is passed on to the customer. It is possible to have a continuous information flow from the origin to the end customer, if requested.

5   IS Integration Extent and Value Configuration

5.1   IS Integration Industries

Table 1 presents a summary of IS integration extent. Generally, the extent of IS integration is closer between farmers and food producers then between food producers and grocery chains and their retailers. The IS integration between food producers and the grocery chains relates mainly to the demand for order and delivery. There is also a flow of information governing invoicing and payment for the products. To this end EDI solutions are de facto standard for all involved parties. There is little or no IS integration dealing with, for instance, sales data from the grocery to the food producers. Thus the grocery chains keep the producers in uncertainty by not sharing sales data. The business logic between retailers and food producers is based on market mechanism without any overall governance. The final link between retail chain and end-customer IS integration through the use loyalty cards and cash register data. But not to precede the analysis we begin with the four facets of IS integration extent: Volume, Breadth, Diversity, and Depth.

IS integration volume refers to the extent an industry's information processing is integrated. Looking at the entire food chain we can see that parts of the information processing is integrated. For instance, between farmers and food producers there is a high degree of information processing to make the farmers more efficient (e.g. optimize the use of fertilization and pesticides) and effective (e.g. quality of the products. The information processing entail feedback loops where the farmers receive feedback on quality of the products and also suggestion of how to improve their internal activities. The integration is based on collaboration between the farmers and the food producers governed by contracts. The farmers also have vertical information processing with external quality agencies, e.g. milk and pork production. When looking at the information processing from the food producers' point of view and upward the food chain to the grocery chains and the retailers another picture emerges.

The integration is not as tight. It is mainly concerns order, delivery and payment. But, between the grocery chain and retailers the integration becomes tight again. The end customers are also integrated through loyalty cards.

Table 1. IS integration extent of the Swedish food industry case

Extent	Milk	Meat	Pea	Sugar
Volume	High	Moderate	Low	Low
Diversity	High	Moderate	High	Low
Depth	Moderate	Moderate	High	Low
Breadth	High	High	Moderate	Low
Volume	High	Moderate	Low	Low

IS integration breadth refers to the scope of purposes for which IS are integrated. The farmer's use IS to control their core activities, such as harvesting, fertilization and feeding. IS are in most cases embedded in the production technology, such as tractors with GPS navigation and smart boxes, and automatic feeding for cows and pigs. Looking at the relationship between farmers and food producers there is high degree of IS integration breadth. These systems are to a large extent provided by the food producers to the farmer. Different IS solutions supports production planning, delivery planning, and quality assurance. There are also IS support for administrative processes, such as invoicing and payments. Except for the pea flow, which is ran by the food producer. Continuing up the food chain the IS integration breadth decreases as only the functional and not operational activities are integrated. When it comes to the grocery chains and retailers the IS integration breadth increases again. The grocery chains provide their retailer with integrated IS for all their activities including cash terminals and loyalty cards.

IS integration diversity, i.e. the degree of IS utilization in different types of business processes. Staring with the pea flow, the fertilization and weed control (the only activities performed by the farmer) is fully integrated with the tractors GPS supported smart card. Data on soil quality and weeds is continuously updated into the smart box, which then controls the fertilization and the use of pesticides based on current data and historical data. The smart box actually controls the tractors when it is out on the fields. The sowing date determines harvest and the closer the harvest the closer the food producer monitors the quality of peas. When it is time the food producer harvest and freezes the peas. The pork and milk flow has similar IS based integration. Feeding of the animals is done through computer support and the process is transport to the food producers and the external quality agencies. Input from the food producers and the external agencies directly influence what the animals are fed. Traceability of both milk and pork seem to be the main drivers. Delivery plans are written in the contracts between the farmer and the food producer. The farmer gets reminders through SMS. Sugar on the other hand is one of the few crops that the farmer actually has some own control off. The business processes integrated here are the same as for the pea flow, but the delivery is supported by a web-based system. The batch production mode with low product sensitivity explains the low need for stronger integration. Upwards the IS integration stops except for order, delivery and payment processes, expect between the grocery chain and the retailer.

IS integration depth, i.e. the use of IS on different hierarchical levels. The farmers' just use IS for transactional support on an operational level. But the food producers' and the grocery chains utilize ISs at all levels (operational, tactical and strategic).

5.2   Value Configuration in Industry

Analyzing the food chain from a value configuration perspective two main value configurations emerge. In the beginning of the food chain we can identify a value chain model, but looking at the end we have a value network. The two value configurations are not ideal, but they both have characteristics that corresponds to other value configurations. This is in line with that any real world cluster of actors will have features of several value creation logics [23].

At the top of the food chain, including grocery chains, retailers, and end customers the value configuration primarily corresponds to a value network. The value creation logic is actually about orchestrating the network of customers and suppliers. The grocery chains and retailers are providing a market, where suppliers of food meet consumers of food. In that sense it is about linking customers. In relation to the primary activities, network promotion and contract management, service provision, and infrastructure operation, a core activity is attracting potential customers and suppliers to participate in the network. The service-provisioning concept (associated with establishing, maintaining, and terminating links between customers and billing for value received) needs to be interpreted in a slightly different by viewing the retail stores opening hours and location as service provision where links between customers are established maintained and terminated. The final primary activity, infrastructure operations is the running of retails stores (the market) and keeping the cash registrar working. In addition for the grocery chains and the retail stores a key activity is inbound and outbound logistics. However, there is no conversion of inputs to outputs. When considering the relationship between the activities they are carried out simultaneously and in parallel, which is consistent with the value network. The interdependency of activities is pooled and sequential. The inbound and outbound activities are sequential in nature. The last and final point is related to the cost and value drivers that are both based on scale and capacity utilization.

At the start of the food chain from farmers to food producers, we find several similarities and some differences. The four food chains are all based on a value chain logic converting inputs (seeds and food) through feeding, fertilization, and harvesting into final products (peas, sugar beets, milk, and pigs). The relationship between the activities is sequential, but there are also a number of iterations and feedback loops between the farmers and food producers. The interdependency is pooled, and sequential. Scale and capacity utilization drive cost and value. The food producer relies on value chain logic and traditional primary activities, such as inbound logistics, operations, outbound logistics, sales, and marketing. The relationship between inbound logistics (harvesting) and operations (freezing) is sequential and the interdependency is sequential. Cost drivers are based on scale and capacity utilization. Value on the other hand is based on reputation.

Peas and sugar flows are produced in batch production with harvest ones a year. Sugar beets are not as sensitive as peas regarding when to harvest them or where to store them before final sugar refinery process. The value creation logic is also based on refining inputs (seeds) to output (sugar beets). Milk and pork production, on the other hand, is different in that the production mode is continuous which creates high degree of interdependency with the customer. A continuous process is built on a tight integration between the involved actors, which is supported by IS integration. The interdependency between activities is sequential. The sequential flow is also vertically integrated with external agencies. The external agency supports the milk farmer with information to improve the quality. In addition milk farmers are the farmers that are most advanced in their use of IS, basically the entire process is monitored and controlled with the assistance of IT. IS integration between farmers and food producers are mainly related to "production" data, with complementary support of secondary processes. The farmers and the food producers are tied to each other with long-term contracts. Thus, farmers and food producers collaborate with each other to reach mutual benefits and thereby have a tight integration. The milk producers have contracts with different local grocery chains and larger retailer. They deliver different milk products on a regularly basis.

In summary, the industry-wide food chain has the shape of a sandglass (Figure 1). At the beginning a great number of farmers creates the raw material for the industry. For each of our empirical subcases it can be claimed that one major actor dominates the food chain. In addition, each of the food flows has just one major food producer – leading to an almost monopolistic position situation, cf. the milk flow. The theme has been noticed being typical for the food industry [22], starting with a large number of farmers and suppliers, in the middle a small number of producers and distributors, ending with a large number of consumers. The farmers and food processors have relations ranging from almost pure value chain logic (sugar) to more co-creation logic (pea). Together the production cluster forms a unit in the value network dominated by the grocery chains.

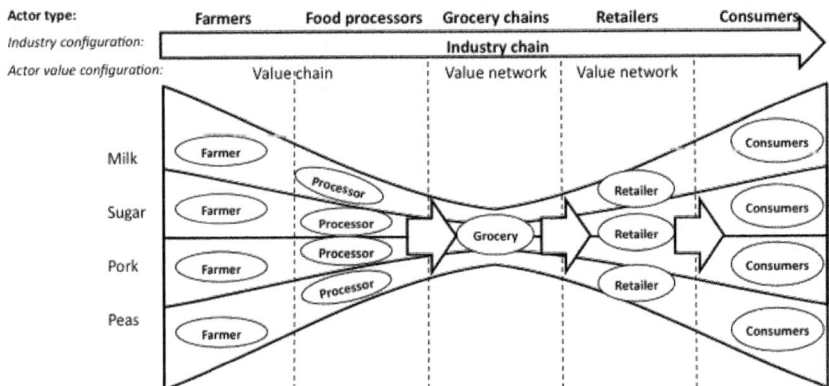

Fig. 1. Industry-wide food chain integration

6   Discussion: Drivers and Inhibitors for Industry IS Integration

Our analysis of the relations between farmers and food processors showed that extent of both organizational and informational integration varied from minor (between sugar farmers and processor) to almost fully integrated (between pea farmers and processor). Consolidating this finding with the value configuration analysis shows that the level of integration corresponds well to the actor's position on a continuum between ideal value chain logic and ideal value network logic. In other words, the more network like the production, the more integrated. Most integrated is the milk production. Thereafter follow peas, pork, and fourthly the production of sugar beets. Interestingly there are two "incompatible" value creation logics, value chain and value network, in the same industry. This change of value creation logic is at the heart of the rupture in IS integration.

The value configuration analysis showed that dependency between the actors was related to the sensitivity of what was produced. Food products are sensitive to heat, coldness, time, or sun and will finally turn bad. The sensitivity of food products is one of the key distinguishing features of the food industry. Milk and peas are compared to pork and sugar more sensitive products. The need for tight monitoring of sensitive products has made the food producers to develop and diffuse IS to their suppliers – who do not have the resources to develop their own information systems.

Dependency between farmer and producer was in the four subcases also related to the production mode, i.e. whether the production is in batches or a continuous process. A continuous production poses different requirements on IS integration than batch production, since there is a need for a frequent communication between farmers and food producers to track delivery and quality. In particular the milk farmer needs quick feedback on the quality – especially if the milk contains certain hazardous bacteria. Arranging the four products in terms of batch/continuous production mode gives that milk followed by pork are the products closest to a continuous flow, while peas and sugar are close to an ideal batch mode production with harvest and processing once a year. Thus, through the mediating state of increased dependency product sensitivity and production mode are drivers of IS integration in the food industry. This conclusion is in line with it resembles the general conclusion that the unique features of an industry drives the IS integration [5].

The analysis of the relations between food producers and grocery chains showed that there was a significant rupture in the IS integration between these actors. The farmers and food processors were at least partly integrated, and likewise were the grocery chains and the retailers on their side. Previous research had shown that different value creating logics have different cost and value drivers according to the type of activities involved and the interdependencies between them. Where multiple logics coexist, the different cost and value drivers may generate tensions [7]. We see that the different value creation logics of the food industry affect the IS integration extent by the dimension of integration depth; the only information exchanged digitally between producer and grocery chains are orders and invoices as the actors only share the functional and not the operational processes.

A fourth important influencing factor is the presence of what we have labeled as value chain captains. There is no overarching control organization that looks out for the entire chain's best interest. Farmers and food producers seem to benefits mutually from their IS integration collaboration, but the retail store and retail chains do not perceive benefits to themselves by collaborating with the food producers. So, there is only ISI on administrative level for order, invoicing and payment – aiming at efficiency gains. Thus, comparing IS integration in internal supply with information in an industry-wide supply chain there is besides the lack of common management level described above, logically also the issue of asynchronous savings by integration efforts. So, in the light of the disjoint economic responsibility and asynchronous gains and costs, we see the role of the value chain captains. The captains are using their dominant positions to enforce IS integration that lays in their direct interest. Very often the costs have to be carried by the smaller actor in the supply chain, while savings mainly are made within the realm of the captain. Backward integration is also more prominent than forward integration in the four cases. Backward integration is associated with efficiency gains in for example reduced inventory, faster time to market, and more reliable output [11]. Forward integration is associated with decreased demand uncertainties, development of market specific strategies, quality assurance and lock-in effects [9]. Problems with proving positive financial impact of forward integration may make companies further down the supply chain more reluctant to IS integration than companies near the end customer. The question to ask is thus whether this is due to benefits of forward integration are fewer or just harder to proof in numbers.

By the value configuration and IS integration extent analysis, we identified four factors explaining industry IS integration. Figure 2 summarizes the explaining factors. High degree of product sensitivity and continuous production mode is positively affecting or demanding IS integration (arrow a and b). Differences in value creation logic are influencing negatively (arrow d) IS integration, but the effects are limited by the presence of value chain captains (arrow c) that can enforce integration. Product sensitivity is a unique industry factor. We assume that similar factor exists in other industries industry, c.f. [5]. Production mode is not an industry specific factor, but it is

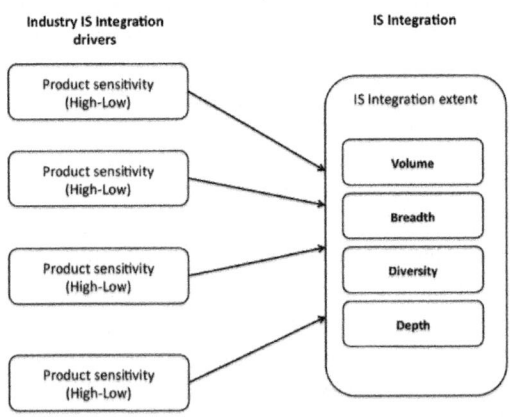

Fig. 2. Explanatory model

an influential factor driving IS integration and is related to the core activities of a business. The lack or presence of value chain captains is a managerial factor applicable to all fragmented industries with differentiated value creation logics.

7   Conclusion

This paper develops an explanatory framework for describing and explaining IS integration in industries, based on value configuration analysis [23] and integration extent [17]. We identify product sensitivity, production mode in the form of batch versus continuous production, differences in value creation logic and lack of value chain captain as four factors explaining the current state of integration in the food industry. Applicability to other industries is dependent on the presence of the mechanisms linking factors to impact described in the paper. Extrapolating the findings from this study industries with sensitive products are likely to be more integrated than non-sensitive industries. For instance, high tech products, such as mobile phones and computers, are sensitive to time, since they rapidly lose value on the market. So also industries with continuous production mode and industries that are centred on one or a few major actors who can decide the terms of doing business, as the automotive industry.

Returning to the outset of this paper, the research was partly founded upon the findings that industries were to a varying degree integrated in there IS [5]. However, it was not investigate further what caused this difference and by which mechanisms. We found four industry-specific factors that influence IS integration in the food industry. We have also tried to explain how the mechanisms work, which is essential in order to understand if and how the factors influence also in other industries.

References

1. Adelberg, A.H.: Management Information Systems and Thier Implications. Management Accounting 53, 328 (1975)
2. Al Mosawi, A., Zhao, L., Macaulay, L.: A Model Driven Architecture of Enterprise Application Integration. In: Proceedings of HICSS'39 (2006)
3. Alsene, E.: The Computer Integration of the Enterprise. IEEE Transactions on Engineering Management 46, 26–35 (1999)
4. Barki, H., Pinsonneault, A.: A Model of Organizational Integration, Implementation Effort, and Performance. Organization Science 16, 165–179 (2005)
5. Bhatt, G.D.: An Empirical Examination of the Effects of Information Systems Integration on Business Process Improvement. International Journal of Operations & Production Management 20, 1331 (2000)
6. Blumenthal, S.C.: Management Information Systems: A Framework for Planning and Development. Prentice-Hall (1969)
7. Bygballe, L.E., Jahre, M.: Balancing Value Creating Logics in Construction. Construction Management and Economics 27, 695–704 (2009)

8. Carroll, J.M., Swatman, P.: Structured-Case: A Methodological Framework for Building Theory in Information Systems Research. European Journal of Information Systems 9, 235–242 (2000)
9. Childerhouse, P., Hermiz, R., Mason-Jones, R.: Information Flow in Automotive Supply Chains–Present Industrial Practice. Industrial Management & Data Systems 103, 137–150 (2003)
10. Eisenhardt, K.: Building Theories from Case Study Research. Academy of Management Review (1989)
11. Hedman, J., Kalling, T.: The Business Model Concept: Theoretical Underpinnings and Empirical Illustrations. European Journal of Information Systems 12, 49–59 (2003)
12. Henningsson, S., Carlsson S.A: The DYSIIM Model for Managing Is Integration in Mergers and Acquisitions. Forthcoming in Information Systems Journal (2011) (available online)
13. Henriksen, H.Z.: Motivators for Ios Adoption in Denmark. Journal of Electronic Commerce in Organizations 4, 25–39 (2006)
14. Konsynski, B.R.: Strategic Control in the Extended Enterprise. IBM Systems Journal 32, 111–142 (1993)
15. Linthicum, D.: Enterprise Application Integration. Addison-Wesley, Massachusetts (1999)
16. Markus, M.L.: Paradigm Shifts - E-Business and Business/Systems Integration. Communication of the AIS 4, 1–45 (2000)
17. Massetti, B., Zmud, R.W.: Measuring the Extent of Edi Usage in Complex Organizations: Strategies and Illustrative Examples. MIS Quarterly 20, 331–345 (1996)
18. Neureuther, B.D., Kenyon, G.N.: The Impact of Information Technologies on the Us Beef Industry's Supply Chain. International Journal of Information Systems and Supply Chain Management 1, 48–65 (2008)
19. Porter, M.E.: The Competitive Advantage: Creating and Sustaining Superior Performance (1985)
20. Ramirez, R.: Value Co-Production: Intellectual Origins and Implications for Practice and Research. Strategic Management Journal 20, 49–65 (1999)
21. Rhee, M., Mehra, S.: Aligning Operations, Marketing, and Competitive Strategies to Enhance Performance: An Empirical Test in the Retail Banking Industry. Omega 34, 505–515 (2006)
22. Salin, V.: Information Technology in Agri-Food Supply Chains. International Food and Agribusiness Management Review 1, 329–334 (1998)
23. Stabell, C.B., Fjeldstad, Ø.D.: Configuring Value for Competitive Advantage: On Chains, Shops, and Networks. Strategic Management Journal 19, 413–437 (1998)
24. Tatari, O., Castro-Lacouture, D., Skibniewski, M.J.: Current State of Construction Enterprise Information Systems: Survey Research. Construction Innovation: Information, Process, Management 7, 310–319 (2007)
25. Themistocleous, M., Irani, Z., Love, P.E.D.: Evaluating the Integration of Supply Chain Information Systems: A Case Study. European Journal of Operational Research 159, 393–405 (2004)
26. Thompson, J.D.: Organizations in Action: Social Science Bases of Administration. Transaction Publishers, New York (1967)
27. Weill, P., Broadbent, M.: Leveraging the New Infrastructure. Harvard Business School Press, Boston (1998)
28. Yin, R.K.: Case Study Research. Sage Publications, Thousand Oaks (1994)

Bridging Research and Innovation by Applying Living Labs for Design Science Research

John Krogstie

Norwegian University of Science and Technology
krogstie@idi.ntnu.no

Abstract. In this paper we provide a framework for how to combine design science research with a Living Lab approach. Whereas Living Labs have a main focus on innovation, it is also important to involve researchers that need to follow a more rigid research approach to be able to produce research papers. The framework is illustrated through reports from a case using the combined framework in connection to research and innovation in the Wireless Trondheim Living Lab (WTLL). WTLL focus on research and development of mobile applications and services. The case, following the development and design science research related to one such service, MSIS (Mobile Student Information System)/Campus-Guide, provides evidence on one way these approaches can be combined, enabling more involvement of researchers in innovation processes and vice versa. The generalisability of the approach is not proved though, and further research will look on how we can utilize the described approach in other settings.

1 Introduction

According to Følstad [7] the term 'Living Lab' has been used over the last 20 years for varying approaches for involving users in innovation and development. Common traits to these approaches are:

- To provide insight into unexpected ICT uses and new service opportunities
- To evaluate or validate new ICT-solutions with users
- To experience and experiment with ICT solutions in contexts familiar to users
- To conduct medium or long-term studies involving users

In our view, an important aspect of Living Labs is experimentation and also co-creation with real users in real life environments, where users together with researchers, companies and public institutions work together in the development of new solutions, new products, new services or new business models.

Although you can have Living Labs on many different areas, in practice we see that many have a strong ICT-component [7], either by looking at an application area that is dependent on the novel use of ICT for doing innovation, or that the innovations is within the ICT-area itself. According to [12], there are two paradigms in applied

C. Keller et al. (Eds.): SCIS 2012, LNBIP 124, pp. 161–176, 2012.

ICT and information systems research: behavioral science and design science. Behavioral science develops and verifies theories that explain or predict human behavior or organization. Design science aims to improve or extend the human and organization capacities by building new artifacts. Hevner et al. [12] writes that "in the design science paradigm knowledge and understanding of a problem domain and its solution is achieved in the building and application of the designed artifact". They also comment that the goal of behavioral science research is truth, whereas the goal of design science is utility. It is safe to say that this approach relates more to providing utility (value), and we also find that a lot of contemporary ICT research to be design science oriented. On the other hand, when we look at the activity and members of ENoLL - European Network of Living Labs, the main focus appear for many of them to be rather on innovation than basic research. Having done design science research in the area of mobile ICT for many years on the other hand, it is striking how much research of this type do not come longer than the prototypes necessary to perform evaluation so as to be able to develop a master or PhD-thesis. When we look at current theoretical research basis for Living Labs, we find the use of co-creation, STS (Science and Technology Studies), Human computer interaction/Human factors and test and experimentation platforms [7], which are all relevant research approaches, but not necessarily those being appreciated the most in engineering research. Another research approach that shares some of the ideas of intervention as design science is action research [3], but given our engineering setting, we have more experience using the design science research thus in this paper discuss the opportunity to combine design science research with the innovation focus of Living Labs, in a way making it even more attractive for researchers in the ICT engineering field to take part in Living Lab activities, and also provide better scientifically founded results from the evaluation that should be also useful for those primarily oriented towards innovation to have confidence in the results.

In the next section, we present relevant methodological frameworks for design science and living lab activities. Section three describes briefly Wireless Trondheim Living Lab (WTLL) [1], which is the concrete environment for attempting this combination of design science research and living lab methodology. A case of utilizing WTLL in design science research (both for producing and evaluating artifacts, but also improving the scientific rigor of this type of research) is described in section 4, before concluding the paper.

2   Methodological Frameworks

Our approach to Living Lab activities is based on five key principles. These are: Openness, Influence, Realism, Value and Sustainability [4].

- **Openness:** In open innovation literature the perspective of openness concerns firms driving innovation processes to develop new products, services or reach new markets. However, openness can also be discussed on an individual, team or organizational level. In these cases openness concerns how to support open mindsets on an individual or team level or openness and knowledge transfer between different levels in an organization.

- **Influence:** A key aspect of the influence principle is to view different types of users and other stakeholders as active and competent partners and domain experts. As such their involvement and influence in innovation and development processes is essential. Equally important is to base these innovations on the needs and desires of potential users, and to realize that these users often represent a hetero-geneous group. This means utilizing the creative power of those involved in the Living Lab, whilst facilitating their right to influence these innovations. Influence is achieved by having the appropriate level of participation. Based on the discussion by Mumford [21,22] we can identify a number of different more detailed possible reasons for having participation, partly based on the power position of the stakeholders.

1. **Morally right:** This is the classical reasoning behind participation, based on a vision of a common good (e.g. justice and freedom) and how universal involvement in decision taking could help ensure this.
2. **Educational:** Involvement might provide understanding and knowledge among those participating that can assist to more effectively realize the objectives of the change.
3. **Improved ownership:** Ensures better motivation among stakeholders, resulting in better take-up of the change. Focus on that by being involved in the process the stakeholders will be more willing to take the changes produced in use.
4. **Leveraging of power:** Unions for instance may encourage participation because they see it as a lever for increasing shop-floor control over the work situation and contribute to industrial democracy.
5. **Protect against poor solutions:** In a company, employees might see participation as a way to prevent things that they believe to be undesirable from happening (i.e. being made redundant or deskilled).
6. **Transparency:** Ensures that the decision-making process behind the change is (perceived to be) open and trustworthy (i.e. not based on hidden agendas).
7. **Emancipation:** Enables those participating to feel free, be their own masters, and in control of their own destinies.
8. **Character-building:** It assists people to develop active, non-servile characters and democratic personalities, and also enables them to broaden their horizons and appreciate the viewpoints and perspectives of others.
9. **Improved solution:** Though participation more relevant knowledge is available and thus a better overall solution can be provided.

- **Realism:** One of the cornerstones for the Living Lab approach is that innovation activities should be carried out in a realistic, natural, real life setting. Orchestrating realistic usage situation is seen as one way to generate results that are valid for real markets in Living Lab operations
- **Value:** Living labs shall produce value for those involved. Value can be looked upon relative to the reasons for stakeholders to have influence. Based on the goals of those using resources to perform the change we can briefly highlight these as:

- Ensure economic gain
- Ensure personal gain
- Ensure organizational (business) gain
- Ensure societal gain

- **Sustainability:** Sustainability refers both to the viability of a Living Lab and to its responsibility to the wider community in which it operates. Focusing on the viability of the Living Lab highlights aspects such as continuous learning and development over time. Here, the research component of the Living Lab plays a vital role in transforming the everyday knowledge generated into methods and theories.

Since the early 1990s, design science has got more and more interest and attention from researcher in the information systems field. It has become a new way of creating and studying phenomena, where the understanding comes from building solutions addressing identified problems. More specifically, previous research [12, 17, 23] not only addressed the importance and value of design science, but also provided guidance and methods to define design science in information systems research.

A focus on design science is the building and evaluation of artifacts. Four types of design artifacts are identified and listed in Table 1.

Table 1. Design Science Artifacts [17]

Design Artifact	Description
Construct	Constructs or concepts from the vocabulary of a domain. They constitute a conceptualization used to describe problems within the domain and to specify their solutions.
Model	Is a set of propositions or statements expressing relationships among constructs. A model can be viewed simply as a description, that is, as a representation of how things are.
Method	Is a set of steps (an algorithm or guideline) used to perform a task. Methods are based on constructs and models when solving problems.
Instantiation	Is the realization of an artifact in its environment. It shows that constructs, models, or methods can be implemented in a working system.

Hevner et al. [12] indicated that researchers should follow seven guidelines in order to maintain the quality of the research and reach a good understanding of the results of design science. The seven guidelines are briefly described in Table 2. Concerning the design evaluation methods [12] described five different types of methods: *observational, analytical, experimental, testing,* and *descriptive.*

A concrete framework for design science is described by Peffers et al. [23]. The framework has four possible entry points depending on the existing knowledge of the problem, goal, and artifact before commencing the research (Fig. 1, bottom). In a problem-centered initiation, the problem is not known, and knowledge about the domain must be accumulated so that the problem and motivation for solving the problem

Table 2. Design Science research guidelines [12]

Guideline	Description
Guideline 1: Design as an Artifact	Design-science research must produce a viable artifact in the form of a construct, a model, a method, or an instantiation.
Guideline 2: Problem Relevance	The objective of design-science research is to develop technology-based solutions to important and relevant business problems.
Guideline 3: Design Evaluation	The utility, quality, and efficacy of a design artifact must be rigorously demonstrated via well-executed evaluation methods.
Guideline 4: Research Contributions	Effective design-science research must provide clear and verifiable contributions in the areas of the design artifact, design foundations, and/or design methodologies
Guideline 5: Research Rigor	Design-science research relies upon the application of rigorous methods in both the construction and evaluation of the design artifact.
Guideline 6: Design as a Search Process	The search for an effective artifact requires utilizing available means to reach desired ends while satisfying laws in the problem environment.
Guideline 7: Communication of Research	Design-science research must be presented effectively both to technology-oriented as well as management-oriented audiences

Table 3. Design evaluation methods [12]

Evaluation methods	Description
Observational	Case study: Study artifact in depth in business environment
	Field study: Monitor use of artifact in multiple projects
Analytical	Static analysis: Examine structure of artifact for static qualities (e.g. complexity)
	Architecture analysis: Study fit of artifact into technical IS architecture
	Optimization: Demonstrate inherent optimal properties of artifact or provide optimality bounds on artifact behavior
	Dynamic analysis: Study artifact in use for dynamic qualities (e.g. performance)
Experimental	Controlled experiment: Study artifact in controlled environment for qualities (e.g. usability)
	Simulation: Execute artifact with artificial data
Testing	Functional (black box) testing: Execute artifact interfaces to discover failures and identify defects
	Structural (white box) testing: Perform coverage testing of some metric (e.g. execution paths) in the artifact implementation
Descriptive	Informed argument: Use information from the knowledge base (e.g. relevant research) to build a convincing argument for the artifact's utility
	Scenarios: Construct detailed scenarios around the artifact to demonstrate its utility

can be established. In an objective-centered initiation the problem is known and articulated, and objectives of a solution must be made clear, and thus suggest requirements for the artifact. In a design and development-centered initiation the artifact is developed based on already existing goals and requirements. In a case where the research is client or context initiated, the artifact already exists and the research task is to demonstrate its utility in a given context. Depending on the entry-point, different research methods are relevant.

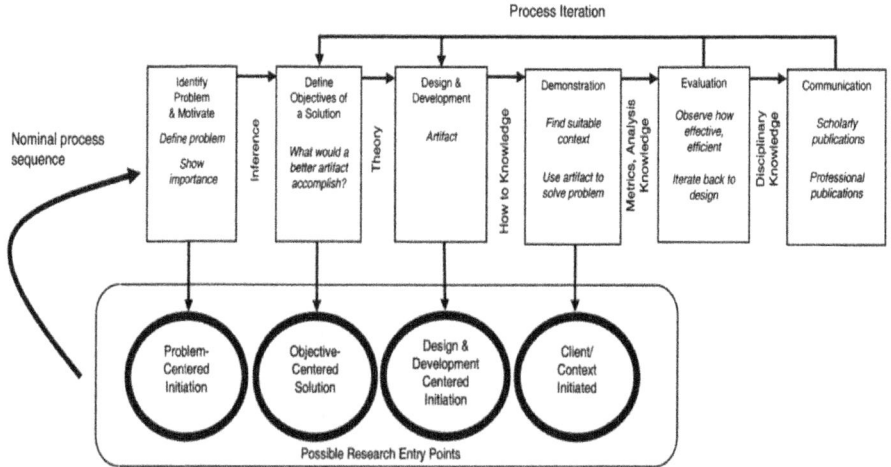

Fig. 1. Design science research method process model [23]

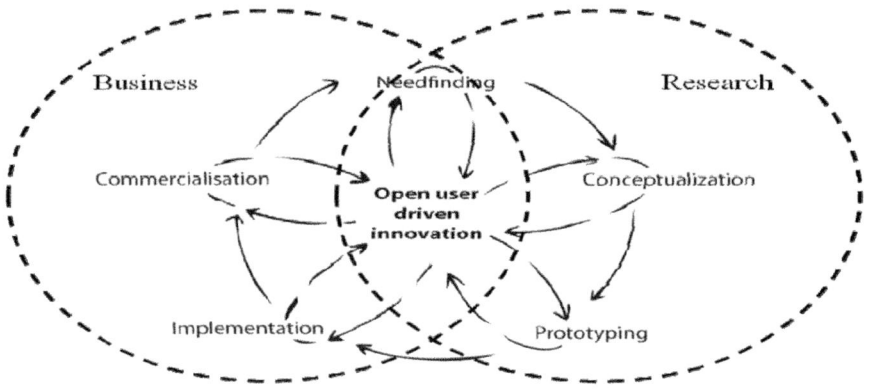

Fig. 2. Interaction between research and exploitation in user-driven and open innovation (based on [16])

The design science research approach described above can be combined with the innovation method provided in a Living Labs setting (figure 2). Five types of activities are identified, which does not necessarily follow each other in sequence as will also be illustrated in the case study presented in section 4.

- **Needfinding:** Identify the high-level needs for a new system among potential stakeholders and users.
- **Conceptualization:** Develop more concrete scenarios, frameworks, requirements and architectures for systems that are to support the identified goals and needs. Relative to the artifacts listed in table 1, this relate to constructs and models.
- **Prototyping:** Develop an instance of a system that can be evaluated under controlled circumstances.
- **Implementation:** Develop a stable full version of the instantiation that can be used in an unrestricted manner, thus evaluated in its business environment.
- **Commercialization:** Develop the system into a marketable product, including a sustainable business model and necessary operating support for long term usage and evolution of the offering.

Approaches and methods used for need-finding and conceptualization in figure 2 can help ensure the industrial relevance (Guideline 2 in table 2) of the solution looked upon. Through prototyping one develops instantiation-artifacts (cf. table 1), which might be implemented as basis for later commercialization either directly or to elicit the requirements to the implementation (as another instantiation-artifact). Research tasks are primarily part of need-finding, conceptualization and prototyping, whereas innovation warrants work done on implementation and commercialization also. Also in these phases, scientific evaluation methods can be applied, having a client/context-initiated entry point (cf. figure 1). Business and research interests often meet during need-finding workshops, and the business-side have a major role in implementation and commercialization. We will see in more detail in section 4 how theses frameworks can interplay.

3   Wireless Trondheim Living Lab

Wireless Trondheim Living Lab [1] is a research and development infrastructure in mid-town Trondheim made possible through the joint efforts of the Norwegian University of Science and Technology (NTNU), the city of Trondheim, the Sør-Trøndelag County Council, SpareBank 1 Midt-Norge, Adresseavisen and Trondheim Energiverk. In addition NTNU has over the last four years developed a wireless broadband net on campus, that is integrated with the wireless public service outdoor broadband and using the same technology as in the Trondheim Mid-town network. The combined network includes around 1800 Wi-Fi base stations. More than 5,000 users have been connected to the network at the same time, which makes the combined wireless network one of the largest in the world. Approximately 1/4th of Trondheim's inhabitants have free access to the network. Foreign students and employees of Eduroam-member universities (http://www.eduroam.org/) also have free access. This includes most Norwegian universities, but also a large number of in particular European universities. Others, including residents and tourists have the possibilities for cheap access. The Wireless Trondheim Living Lab includes three parts:

- The access network described above managed by Wireless Trondheim LtD.
- A service research and development lab.
- A networking lab or the "Street'n Roof Lab": This features its own physical infrastructure in parallel to the access network

The infrastructure supports several SSIDs allowing different ISPs to offer their services in the same network, sharing the costs. Currently five SSIDs are in use.

Wireless Trondheim LtD offers outdoor coverage and in addition coverage for most cafés and some malls. The coverage is all based on an advanced Cisco Wi-Fi platform. This is a well-suited platform for testing of new and innovative location and context-oriented service because the platform supports:

- Mobility – the user can move around in the coverage area without losing connectivity. The Cisco deployment allows layer 2 mobility handling supporting handoffs at city traffic speeds.
- High capacity – every access point has at least 10 Mbit/s symmetric connectivity to the backhaul fiber-network offering the possibility to experiment with services demanding high bandwidth.
- Location information – the network can gather location information about the users and offers the possibility of presenting services depending on the current location of the user using the CISCO Mobility platform. Open APIs returning the users location are established.
- Security – the network supports all well known standards for security in Wi-Fi including WPA/WPA2 allowing services with a high demand for security.

A large variety of context-aware mobile services have so far been experimented with. In addition to look at general frameworks for context-aware services, we are developing, testing and investigating the acceptance and diffusion of a number of services, including location-based services. A specific Mobile System Acceptance Model (MSAM) [8] has been developed by us in connection to this to be able to foresee the intention to use new mobile applications and services. Particular services include:

- Services for tourist, supporting both planning using a PC-platform, mobile support during the trip, and support for user-generated contents during and after the trip. This includes the use of context aware recommender systems.
- Personalized shopping oriented services utilizing profile information and the use of semantic web technologies [11].
- Services utilizing presence information [13].
- Mobile news services, including new delivery and commercials on mobile devices.
- Services for mobile workers [25].
- Mobile student information services [2].
- Mobile health services, including mobile health monitoring [10] and for tracking operating equipment and person in a hospital setting [6, 15].
- Mobile learning services [13].
- Services within entertainment, art, and culture, including social multi-player mobile games [26].

4   MSIS and the Campus-Guide - A Case of Applying Wireless Trondheim Living Lab for Design Science Research

As indicated above, we have experimented with a number of mobile applications and services. One of these relate to mobile systems for students as a type of a campus information system [1]. Campus Information System for students is defined as "An interrelated group of information resources, accessible by computer through the campus institutional external and internal web environment, that a university places at the disposal of its users to enable them to consult it and/or provide a selection of significant and relevant data, in the wide context of their university life in its academic, administrative and social senses, in order to improve student's knowledge base" [5].

The system for students' information (originally called MSIS - Mobile Student Information System) was one of the main artifacts that have been developed in this work. The follow-up commercial implementation of the Campus-Guide is the second. In addition, MSAM as mentioned above has been developed and evolved in parallel, but will not be looked upon here in detail. The MSAM instrument measures different facets of a mobile information service, some taken from standard technology acceptance models such as the perceived usefulness, ease of use, and intention to use, but also including aspects relating to the mobile context and user characteristics developed particularly as part of MSAM. Note thought that whereas the artifact we are looking at is particularly related to the increase of value, for the sustainability of a living lab, it is important that knowledge is captured also in more elaborated models like MSAM. Below the main activities according to Fig 2 are briefly described. More detailed result from the different activities are presented in the referenced works, here we can only provide a high-level overview due to space limitations.

4.1   First Need-Finding

The first need-finding activity was performed as a survey among members of the target user group (students at the university) [18]. Although with a suspicion that there was a potential for improvement in provisioning of up to date student information, one can classify this as a problem-oriented initiation of the design science research (cf. Fig. 1). The goal of the survey was to identify shortcomings and issues with the way information currently was communicated to the students, and gather feedback regarding what services and functionality that the students felt would be important in such application. An electronic questionnaire was created to enable rapid distribution and computer aided analysis of the gathered data. It was regarded as more convenient for the participant to complete the survey online in their spare time instead of having to hand in a piece of paper. When planning a survey, the methods to use should always be decided in light of your target audience [20]. In this project, the 89 respondents consisted mainly of technology students well familiar with computers. There are several alternatives for performing need-finding, e.g. the use of focus-groups [7]. This technique was not used at this stage in the case.

The main conclusions from the survey where:

- It is desired to consolidate the information from the multitude of channels into a single place.
- There is a need for more personalized information, customized to the individual student's curriculum. I.e., the information services should be more user-centric.
- The information should be presented through a user-friendly interface, with intuitive navigation.
- The most useful services are likely to be a news/notifications board, a schedule (lecture plan), and a service for locating resources and places on campus.
- The framework should be flexible enough to support development of clients for different platforms, e.g. combine a desktop application and a mobile application.

4.2   First Conceptualization

Based on the first need-finding activity, and a literature study, a conceptualization including development of artifacts such as usage scenarios, system requirements, and an implementation architecture was developed.

4.3   First Prototype

A prototype of MSIS was developed based on the requirements in the first conceptualization [19]. This version of MSIS consisted of three parts: a lightweight client application for deployment on mobile devices, a Web-based portal for system configuration, and a backend server which provides database storage, business logic, and a number of public web services.

Three basic functions offered by the system were:

- **Location Finder:** Allow users to search for different type of locations on campus, e.g. lecture rooms, computer labs, dining halls. It provided a short description of the location with an option to show the position of the location on a map.
- **Lecture Planner:** Allow users to view their lectures for a given day.
- **Announcement:** News, notifications, and other information relevant to the user are published on an announcement board. The list supports sorting according to different "flags," such as importance or category.

Figure 3 shows screenshots of the MSIS main menu and the location finder service as they appear on a Windows Mobile 6 Professional emulator.

First design evaluations were through traditional testing, and through descriptive scenarios (cf. table 3). Then a group of 25 university students were invited to participate in the experimental evaluation of the system. Using students in the evaluation scores in this case OK on realism and later influence. The pilot group consisted of students from various study programs, including students with both technical and non-technical background. Fifteen of the participants were students majoring in computer science, whereas the other 10 participants were students with non-computer science background. Most of the survey participants had at least one mobile device and had some previous experience with mobile services. Students at all levels participated, ranging from first-year undergraduate students to senior graduate students.

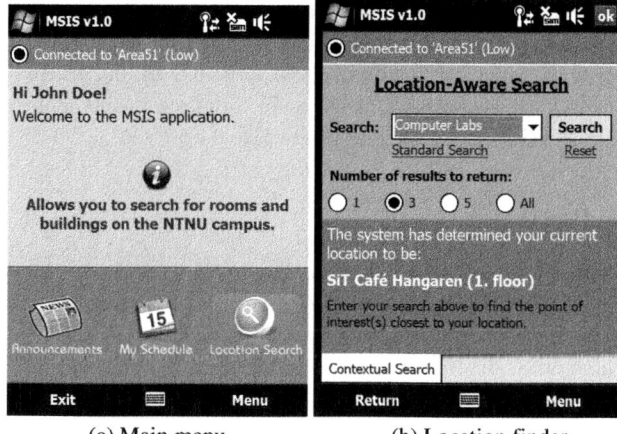

(a) Main menu   (b) Location finder

Fig. 3. Screenshots of the Mobile Student Information Systems (MSIS)

A paper-based survey was distributed to the sample. Prior to completing the survey, all pilot subjects were provided with an information sheet describing MSIS and a mobile device with MSIS installed. This way, all participants got some basic ideas about the mobile service. After using MSIS according to two specific realistic scenarios in the university campus environment for around 45 minutes, the survey was distributed to all participants. The first scenario referred to the location finder and map services within campus, whereas the second scenario referred to the course schedule service. Respondents were also informed that the data being collected was part of a research study. After filling out the survey, the pilot subjects returned the completed survey to us. In addition to include feedback on usability of the system for later development, this evaluation was used to verify MSAM, originally developed based on experiences from another mobile application [14], and giving indication on the likely acceptance of a MSIS-type application.

4.4   Second Need-Finding

In addition to evaluate the artifact and it's likely acceptance, the first prototype pointed to additional needs, in particular relative to support not only access to the administrative information on courses, but also supporting the overall learning process. Iteration is a main guideline in design science research and on this basis a second iteration was started, with the focus on mobile learning [9]. Here a survey among 50 students was performed to gather more detailed needs relative to such a service (anchoring the problem relevance through an objective-centered entry point).

4.5   Second Conceptualization

Based on the prototype of the first iteration and the result from the second need-finding, support for a more comprehensive system was devised, including first a conceptualization through development of new construct and model-artifacts such as additional scenarios and requirements. The architecture from the first iteration was kept, although with some extensions in how it would be integrated with additional sources of information, including linkage to information in the central learning management system (LMS) used at the university [1].

4.6   Second Prototype

The second prototype is described in [1]. Briefly, in addition to services in the first prototype, it included services incorporating twitter and RSS-feeds, email, and group-services supporting collaborative learning, as well as access to learning objects.

Also here the first evaluation was through technical testing and the use of descriptive scenarios. To measure the expected take-up of the second MSIS-prototype and its services, an acceptance test was performed. A user-driven experimental evaluation of the MSIS service was conducted among a group of 79 NTNU students. The utility and usability of the system were evaluated by applying experimental evaluation methods in the campus-environment. The user tests identified a number of issues with the initial design, and suggested ideas for enhancements which have been implemented in the current version of the system.

4.7   First Implementation

Based on the experiences from the two prototype-iterations, Wireless Trondheim LtD developed a service to be generally available. Whereas the prototypes was developed on the Windows Mobile platform, a change of platform was done to be able to provide the Campus-Guide (as it is now called) on the most widely used platforms (including Android and iPhone). From being done by Master and PhD-students, the implementation was now also done within the Wireless Trondheim LtD, to ensure continuity of knowledge relative to the solution. The starting point was design and development-centered, only included a subset of the functionality of MSIS, focusing on those services evaluated to be of most use, to ensure that it was possible to come up with a stable solution quickly. This included in particular in-door navigation possibilities. 100 persons were invited as beta-testers of the first implementation to provide additional input, providing an observational evaluation (cf. table 3).

4.8   Second Implementation and Commercialization

A second implementation of the Campus-Guide was performed in the summer of 2011, being released for general (commercial) use August 30, 2011. Additional observational evaluation of long-term use will be done, again utilizing the MSAM-model to also get research results from the use of the commercially available systems, and potentially identifying new needs for later versions both of the prototype system (MSIS) and the commercial implementation (Campus-Guide). The implementation thus enhances sustainability and realism through ensuring continued openness. The core of the Campus-Guide with focus on supporting in-door navigation has also instilled interest both from other universities, but also from organizations support indoor wayfinding and navigation in large building complexes (such as shopping malls, airports, and hospitals), taking a client/context initiating entry point (cf. figure1). At the time of writing a new spin-off company is being established relating to such solutions, establishing value both for current and new users and business value.

4.9   User-Driven Innovation as Design Science

Looking back at the guidelines for design science [12] we can observe the following:

Design as an artifact – The research must produce a viable artifact in the form of a construct, a model, a method or an instantiation. The main artifacts has underway been instantiations of the MSIS/Campus-Guide system, although also constructs and models are developed [1, 8].

Problem relevance – The research has to develop technology-based solutions for an important and relevant business problems.   Problem relevance was established through the need-finding activities [18], and confirmed through the evaluations of the different prototypes and implementations [1, 8]. Based on this, we can claim that the application developed will provide help to enhance the student experience with the mobile student information system.

Design evaluation - The utility, quality, and efficacy of a design artifact must be rigorously demonstrated via well-executed evaluation methods. As describe above the different versions of the artifacts were evaluated through testing, descriptive scenarios, experiments [8, 9, 19], and observational case studies to verify the quality and utility of the application and the services provided to the students. Evaluation was done both relative to usability and technology acceptance [8].

Research Contributions – The research must provide clear and verifiable contributions in the areas of the design artifact, design foundations, and/or design methodologies. As indicated, a number of papers have been produced so far based on this work, both relative to the MSIS-system [1] and the usage and development of MSAM [8].

Research Rigor – The research relies upon the application of rigorous methods in both the construction and evaluation of the design artifact.   During the work, a number of research methods have been used, including survey research, usability testing, and acceptance model evaluations, using established techniques for the different types of research [8, 9, 19]. Different types of research methods are used at different steps in the innovation model as described in 4.1-4.8.

Design as a search process - Requires utilizing available means to reach desired ends while satisfying laws in the problem environment. Design as a search process motivates the use of iteration as a research methodology. As indicated above (e.g. in 4.4-4.6), a number of iterations are performed, developing new versions of the artifacts through gathering experiences from earlier versions.

Communication of research – The research must be presented effectively both to technology-oriented as well as management-oriented audiences. The work has been presented through a number of reports and papers (both in conferences and journals [1, 8, 9]. It has also been presented in a number of more industrial events. As the artifact is now being taken over into a commercial phase, there is a challenge to be able to continue the research work relative to this. In WTLL this is addressed through the close cooperation between the university researchers and the Wireless Trondheim LtD and related spin-off companies. Since MSIS and the Campus-Guide is on different implementation platforms, we also envisage to keep the prototype of MSIS (which has so far a much richer functionality than the Campus-Guide) and experiment with related type of functionality for mobile applications on new versions of this.

5   Conclusion and Further Work

In this paper we have illustrated how we methodologically and in practice can combine a design science research with the more innovation-oriented tasks of open and user-driven innovation, and by this achieving both research results and innovation results. We have for many years done design science research in the university setting relative to mobile application and services, but very often this results only in prototypes that are evaluated and then left when the master or PhD-student finishes.

An important learning from this, is that it is possible to combine the more research-oriented work (which has scientific publication as a main goal) with the more innovation-oriented goal of bringing new applications to the market (where you in essence do not care about scientific publication), creating value in the economical sense of the word. There are several aspects of the presented approach that can make these results hard to generalize though:

- The set-up of Wireless Trondheim Living Lab, with a research-oriented university-partner (NTNU) and a more innovation oriented commercial partner (Wireless Trondheim LtD) that has as part of its business model to also contribute to research projects. When not having this mix of interests and competences, it can be hard to argue for the necessary rigor in how e.g. evaluation is done to ensure that the results from the evaluation have a scientific value (and not only a commercial value), and can be the basis for scientific publications. Scientific publication might also at times be at odds with commercial interests, although in a Living Lab environment where one of the core values are openness, one need to handle aspects related to IPR in these type of situations anyway.
- The type of system and stakeholders (students) might make this type of combined research and innovation easier than e.g. a commercial service for another type of users (e.g. a financial service for business users), since in our case it might be easier to get the users both involved in research tasks and as more traditional users of a new service.

In later work we will investigate this approach also for different types of services. As indicated in Section 3, a large variety of services is experimented with, although so far primarily being kept in the research phases. Where a bridge from the research phases to the business phases has happened, we have in most cases lost the contact with the business implementation and commercialization. We also cooperate with other living labs in Nordic and European projects and networks (in ENoLL in general, and the Apollon-network in particular), and will investigate the more general applicability of this approach through our involvement in these settings, looking upon it in relation to e.g. the FormIT-methodology [24].

References

1. Andresen, S.H., Krogstie, J., Jelle, T.: Lab and Research Activities at Wireless Trondheim. In: 4th International Symposium on Wireless Communication Systems, Norway (2007)
2. Asif, M., Krogstie, J.: Mobile Student Information System. Campus Wide Information Systems 28, 5–15 (2011)
3. Avison, D., Lau, F., Myers, M., Nielsen, P.A.: Action Research. CACM 42(1) (January 1999)
4. Bergvall-Kåreborn, B., Ihlström Eriksson, C., Ståhlbröst, A., Svensson, J.: A Milieu for Innovation - Defining Living Labs. In: The 2nd ISPIM Innovation Symposium - Stimulating Recovery - The Role of Innovation Management, New York, USA, December 6-9 (2009)
5. Cobarsí, J., Bernardo, M., Coenders, G.: Campus information systems for students: classification in Spain. Campus - Wide Information Systems 25, 50–64 (2008)
6. Dahl, Y., Svanæs D.: A Comparison of Location and Token- Based Interaction Techniques for Point-of-Care Access to Medical Information. Personal and Ubiquitous Computing. (2008)
7. Følstad, A.: Living Labs for Innovation and Development of Information and Communication Technology: A Literature Review. The Electronic Journal for Virtual Organizations and Networks 10 (2008)
8. Gao, S., Krogstie, J., Siau, K.: Development of an Instrument to Measure the Adoption of Mobile Services. International Journal of Mobile Information Systems 7(1) (2011)
9. Gao, S., Krogstie, J., Asif, M., Kuadey, N.:An Empirical Study of Mobile Information Services Adoption at a Norwegian University. Paper Presented at the International Conference on Electronic Business, Shanghai, China (2010)
10. Haugros, H., Overå, S., Krogstie, J., Strømme, Ø.: A home-based health monitoring system: An implementation and evaluation. NOKOBIT, Kristiansand, Norway (2008)
11. Hella, L., Krogstie, J.: Personalization by Semantic Web Technology in Food Shopping. Paper Presented at the WIMS 2011, Sogndal, Norway, May 25-27. ACM press (2011)
12. Hevner, A.R., March, S.T., Park, J., Ram, S.: Design Science in Information Systems Research. MIS Quarterly 28, 75–105 (2004)
13. Kofod-Petersen, A., Griff Bye, G., Krogstie, J.: Implementing a context-sensitive mobile learning system. In: Proceedings of the IADIS International Conference on Mobile Learning IADIS (2009)
14. Kofod-Petersen, A., Gransæther, P.A., Krogstie, J.: An empirical investigation of attitude towards location-aware social network service. International Journal of Mobile Communications 8, 53–70 (2010)
15. Landmark, A.D., Seim, A.R., Toussaint, P.J.: Use of Events in Clinical Software. SMIT (2010)

16. Living Lab Toolbox (2009), http://www.lltoolbox.eu/ (last accessed February 9, 2012)
17. March, S.T., Smith, G.F.: Design and natural science research on information technology. Decision Support Systems 15, 251–266 (1995)
18. Moe, S.P.: Mobile student information system (MSIS), Depth Study, Norwegian University of Science and Technology (2008)
19. Moe, S.P.: Design and Evaluation of a User Centric Information Systems; Enhancing Student Life with Mobile Computing, Master Thesis, Norwegian University of Science and Technology (2009)
20. Mordal, T.L.: Som man spør, får man svar: arbeid med survey-opplegg. Universitetsforlaget (2000)
21. Mumford, E.: Designing Human Systems for new technology: The ETHICS Method, Manchester Busines School (1983)
22. Mumford, E.: Participation–from Aristotle to today. In: Trends in Information Systems. North-Holland An Anthology of Papers from Conferences of The IFIP Technical Committee, vol. 8, pp. 303–312. North-Holland Publishing Co., Amsterdam (1986)
23. Peffers, K., Tuunanen, T., Gengler, C.E., Rossi, M., Hui, W., Virtanen, V., Bragge, J.: The Design Science research process. In: Proceedings of DESRIST, pp. 83–106 (2006)
24. Ståhlbröst, A., Bergvall-Kåreborn, B.: Living Labs – Real-World Experiments to Support Open Service Innovation. In: eChallenge, Firenze, Italy, September 26-28 (2011)
25. Sørensen, C.F., Wang, A.I., Conradi, R.: Support of Smart Work Processes in Context Rich Environments. In: Krogstie, J., Kautz, K., Allen, D. (eds.) MOBIS 2005. IFIP, vol. 191, pp. 15–30. Springer, Boston (2005)
26. Wang, A.I., Sorteberg, E., Jarrett, M., Hjemås, A.M.: Issues Related to Mobile Multiplayer Real-time Games over Wireless Networks. In: The 2008 International Symposium on Collaborative Technologies and Systems (CTS), Irvine, California, USA, May 19-23 (2008)

Author Index